Socrates Henkel

History of the Evangelical Lutheran Tennessee Synod

Socrates Henkel

History of the Evangelical Lutheran Tennessee Synod

ISBN/EAN: 9783337042998

Printed in Europe, USA, Canada, Australia, Japan

Cover: Foto ©ninafisch / pixelio.de

More available books at **www.hansebooks.com**

HISTORY

OF THE

EVANGELICAL LUTHERAN

TENNESSEE SYNOD,

EMBRACING

AN ACCOUNT OF THE CAUSES, WHICH GAVE RISE TO ITS ORGANIZATION; ITS ORGANIZATION AND NAME; ITS POSITION AND CONFESSIONAL BASIS; OBJECT OF ITS ORGANIZATION; WORK, DEVELOPMENT, AND VARIOUS SESSIONS; ITS POLICY; AND ITS FUTURE.

BY

SOCRATES HENKEL, D. D.

NEW MARKET, VA.:

HENKEL & CO., PRINTERS AND PUBLISHERS.

1890.

PREFACE.

Some years ago, the author was requested, by the Evangelical Lutheran Tennessee Synod, to prepare, for publication, the history of this Synod. This seemed to be necessary, in order to present the Synod in its true light before the Church and the world. Some years were spent in securing proper data or material for that purpose. Recourse was had to different sources, as, the Minutes of this Synod and of other Synods, as well as to some of the most reliable and intelligent members of the Church, who were present during the trials and conflicts which gave rise to its organization, and to other reliable sources. The object was to present the true, historical facts, in a fair, impartial manner, without any disposition to reflect unnecessarily on any one, or to perpetuate strife or contention. An honest, faithful statement seemed to be necessary in order to perpetuate the facts.

Whatever discrepancies may appear in some portions of this history, in regard to style, punctuation, &c., may be accounted for on the ground, that such portions were quoted in a general way, as they appeared on the records from which they were taken. The differences which appear in the elements and styles of the obituaries, result from the fact, that they are made up, with few exceptions, from the Minutes of Synod and church journals, nearly, in most instances, as their authors presented them.

In the preparation of this work, care was taken to give such facts and matters as are best calculated to promote the highest interests of the Church, and to give them due prominence in a plain, simple way. Facts and sound principles should be maintained and perpetuated. Truth is what is needed. There is too much cant, prevarication, and hypocrisy.

This work is now humbly submitted to an impartial public, to determine how well and faithfully its author has accomplished the object contemplated, with the hope, that it may prove a blessing in the department for which it is intended, and promote the best interests of the Redeemer's Kingdom.

S. H.

New Market, Va., 1890.

CONTENTS.

CHAPTER VI.

ITS POLICY.

CHAPTER VII.

ITS FUTURE.

HISTORY

OF THE

EVANGELICAL LUTHERAN

TENNESSEE SYNOD.

CHAPTER I.

THE CAUSES WHICH GAVE RISE TO ITS ORGANIZATION.

THE causes which gave rise to the organization of the Evangelical Lutheran Tennessee Synod, in the year 1820, will be found chiefly in the position which the Church occupied, at that time, in regard to doctrine and practice. Hence, it will be necessary, in the outset, to take a brief view of the condition of the Church, in these respects, during that period.

The most authentic records seem clearly to indicate that the Church generally adhered closely to the doctrines and principles of the Bible, as set forth and confessed in the Unaltered Augsburg Confession and her other Symbolical Books, until towards the close of the eighteenth and the beginning of the nineteenth century.

They were Lutherans,—just what their name indicated. The first Swedish colonists even, who settled in this country, based themselves firmly on the Augsburg Confession and Luther's Catechism. For a number of years every effort to preserve these doctrines in their purity and simplicity, was made. The instructions to the Governor were: "Before all, the Governor must labor and watch, that he render, in all things, to Almighty God, the true worship which is his due, the glory, the praise, and the homage that belong to him, and take good measures that the Divine service is performed according to the true Confession of Augsburg, the Council of Upsal, and the ceremonies of the Swedish Church, having care that all men, and especially the youth, be instructed in all parts of Christianity, and that a good ecclesiastical discipline be observed and maintained."—*Schaeffer's Early History, p. 15.*

In accepting the aid offered by the King of England and the English Society, the Salzburg refugees made it a condition, "that they should be protected in the free exercise of their holy religion, as contained in the Augsburg Confession, and the other Symbolical Books of the Evangelical Lutheran Church, of which they professed to be members."—*Dr. Mann's Lutheranism in America, p. 117.*

Neither did Muhlenberg and his co-laborers teach any other doctrines, nor endeavor to establish, in this country, any other system of faith, than that inculcated in the Lutheran Confessions and Catechisms. "The Lutheran Church in America was, from the beginning, built upon the old foundation of the Gospel, as interpreted by the collective body of the Symbolical Books; and ministers and parochial school-masters were required to preach and teach in accordance with them."—*Dr. Mann's Lutheranism in America, p. 112.*

"When St. Michael's Church, in Philadelphia, was founded, in 1743, it was publicly proclaimed: 'The corner-stone of this church has been laid, with the design that in it may be taught the Evangelical Lutheran doctrines, according to the apostles and prophets, as contained in the Unaltered Augsburg Confession, and all the other Symbolical Books.'"—*Halle Nachrichten, p. 288.*

"In the year 1748, the ordination of Rev. N. Kurtz occurred, the Swedish pastors joining in the performance of the solemn rite; but before it was performed, a declaration was exacted from the candidate 'that he would adhere to the pure doctrine of our Evangelical Church, according to the Word of God and our Confessions of Faith.' The year preceding, Brunnholz re-dedicated a church, as 'an Evangelical Lutheran Church, according to the foundation of the prophets and apostles, and our Symbolical Books.'"—*Halle Nachrichten, p. 252.*

"In 1760, Paul D. Pryzelius was admitted into the Synod, after having made the following declaration: 'I sincerely promise, before God, the Searcher of hearts, that I will teach nothing to my congregations, except what is well founded in the canonical books of the Old and New Testaments, and to conform, in all my sermons, and in all my public and private instructions of the Holy Sacraments, to our Symbolical Books.'"—*Halle Nachrichten, p. 856.*

"In 1761, Muhlenberg gave direction for the form of the deeds for the newly begun church at Barren Hill, to the effect that they be 'prepared in such a way as forever to devote the church to the Evangelical Lutheran doctrine, according to the foundation of the Apostles, and the teachings of the Unaltered Augsburg Confession.'"—*Halle Nachrichten, pp. 864 and 1182.*

"In the Constitution for the Philadelphia congregation (1762,) which became the model for many others, the first article required the minister to teach according to the Unaltered Augsburg Confession."—*Halle Nachrichten, p. 762.*

About the close of the eighteenth century and the beginning of the nineteenth, the fathers who had immigrated to this country, and done the hard and difficult work of the pioneer, had passed from this realm to that beyond the skies, to enjoy their rest and their rewards. Their fidelity to the Confessions of the Church and her Scriptural services, their arduous, conscientious, energetic labors in establishing and building congregations, their faithful Gospel preaching and careful catechetical instruction, their zealous family devotion, and their pious walk and conduct, had passed, and well nigh escaped the memory of the survivors.

Great political changes grew out of the results of the Revolutionary War. These, under the changed condition of things, together with other pernicious influences, which found their way into this country, proved disparaging to the Church and her work, leaving Christianity in a very precarious state, vacillating to and fro, with very little definite or fixed policy or principles. Under this new and unsettled condition of things, Liberty, Freedom, the all-absorbing element of that day, exaggerated and carried beyond its proper sphere or domain, resulted in ignoring almost every thing that was definite, fixed, or established. It seems, in fact, that there was scarcely any positive Christian faith really recognized, and that almost every trace of a true and living churchliness was obliterated.

Pietism and Rationalism prevailed to an alarming extent in Germany and other countries. The former, inaugurated by Spener,—a man of distinguished talents and rare learning,—for the purpose of reviving, in the Church, greater zeal for vital piety and practical Christianity, was afterwards carried beyond its contemplated object by Franke, a very zealous and able minister, and thus, amidst the agitation, it finally resulted in fanaticism, as well as in a perversion of many of the leading doctrines of the Church, and in ignoring, to a greater or less extent, her true Confessions.—*Kurtz's Church History, pp. 198, 199. 240.*

The controversy between the Orthodox and the Pietists concentrated especially around the doctrines of Regeneration, of Justification, of Sanctification, of the Church, and of the Millennium. Page 242. Some of the ministers who immigrated to this country were of the Halle, Frankean, Pietistic school, and they came imbued with that spirit, to some extent, and infused it in some parts of the Church; and, hence, it is, that we still see it occasionally cropping out, in certain sections, in its heterodox, fanatical elements.

The latter, Rationalism, in the language of Kurtz's Church History, p. 276, crept into the Protestant theology of the continent, especially of Germany. The extremes of Pietism, it appears, prepared the way for Rationalism, the other extreme. One extreme usually results in another, in the opposite direction. Fanaticism generally ends in skepticism. This pernicious, disturbing element, Rationalism, also found its way to North America, and exerted a very baneful influence over the people in regard to the teachings of the Bible, as presented in the Confessions of the Church. The tendency was to yield or compromise nearly everything that was positive or definite, until, as Dr. Krauth said, in speaking of the condition of the Evangelical Lutheran Church, at the close of the eighteenth and the beginning of the nineteenth century, "We had a weak, indecisive pulpit, feeble catechisms, vague hymns, and constitutions which reduced the minister to the position of a hireling talker, and made Synods disorganizations for the purpose of preventing anything from being done." Unionism followed in the wake.

On the 13th day of November, 1787, "The Corpus Evangelicum, or Unio Ecclesiastica," was organized in South Carolina, "composed of Lutheran and German Reformed ministers, together with lay-deputies from the churches belonging to both denominations."—*Bernheim's History, &c., p. 289.* But this organization did not long continue, as must be the case with any union not based on agreement in doctrine and principles. Failure and trouble are written on the face of any such attempt.

A few years after the death of Rev. Dr. Muhlenberg, which took place October 7, 1787, the Ministerium of Pennsylvania changed its confessional basis, to the disparagement of the Confessions. In a paper "on the Lutheran Church in America," Dr. Mann says: "While the constitution of the Ministerium of Pennsylvania, prepared under Muhlenberg's auspices, is based upon the Confessions of the Lutheran Church, in that published a few years after his death, they are entirely ignored;" and Lutheranism continued to degenerate more and more, till a reaction was brought about.

In the year 1817, a new hymn-book, called Gemeinschaftliche Gesangbuch, intended for the Lutheran and Reformed Churches, published by Schaeffer & Maund, of

Baltimore, Md., was introduced, and after examination by all the Lutheran and Reformed Synods in the United States of America, at that time, its use in all the congregations was authorized. See "*Comprehensive Account of the Rise and Progress of the Blessed Reformation of the Christian Church. By Dr. Martin Luther.*"* Prepared by Rev. G. Shober, of the North Carolina Synod. Pp. 146, 147.

In speaking of this new hymn-book, Rev. Shober says: "This meritorious undertaking paves the way to universal harmony, union, and love among our Lutheran and Reformed Churches, removing all the obstacles which hitherto prevented that happy effect, and establishes a uniformity in that part of divine worship which cannot fail to be highly gratifying to all those who consider brotherly love an indispensable attribute of Christianity."

No doubt, this insidious course produced, to a considerable extent, for the time being, the effect which the author of those lines so much desired,—for the songs and services used in worship exert great influence. But whilst it was doing this, it was aiding in engendering and cultivating a spirit which, as the child of an unjustifiable compromise of principles, ultimately resulted in ignoring some of the most vital and fundamental doctrines and elements of the Church, leaving her in that latitudinarian state of indifference and laxness in regard to almost every thing that was regarded as positive and definite, in which she appeared about the beginning of the nineteenth century, without helm or rudder,—a deplorable wreck, requiring years for its restoration.

It may not be inadmissible to call attention here to the great religious revival which swept over the United States in 1800 and 1801, not that the Evangelical Lutheran Church gave it any special countenance at that time,—at a

*If occasions for referring to the above work, in writing this history, present themselves, we shall indicate that work by the title, Luther, as "Luther" is the name which appears on the back of the book.

later period this delusive system or plan of operation was introduced in some portions of her territory,—but to show the unsettled, unchurchly state of religion, in general, in this country, at that time.

In regard to it, Rev. Storch, of North Carolina, writes: "By the side of this pestilence (infidelity), there prevails now, for over a year, a something, I know not what to name it, and I should not like to say *Fanaticism.* Christians of every denomination assemble themselves in the forest, numbering four, six and sometimes ten thousand persons; they erect tents, sing, pray, and preach, day and night, for five, six, and eight days. I have been an eye-witness to scenes in such large assemblies, which I cannot explain. I beheld young and old, feeble and strong, white and black, in short, people of every age, position, and circumstance, as though they were struck by lightning, speechless and motionless; and, when they had somewhat recovered, they could be heard shrieking bitterly, and supplicating God for mercy and grace.

"After they had thus spent three, and many even more, hours, they rose up, praised God, and commenced to pray in such a manner, as they never were wont to do, exhorting sinners to come to Jesus, &c. Many of those who were thus exercised, were ungodly persons before, and we can now discover a remarkable change in them. Even deists have been brought to confess Christ in this way. Thus this thing continues even to this hour.

"Opinions are various in regard to it; many, even ministers, denominate it the work of the devil; others again would explain it in a natural way, or in accordance with some physical law; whilst others look upon it as the work of God."—*Rev. Dr. Bernheim's History of the Lutheran Church in the Carolinas, pp. 351, 353.*

In the Minutes of a Conference, held in Rader's Church, Rockingham County, Virginia, in 1806, Rev. Paul Henkel says relative to this revival:

"Towards the close of the year 1801, there occurred a mighty waking up of religion among the English people in Guilford and Orange Counties, N. C., which caused our German people to understand the true worth of the Gospel. Both the pastors and their people were surprised; for it appeared exceedingly strange to those who were well acquainted with the order of salvation, that true conversion should consist in such a way as declared by these people; that true faith should originate in such sermons, as caused such corporeal convulsions, such representations of the devil, death, and hell; the fearful and awful expressions of lightning, thunder, hail, fire, and brimstone against the sinner, deprived many of their senses, and prostrated them in fainting fits.

"As the like proceedings were upheld and defended by so many English preachers, and as many had declared that by means of such workings they had received true and reliable witness of the pardon of their sins and of the new birth, many of us hesitated to contradict such proceedings, although they were thought to be so contrary to the doctrines of the Gospel. Many passages of Scripture were pointed out as opposed to these outward manifestations; but many good meaning persons defended them as Scriptural, whereupon the important question arose among them: 'Must we not also experience the same thing in order to be saved?' The people became anxious and concerned, were much affected and distressed, and pressed upon their pastors to decide this matter for them, who were unwilling to do this without due consideration and the fullest assurance.

"The German ministers were at first divided in their opinions on this subject; nevertheless, it drove them to more intimate communion with each other in their official acts, and they have thus the opportunity to investigate this matter more closely."

This course of procedure, that is, this revival theory, also had a tendency to divert the mind from the regular Means of Grace as set forth in the Word of God, as well as from a reliance on the promises contained in Divine Revelation, to a dependence on the feelings or emotions, for salvation, thus disparaging, to a greater or less extent, the true doctrines of the Holy Scriptures, and leaving the Church in a state of distraction, in regard to some of the most vital features of sound Scriptural theology.

In the year 1794, Robert Johnson Miller,—a licentiate of the Methodist Episcopal Conference,—was ordained, by Lutheran pastors, of Cabarrus and Rowan Counties, North Carolina, on petition from White Haven Church, Lincoln County, North Carolina, really as a minister of the Protestant Episcopal Church in America, under obligations always to obey the Rules, Ordinances, and Customs of that Society of Christians; as his ordination certificate will show,—on the opposite side of which the Lutheran ministers give their reasons for ordaining a man who was attached to the Episcopal Church, as a minister of that denomination.—See *Bernheim's History of the Lutheran Church in the Carolinas, pp. 338, 339.*

As such, he labored in connection with the Lutherans of North Carolina, and after the organization of the Evangelical Lutheran Synod in that State, in 1803, he continued to labor in that Synod till 1821, when he severed that connection, and was ordained in Raleigh, N. C., to deacon's and priest's orders in the Episcopal ministry. In his former connection, even as an Episcopalian, he labored for a period of twenty-seven years.

According to the Journal of the Episcopal North Carolina Convention of 1818, it seems that previous to the year 1816, there was no Episcopal clergyman in that State, and but one congregation in which the worship of that church was performed. Hence it was, that the said Miller thought it his duty to form a temporary connection with the Lutheran Church. He was a man of quite respectable attainments, energy, zeal, and perseverance, and did much missionary work among the Lutherans. But it is not unreasonable to conclude that such connection and policy had a tendency to looseness in doctrine and practice, as well as to unionism.

In 1821, a move was made to effect a fraternal union between the North Carolina Synod and the Protestant Episcopal Convention of North Carolina. At the Episcopal Convention, held in Raleigh, April 28, 1821, which Rev. Robert J. Miller attended with a view to connect himself fully with the Episcopal Church, "to which he really belonged, having been ordained by Lutheran ministers of North Carolina, as an Episcopal minister, and was the pastor of an Episcopal congregation, White Haven Church, in Lincoln County," he proposed the establishment of such a union. His proposition was accepted, and received the proper action on the part of the Episcopal Convention, to consummate the contemplated union. At its meeting in Lau's Church, Guilford County, North Carolina, June 17, 1821, the Lutheran North Carolina Synod accepted the proposition, and the delegates of the Episcopal Convention being present, the union was completed. At the next Episcopal Convention, held in Raleigh, April 18, 1822, the proceedings were ratified. But it seems this union did not long continue. "For, after the year 1823, nothing more appears concerning the fraternal relations of these two bodies."—See *Bernheim's History, &c., p. 457.*

In 1810, Gottlieb Shober, a Moravian, was ordained by the Lutheran Synod of North Carolina, but it seems, that, in some way, he also retained his connection with the Moravians. He resided all his life in Salem, North Carolina, and labored in some Lutheran churches in its vicinity.—In regard to him, Bernheim's History, pp. 441, 442, says: "Rev. Shober was no Lutheran, he was a member of the Moravian Church, and never disconnected himself from communion with the same; he lived and died as a member of that church. This information the writer received from his own daughter, the widow of Bishop Herrman. He merely served the Lutheran Church in the capacity of one of its ministers, being pastor of several neglected Lutheran congregations in the vicinity of his place of residence." It is not unnatural to conclude, that such connection and labor would ultimately result, to some extent, in disintegration and disturbance.

During the meeting of the Evangelical Lutheran Synod of North Carolina, in 1816, it was resolved that the Secretary, Rev. Shober, "compile all the rules adopted by this Synod, and publish them in the English language." In accordance with this resolution, the secretary prepared and laid before Synod in 1817, a manuscript compilation entitled: "Comprehensive Account of the Rise and Progress of the blessed Reformation of the Christian Church, By Dr. Martin Luther, actually begun on the 31st day of October, A. D., 1517; interspersed with views of his character and doctrine, extracted from his books; and how the Church, established by him, arrived and progressed in North America,—as also, the Constitution and Rules of that Church, in North Carolina and adjoining States, as existing in October, 1817."

This work also contains a translation of twenty-two articles of the Augsburg Confession. The translation used, is, according to a statement made by Rev. Dr. Beale M. Schmucker, in a little work entitled, "English Translations of the Augsburg Confession," that of Dr. E. L. Hazelius, with all its omissions and notes. In the tenth article, the word *true* is omitted, and the article is accompanied with a foot-note, which perverts the true sense, and so modifies it, as to make it acceptable to the various denominations; and so too, in regard to the eleventh article. Really, the translation is very defective.

According to the first article of the Constitution of the North Carolina Synod, as presented in that book, the first twenty-one articles of this translation of the Augsburg Confession, are made the point of union, and the ministers entering that Synod were pledged to the same.

In that book, the Rules, made by that Synod in 1817, for its government, appear. In the eleventh one of these

Rules, page 172, the New York Liturgy is designated as one of the Symbolical Books of the North Carolina Synod.

Whilst that work, compiled by Rev. G. Shober, approved by the North Carolina Synod, and familiarly called "Luther," conforms in some respects to sound Lutheran principles, its general tone and tenor are compromising and unionistic, with a tendency to latitudinarianism and looseness in doctrine, rather ignoring the true Confessions of the Church, and disparaging her distinctive features, with a view to effect a kind of general, fraternal union with the different denominations. This is evident from the following remarks which the author, Rev. Shober, makes in the conclusion of his book, called Luther, page 210:

"I have attentively examined the doctrine of the Episcopalian church, and read many excellent authors of the Presbyterians, know the Methodist doctrine from their book, 'Portraiture of Methodism,' and am acquainted with the Baptist doctrine so far as they admit and adore Jesus the Savior.

"Among all those classes who worship Jesus as a God, I see nothing of importance to prevent a cordial union; and how happy would it be if all the churches could unite, and send deputies to a general meeting of all denominations, and there sink down upon the rock Jesus, and, at the same time, leaving to each their peculiar mode and form; this would influence all the Christians to love one another when and whersoever they meet, and they would commune together."

Again, pages 211, 212, he says:

"I think my sentiments and experiences are as orthodox and Calvinistical as need be, and yet I am a sort of speckled bird among my Calvinist brethren. I am a mighty good church man, but pass among such as a Dissenter *in prunello.* On the other hand, the Dissenters, many of them I mean, think me defective either in understanding or in conscience, for staying where I am. Well, there is a middle party, called Methodists, but neither do my dimensions exactly fit them; I am somehow disqualified for claiming a full brotherhood with any party; but there are a few among all parties who bear with me, and love me, and with this I must be content at present."

It requires no great acuteness to see how such loose, unguarded sentiments vitiated and corrupted the Church, and how they soon afterwards began to crop out everywhere, and still come to the surface in some sections.

Now, in view of all these vitiating, corrupting, and disintegrating influences which were brought to bear on the Church during that period, it takes no very great stretch of mind to see the indefinite, unsettled, lax, disintegrated, and dilapidated condition of the Church in regard to doctrine and practice at the time of the rupture in the North Carolina Synod, in the year 1820. Nor is it any wonder that, in view of such influences, such a state of disintegration and dilapidation should exist, and result in the trials and troubles which followed. For, at that time, according to all the facts in the case, there was not a Synod in North America that unreservedly recognized and acknowledged the full, Unaltered Augsburg Confession, much less the other Symbolical Books.

In view of such compromising, unionistic proclivities and unchurchly deviations and divergencies, differences in regard to doctrine and practice arose among some of the ministers of the North Carolina Synod, and they were more and more agitated. There were conflicts in the pulpit, in the congregation, and in the family. One of the leading ministers charged Rev. David Henkel with teaching doctrines contrary to the position of the Church. To defend himself against such unfounded charges, the latter appealed to a Latin copy of the Book of Concord, which he had in possession. That gave him a decided advantage, in some respects, in the estimation of many of the people, who were not willing to acquiesce in the extreme, latitudinarian views inculcated by the former. To counteract this increasing advantage, that minister called into question the correctness of these translations from the Latin. This proved disparaging for a while, but soon afterwards Rev. David Henkel happened to come across a German copy of the Book of Concord, at the residence of a German in South Carolina, with whom he spent a night or two. After much persuasion, the German let him have the book. This he brought with him, rejoicing in his good fortune to get it, to North Carolina.—This he presented, to sustain the correctness of his translations made from the Latin copy of his Book of Concord. For, this the people could read and understand for themselves, and finding that his translations from the Latin copy referred to, were correct, many of the members of the Church took a decided stand in favor of him and his positions, and faithfully defended him and his doctrines against the innovations and false charges of his opponents.

The council of the congregation met, and after considering the matter, one of the Elders, Capt. John Stirewalt, father of the late Rev. Jacob Stirewalt, presented the Book of Concord to the minister, saying, We want to know whether you intend to preach according to this book, in the future. The minister hesitated and evaded, but being pressed, he raised the book up and brought it down on the table, saying, From this day henceforth, I will not: it is nothing but a controversial book. Mr. Stirewalt then raised the book up, and brought it down on the table, saying, From this day henceforth, you won't be our preacher.

The differences in doctrine becoming more apparent, the controversies and conflicts assuming a wider range and more formidable aspects, effecting some of the more vital doctrines of the Church, and the authority of her Confessions being called into question, furnished occasion for rupture and schism, and gave rise to the chief causes or reasons which ultimately resulted in the organization of the Evangelical Lutheran Tennessee Synod; and all that was wanting to bring about the final rupture was a suitable opportunity. The elements were at work, and the opportunity for separation was not long delayed.

In 1818, no Synod was held, in consequence of the fact, that as the Synod, at its session in October, 1817, had, according to its constitution, adopted at that term, changed the time for its annual meetings from October to Trinity Sunday in each year, it was deemed unnecessary to meet in 1818, so soon after the meeting in October, 1817.

Dr. Bernheim, in his History, p. 435, says: "This time of meeting was '*firmly fixed*' (vest gesetzt)." Hence, on account of this change as to the time for the meeting of this Synod being *firmly*, unchangeably fixed, the Synod adjourned to meet on Trinity Sunday, 1819.

During the period of nineteen months which intervened between the meeting in October, 1817, and that appointed for Trinity Sunday, 1819, there was no opportunity for any united, official efforts to calm the conflicting elements in regard to differences in doctrine; and, hence, the breach grew wider and wider.

But notwithstanding the Synod, in its constitution, adopted October, 1817, had changed the time for its regular annual meetings from October to Trinity Sunday in each year, and *firmly fixed* that as the time; notwithstanding it had adjourned to meet on Trinity Sunday, 1819; and notwithstanding the fact that on that day a considerable number of candidates for the ministry were, according to previous resolution of Synod, to be consecrated, the Synod was convened, without regard to the ordination of these candidates, five or six weeks sooner than the time designated in the constitution for the meeting of the Synod, to which Synod had adjourned to meet.

The reasons assigned for this unconstitutional change were, that a communication had been received by the Secretary of the North Carolina Synod from the Secretary of the Ministerium of Pennsylvania, to the effect that there was a general desire among its ministers to effect a more general union, and that as the next meeting of the Ministerium of Pennsylvania was to convene in Baltimore, Md., on Trinity Sunday, 1819,—the same day on which the North Carolina

Synod was to meet,—it was necessary,—if the North Carolina Synod desired to take part, through a delegate or delegates, in considering the propriety of such a move,—to convene the North Carolina Synod sooner than the constitutional time.

Hence it was, that a portion of the ministers of the North Carolina Synod, who were in favor of, possibly, a more general union than the ministers of the Pennsylvania Synod contemplated, even of the different Protestant denominations, according to Rev. Shober's ideas which have been already stated, after some consultation, requested the "President, with the consent of two or three ordained ministers residing in the vicinity," to convene the Synod before the time fixed in the constitution. The interval between the time when the call was made and that of the meeting, was too short to enable ministers at a distance to reach the place of meeting.* At this meeting, Rev. Shober was elected as a delegate to represent the North Carolina Synod in the meeting which took place in Baltimore in 1819. This meeting of the North Carolina Synod was afterwards called the "untimely" or called meeting.

When the time fixed in the constitution of the Synod for its regular meeting, to which the previous regular Synod had adjourned, namely, Trinity Sunday, 1819, came, a minister of Tennessee and several of North Carolina, together with a number of lay-delegates, met at the place appointed for the meeting of Synod, and not finding the President there, the minister from Tennessee sent one of his associates, accompanied by one of the elders of the congregation, to see the President, who was only several miles distant from the church, with a written request that he should come to the church, in order that everything might be arranged and done in a regular, orderly manner. The

---

*In fact, some of the ministers knew nothing of this meeting, or "untimely" Synod, as it was afterwards called, until after it was all over.

President replied that he was not very well, and if he were, he would not go, remarking that the Synod had been already held, and that there was no need for holding it over, or again. He also commanded his Elders not to open the church; yet after the messengers reasoned with him awhile relative to the matter, he agreed that the church might be opened for preaching, but not for any synodical business. At the appointed time the church was opened, and the regular services were conducted and a sermon was preached, after which the Synod met under several shade trees near by, and there being three petitions in due form from Rev. David Henkel's congregations presented, earnestly requesting his ordination to the office of pastor, his lay-delegates demanding it in accordance with the resolution passed at the previous meeting of the Synod, in which it was resolved or ordered, that he and a number of other candidates for the office of the ministry, who had sustained their examinations and were approved, should be ordained at the next meeting of Synod, on Trinity Sunday, 1819. He and another one of that number of candidates who was present, were ordained, in a regular, orderly manner, according to the custom of the Church and the resolution of the Synod.

But afterwards, it seems, some of the ministers who were so strongly in favor of a general union among all Protestant denominations, began to call into question the validity of Rev. David Henkel's ordination, and to invalidate it, whilst they recognized that of the other candidate who was ordained with him at the same time and under the same circumstances. But the other party sustained the ordination of the said David Henkel, asserting that it had taken place strictly in accordance with the act or resolution of the previous regular Synod, which provided for its performance on "next Trinity," 1819, and according to the regulations of the Church. The opposite party, however, contended that the word "Trinity" did not stand in connection with that action or resolution of Synod which appears in the book called "Luther," by Rev. G. Shober, but that the time for ordination was left blank. An examination of the book was demanded, and when it was opened at the place, the word Trinity did not appear at first. But some of those who vindicated the validity of the ordination in question having previously detected the fact that a little piece of blank paper had been pasted over the word Trinity, by some one whom they knew not, after the book was printed and before it was distributed or circulated, as they presumed, took a knife and removed the little paper, and the word Trinity appeared at the right place, in connection with the act or resolution of Synod. After this occurrence, it is stated, that very little more was said about the validity of that ordination. Some of these books are still in existence, with the paper on the word Trinity.

Whilst it is unpleasant to make these statements relative to that ordination, and whilst there is no disposition to reflect on any one, fidelity to the facts demands it.

The controversies in regard to doctrinal differences grew more intense, and assumed a wider range. Strong opposition to the move for the organization of a general union, including different Protestant denominations, which failed in the meeting in Baltimore, Md., on Trinity Sunday, 1819, and resulted in the establishment of the Northern General Synod, at Hagerstown, Md., October 24, 1820, which also afterwards met with opposition on account of its failure to adopt a well defined Doctrinal or Confessional Basis, was worked up and prevailed to a considerable extent.

The persons who became the leaders in these conflicts or differences in doctrine and policy, were Rev. Gottlieb Shober on the part of the unionists and Rev. David Henkel on that of the anti-unionists. The opportunity for the final rupture or separation was furnished during the meeting of the North Carolina Synod, which convened in Lincolnton, Lincoln County, North Carolina, May 28, 1820.

Rev. Dr. Bernheim gives the following description of

these men in his History of the Lutheran Church in the Carolinas, pp. 441, 442, 443:

"Rev. Shober was a man of decided opinions, unyielding in everything which he considered right, as may be seen from a sketch of his life in the Evangelical Review, vol. viii., pp. 412–414; 'with a mind that knew no dissimulation, a lofty independence, an ardent temper, and a character decidedly affirmative, he frequently experienced difficulties and encountered points other than pleasant in his pilgrimage through life, and which a disposition more pliant could have averted.'

"'The lineaments of his countenance gave indications of a strong and active mind.' 'He was one of the most active defenders of (the) General Synod, as he had also been prominent among its early founders.' But Rev. Shober was no Lutheran, he was a member of the Moravian Church, and never disconnected himself from communion with the same; he lived and died as a member of that Church. This information the writer received from his own daughter, the widow of Bishop Herrman. He merely served the Lutheran Church in the capacity of one of its ministers, being the pastor of several neglected Lutheran congregations in the vicinity of his place of residence, Salem, N. C. It may be readily perceived that no compromise could be expected on his part in the difficulties which distracted the Lutheran Church at that time.

"Firm as was the Rev. G. Shober, he found his equal in that respect in Rev. David Henkel, who, though a young man then, was equally as decided and unyielding in his opinions. He was a hard student and well educated, not only in the German and English languages, but also in Latin, Greek, Hebrew, and Theology, all of which he had principally acquired by private study and close application. He was the best informed candidate for the ministry the North Carolina Synod had at that time, and wielded even then a considerable influence in the Church. It is not to be supposed that he would readily yield his opinions to others, or permit himself to be led about at the will of even those who were older than himself, when he believed his cause to be just. In him the Tennessee Synod had a champion who could not be easily overcome. He had a mind that was clear, active, and penetrating; he was quick in discerning an advantage, and not slow in making use of it. These characteristics are gathered principally from his own writings."

When the North Carolina Synod met in regular convention, in Lincolnton, Lincoln County, North Carolina, May 28, 1820, well represented by ministers and lay-delegates, especially of that State, it seems, the occasion and causes for a rupture were fully matured, and the much lamented and deplored separation took place.

The unionistic party, it appears, claiming that they had a majority, made no proposition to the other party, to investigate and adjust the difficulties and differences according to the teachings of the Holy Scriptures, in a friendly, Christian manner, but before they approached the other party who were at the church, they sent one of their ministers to one of the ministers of that party, with two questions. The first one was: "Will you withdraw from the Synod?" The second one was: "Will you submit to the decision of the majority of the ministers and lay-delegates, relative to the controversies and differences?" To these questions no decisive reply was made. He then went to the friends of his opponent and asked the same questions, which they answered in writing, stating: "We will not withdraw from the Synod, nor will we be ruled by a majority, but are ready and willing to investigate and decide every thing according to the teachings of the Augsburg Confession and the Constitution of the Synod, but not otherwise?"

After all his opponents had gathered together, he again approached them, and demanded an oral or verbal answer to the same questions. The questions were answered according to his request. To this answer, he replied with a defiant mien, in a domineering tone: "That is not the thing. I only ask, Will you, or will you not?" They replied, "We will not." He then said: "This is all I want to know," and quickly turned around, and briskly walked away. Then he and his friends came and presented the same questions, and received the same reply as that given before. Their leader then attempted to show, that the Synod was not bound to any fixed or definite regulation, according to which controversies or differences are to be decided, but that such things are to be decided only according to the majority of the votes of the ministers and lay-delegates, and claimed, that they had the majority, and that it is reasonable and just, that their opponents should be thus governed in these matters, but the other party contended, that the doctrines of the Augsburg Confession, which they felt certain could be proved to be in accord with the teachings of the Bible, ought to be of greater consideration, than is the majority of the votes of persons, who are opposed to the doctrines and regulations of the Church.

After a short interchange of words of a similar character, the unionistic party went into the church, and were followed by the other party. The President then delivered a long discourse in the German language, to show what he had heretofore sought to maintain. He was followed by the Secretary in a still longer one, in the English language, in which he endeavored to show, that the Synod was by no means bound, to act according to the Constitution or Regulation of the Synod; and, notwithstanding the fact, that he himself had compiled the work and had it printed, according to resolution and the approbation of the Synod, he still contended, that it was not the intention, that it should be a rule or standard, according to which the members of Synod should be governed in their transactions. He claimed, that it was only a kind of plan or form, which, in the course of time, if deemed necessary, in the future, might be formed or arranged into a rule of order, but for the present, no one needs any thing of the kind.

But the other party showed from the Church Regulation itself, that it was accepted as such a work, having been first examined by a committee of ministers appointed by Synod, and favorably recommended, and afterwards approved by Synod, and handed over for publication.

In regard to this, he replied, that it was not so intended, and, that, for the want of time, he had written it hurriedly and inconsiderately, without previously investigating it properly; hence, every thing must now be regulated and determined by the majority.

The other party regarded that construction of the matter as very singular and unsatisfactory, in view of the fact, that the work was published, on the order and approbation of the Synod, and that an amount of money sufficient to pay for printing and binding 1,500 copies of the work, at a cost of 75 cents per copy, was taken out of the Treasury.

The controversy now turned more directly to differences in doctrine. Some of the unionistic party called into question, and even denied, some of the doctrines clearly taught in the Augsburg Confession; while on the other hand, the other party defended the teachings of said Confession with zeal and earnestness.

In the midst of the discussion of these subjects, so vitally important, one of the officers of the Synod, who was so enthusiastic in regard to his idea of a general union, exclaimed: "Whoever is a right Lutheran, let him follow us out to J. H.'s hotel,"—this was John Harry's hotel,—"there we will begin our Synod!" A reply came from the other side: "Whoever is a real fanatic" (Schwarmer), "let him follow; for you are no true Lutheran preachers; you are fanatics, and to such you belong." They then left the church and went to the hotel, leaving the other party in the church, and there commenced their Synod.*

*It is hardly just to conclude that all those who followed out were in full sympathy with this move and the doctrines of the leader, but were carried along rather by the force of circumstances and their situations.

Those who remained in the church, after some deliberation and consultation, adjourned; and, on the 17th of July of the same year, they, with others, met again in Solomon's Church, Cove Creek, Green County, Tennessee, to organize a synod according to the teachings and doctrines of the Church.

These statements and historical facts are derived from the Minutes of the first meeting of the Evangelical Lutheran Tennessee Synod, which were not printed till 1821, and from intelligent men of irreproachable character and standing, who were present and witnessed the whole procedure.

The chief doctrines about which these conflicting parties differed were, first, in regard to Original Sin; second, The Person and Nature of Christ; third, Baptism; fourth, The Lord's Supper; and strange as it may seem, these very differences still occasionally crop out in some sections of the Church. So deeply was that Pietistical element infused, that it has required much time and patience, and still requires much vigilance, to keep it from coming to the surface too frequently.

It is true, efforts have been made to make it appear that personal difficulties were among the first causes which gave rise to the rupture. The facts will not justify such a conclusion. For these did not occur till after many of the conflicts in regard to differences in doctrine and practice had taken place and been agitated. The truth is, the personal matters referred to by some were not between ministers, but between one minister and a member of the German Reformed Church. That idea seems rather to grow out of an after-thought, to palliate.

CHAPTER II.

THE ORGANIZATION AND NAME OF THE SYNOD.

First Session.

AN open rupture having taken place, on account of differences in doctrine and practice, in the North Carolina Synod, at its meeting in Lincolnton, Lincoln County, North Carolina, May 28, 1820, and those who advocated and favored the *new-measure*, unionistic policy, having withdrawn from the church, as indicated in the preceding chapter of this work, the others, who had determined to adhere closely to the doctrines and principles of the Church, as set forth in her Confessional Writings, after some consultation and deliberation, adjourned, and with others, afterwards, met in Solomon's Church, Cove Creek, Green County, Tennessee, July 17, 1820, to organize a conference or synod, in accordance with the teachings, doctrines, and policy of the Word of God, as set forth in the Confessions of the Evangelical Lutheran Church. This was a time for serious consideration, meditation, and prayer.

The following ministers and lay-delegates were present, on that occasion: Revs. Jacob Zink, of Washington County, Virginia; Paul Henkel, of New Market, Shenandoah County, Virginia; Adam Miller, of Sullivan County, Tennessee; Philip Henkel, of Green County, Tennessee; George Esterly (Easterly), of Green County, Tennessee; and David Henkel, of Lincoln County, North Carolina, who, although he could not be present in person, acquiesced in the object of the meeting, and was recognized as a member. The lay-delegates representing congregations were, from Emmanuel Church, Washington County, Tennessee, John Keicher and Conrad Keicher; from Union Church in the same County and State, Michael Kapp; from Jacob's Church, Green County, Tennessee, John Nehs (Neas), John Ottinger,

Philip Esterly, and John Renner; from Sinking Spring Church, in the same County and State, John Bauer, Frederick Schaeffer, Peter Gabel, and Jacob Hermann; from Solomon's Church, Cove Creek, same County and State, Frederick Gottschall, John Koch, Philip Ebert, and John Froschaur; from three congregations in Sullivan County, Tennessee, Henry Herchelroth and Jacob Deck; from Golden Spring Church, Green County, Tennessee, Nicholas Eley and George Boessinger.

The meeting was opened in a regular, churchly manner, with singing and prayer.

After the adoption of the following basis and regulations, an organization was effected, under the name and title of the Evangelical German Lutheran Tennessee Conference or Synod:

Basis and Regulations.

1. It is deemed proper and useful, that all the business and work, which may come before this Conference or Synod, shall be transacted in the German language; and all the written proceedings in regard to its transactions, which pertain to the general interest, shall be published in the German language.*

2. All teachings relative to the faith, and all doctrines concerning Christian conduct, as well as all books publicly used in the Church in the service or worship of God, shall be arranged and kept, as nearly as it is possible to do, in accordance with the doctrines of the holy Scriptures and

*The reason why we desire an entirely German Conference, is because we have learned from experience, that a conference, in which both languages, the German and the English, are used, the one or the other side will be dissatisfied. If the German is used, the English will understand little, and often nothing in regard to the matter; and if the English is employed, many of the Germans will not understand more than the half of what is said, and hence know not how to act relative to the most weighty matters. Besides, at the present time, we find very few entirely English preachers who accept the doctrines of our Church, or desire to preach them.

the Augsburg Confession. And especially shall the young, and others who need it, be instructed in Luther's Small Catechism, according to the custom of our Church, hitherto. This said Catechism shall always be the chief catechism in our churches. But the Catechism styled the Christian Catechism, which was published in the German and English languages, in New Market, Shenandoah County, Virginia, may also be used in connection, to explain Luther's Catechism.

3. No one can be a teacher or otherwise an officer in the Church, who has not been received into the congregation, according to the order of the Church, and does not lead a Christian life. Whoever desires to be a teacher, shall also take a solemn obligation, that he will teach according to the Word of God and the Augsburg Confession and the doctrines of our Church. Nor can any teacher in our Conference be allowed to stand in connection with any organization in connection with the so-called Central or General Synod, for reasons which shall hereafter be indicated.

4. None shall be members of our churches, except such as have been baptized according to the command of Christ, and confirmed, by the imposition of hands, according to the order of the Christian Church, and participate in the celebration of the Holy Supper.*

5. As to the ranks and grades in the office of teaching, or the ministry, we acknowledge not more than two as necessary for the preservation and perpetuation of the Church; namely, Pastor and Deacon. Pastor is an evangelical teacher, who executes that office fully in all its parts, or performs all the ministerial acts. Such person must be ordained with prayer and the imposition of hands, by one or more pastors, to such office. Besides, he must then also

* If, however, any one, who has been baptized according to the command of Christ, and confirmed to some Christian Church, and can make this appear, desires to commune with us, or to be received into connection with our Church, he shall be permitted to do so, without being re-baptized or re-confirmed.

solemnly affirm, that he will faithfully, according to the Word of God and the doctrines of our Church, perform the duties of that office.

6. A Deacon is also indeed a servant in the Word of God; but he is not fully invested with the ministerial office like the Pastor is. But he is to give instructions in the catechism, read sermons, attend to funerals, admonish, and, if desired, in the absence of the Pastor, to baptize children. He must be an orderly member of the Church, and have the evidence of a Christian conduct. He must, at the desire of the church council, be examined as to his fitness for office by the Synod, and if he is found qualified, he must be consecrated and ordained to that office with prayer and the imposition of hands, by one or more pastors, either at Conference or in one of the congregations in which he labors. Besides, he shall also make a solemn affirmation, in the presence of the whole congregation, that he will faithfully serve in that office according to the instructions given him. But if such Deacon prove so industrious or assiduous in his office as to reach the required attainments and qualifications to bear the office of Pastor, and secures a regular call from one or more vacant congregations, he can be consecrated and ordained to the office of Pastor in the same manner as already indicated.

In regard to the offices in the congregations, they shall be as they were heretofore customary in our Church: Elders, Deacons, &c.

7. At each Conference, pastors shall be named or elected who shall conduct the ordinations, and sign with their own hands all ordination certificates and affix their seals, and see that good order is maintained. They shall also sign all other proceedings of the Conference or Synod; and if for any reason it is desired, all the other pastors and the lay-delegates may also sign them. The preachers and lay-delegates may find it good or useful to appoint or name one of the pastors as chairman, who shall read all that is necessary, make propositions, &c. In the same manner may

one be appointed as secretary. But it is not to be understood that these must serve in these positions throughout all the sessions. Changes can be made, and others can serve, as circumstances require.

8. It was resolved, that annually, on the third Sunday of the month, October, a meeting of Conference shall be held, in the State of Tennessee, or in the western part of Virginia, at such place as the majority of the preachers and lay-delegates indicate. But if it should be deemed necessary, that the said Conference should meet in an adjoining State, it may be held in such State. But the Conference or Synod shall always retain the name Tennessee Conference or Synod; although it may have ministers and lay-delegates also in other States.

9. The Conference shall be composed of preachers and lay-delegates elected by their congregations, as has been the order heretofore, in similar cases; but there shall not be more votes cast by the lay-delegates, than the number of preachers present is. The surplus delegates may be present, and consult and advise with the others.

10. The necessity for each congregation to have a treasury for itself, in which to deposit all the money that each member or other person may freely give, will manifest itself to all. Such moneys shall be used to defray the cost of printing the minutes of the Conference, to aid traveling ministers, and for other purposes which will best enhance the interests of the churches or congregations. The way and manner, in which these treasuries are to be kept, and the disbursements, are to be made, are to be left to the good judgment of the church councils and the ministers acquiescing. The moneys may be gathered at every meeting, each month, or every three months. At every meeting of Conference, the council of each church shall make a report of the amounts thus collected. A treasury for the Conference, is, at this time, deemed unnecessary.

11. It will be found useful for every minister to keep a

record of the number he baptizes, the number of confirmations, and of communicants and funerals, as well as of the German schools in his congregations, so that they may appear in the proceedings of the Conference each year.

12. We also deem it of the highest importance to use all possible diligence to make our children acquainted with all our doctrines in faith, in the German language ; so that we may the more easily give them instruction therein ; and so that the parents especially may be careful to teach their children in regard to these things.

13. None of the teachers of our Conference can take a seat and vote in the present Synod of the State of North Carolina, because we cannot regard it as a true Lutheran Synod.

14. The propriety of preserving and maintaining these principles and regulations of Conference, as here set forth, and of acting according to them, must be apparent to all.—But if, at any meeting in the future, anything may be necessary to be added, it may be done, by a majority of the votes, but in such a manner as not to come in conflict with the design and intention of the foregoing principles.

The name Tennessee was not intended to indicate boundary, but to distinguish this Conference or Synod from other Synods already in existence ; as, the Pennsylvania Synod, the New York, the Maryland, the North Carolina, and the Ohio Synods, and especially the North Carolina Synod. This is evident from statements in its own proceedings, where it is said, "If it become necessary, this Conference or Synod may be held in adjoining States. Again, in the proceedings of its eighth session, in 1827, during which its basis was revised and improved, to make it more clear and simple, it is stated, "This body shall continue to bear the title Evangelical Lutheran Tennessee Synod. But this title shall not be so construed as to give the members who reside in Tennessee any prerogatives or advantages over others ; for this body consists for the most part of members in other States ; but it shall bear this title simply to distinguish it from the North Carolina Synod, which belongs to the General Synod." See Minutes of 1827, page 22.

At first the German language alone was used in the transactions of the Synod, in view of the fact that nearly all the ministers, as well as a large portion of the lay-members, at that time, used that language. At a later date the English language was introduced.

Thus, after agreeing on a basis and regulations, the Conference proceeded to the transaction of such other business as was deemed necessary.

It then set forth its reasons for organizing this Synod. These reasons are based chiefly on the differences in doctrine, as already indicated in the first chapter of this work. Then follows a Dissertation on Holy Baptism, relative to the differences between the conflicting parties, in regard to that subject.

In its proceedings, appears also the constitution or plan of the General Synod, accompanied with objections to, and criticisms on, every article. Then follows a paper, signed by several Evangelical Lutheran ministers, of the State of Ohio, and others, showing why they cannot endorse or adopt the plan or constitution of the General Synod. And finally, appears the Unaltered Augsburg Confession, in its twenty-eight articles, in the German,—perhaps, among the first editions, if not the first edition, ever printed in the United States, in the German language, in its twenty-eight articles.

Among the proceedings of this meeting, we note the following:

1. A resolution, making it the duty of one of the older ministers of that body, annually to visit all the congregations in its connection, in order to look into their condition, and to give wholesome instructions to the younger teachers or ministers and their congregations, as well as cordial admonitions, and to report the result of his visits to the next meeting of Synod.

2. In regard to a petition from a number of persons residing in Cape Cheredo, Missouri, asking a visit on the part of one of the ministers, it was resolved, that Rev. Jacob Zink visit that section as soon as possible and administer to their spiritual wants.

3. That the next meeting of this Conference be held in one of Rev. Adam Miller's congregations, in Sullivan County, Tennessee, beginning on the third Sunday of October, 1821.

4. Jacob Zink and Adam Miller were ordained by the imposition of hands and with prayer.

After regular services and preaching, the Conference adjourned to meet at the time and place indicated.

Thus, among great trials, difficulties, and anxieties, this Synod was organized, and took its position in the Church, depending on its great Head, to guide it in its efforts to maintain, promulgate, and perpetuate the Scriptural, churchly principles and doctrines it so earnestly loved, and to enable it to fill its mission with honor and abiding success.

CHAPTER III.

ITS POSITION AND CONFESSIONAL BASIS.

NOTWITHSTANDING the fact that at the time this Synod was organized, there was probably not a Synod in the United States of America that unreservedly received and acknowledged the Unaltered Augsburg Confession as its confessional basis, nevertheless this Synod laid down the following basis, requiring its ministers or officials in the Church, to make a sacred affirmation, to teach in accordance with it:

1. All doctrines of faith and teachings in regard to Christian conduct, as well as all books used in the public services of the Church, shall be so formulated and arranged as to conform, as nearly as possible, to the teachings of the Holy Scriptures and the Augsburg Confession of Faith.

2. The young and others who need instruction, shall be taught from Luther's Small Catechism, according to the custom of our Church. And this Catechism shall always be the chief catechism in our Church. The Christian Catechism, printed at New Market, Shenandoah County, Virginia, may, however, be used for the purpose of explaining Luther's Catechism.

3. No one shall be a teacher or an officer in the Church who has not been received into the congregation according to the order of the Church, and does not bear a Christian character.

4. Whoever desires to be a teacher, shall make a sacred affirmation or promise that he will teach according to the Word of God, the Augsburg Confession, and the doctrines of our Church.

5. No one who has not been baptized according to the command of Christ, and confirmed by the imposition of hands, according to the order of the Christian Church, and

partaken of the Lord's Supper, shall be a full member of our Church.

This Synod recognized, in its constitution, two grades in the ministry,—Pastor and Deacon. The pastor is authorized to perform every ministerial act; whilst the deacon is allowed only to catechise, preach, and baptize.

In 1827, its constitution was revised, but there were no material changes made in regard to its confessional basis, or in any other respect, except as to arrangement.

In 1828, the constitution appears, in the proceedings, with explanatory remarks, by Rev. David Henkel, but without material changes.

In its revised constitution of 1866, the confessional basis is more fully presented, so as to express more clearly its doctrinal position, as follows:

1. The Holy Scriptures, the inspired writings of the Old and New Testaments, shall be the only rule and standard of doctrine and church discipline.

2. As a true and faithful exhibition of the doctrines of the Holy Scriptures in regard to matters of faith and practice, this Synod receives the three Ancient Symbols: the Apostolic, Nicene, and Athanasian Creeds, and the Unaltered Augsburg Confession of Faith. It receives also the other Symbolical Books of the Evangelical Lutheran Church, viz.: The Apology, the Smalcald Articles, the Smaller and Larger Catechisms of Luther, and the Formula of Concord, as true Scriptural developments of the doctrines taught in the Augsburg Confession.—*Minutes of 1866, p. 19.*

Constitution of the Evangelical Lutheran Tennessee Synod.

(As Revised in 1866.)

ARTICLE I. The name of this Synod shall be THE EVANGELICAL LUTHERAN TENNESSEE SYNOD.

ARTICLE II. The Holy Scriptures, the inspired writings of the Old and New Testaments, shall be the only rule and standard of doctrine and church discipline.

As a true and faithful exhibition of the doctrines of

the Holy Scriptures, in regard to matters of faith and practice, this Synod receives the three Ancient Symbols: the Apostolic, Nicene, and Athanasian creeds; and the Unaltered Augsburg Confession of Faith. It receives also the other Symbolical Books of the Evangelical Lutheran Church, viz.: The Apology, the Smalcald Articles, the Smaller and Larger Catechisms of Luther, and the Formula of Concord—as true Scriptural developments of the doctrines taught in the Augsburg Confession.

ARTICLE III. This Synod shall be composed of regularly ordained ministers of the Evangelical Lutheran Church, and lay-delegates. The lay-delegates shall be appointed by the congregations in connection with this Synod to represent them in the Synodical Meetings.

Each one of these congregations shall have the right to appoint one such delegate who shall have equal rights and privileges with the ministers in transacting the business of Synod.

Every minister desiring to be received into connection with this Synod, shall, on his reception, be required to subscribe this Constitution.

No minister in connection with this Synod, shall be allowed to teach any thing, nor shall Synod transact any business contrary to the confessional basis as set forth in Article II.

No business shall be transacted secretly or under closed doors, unless an unhappy period should arrive, in which the Church would be liable to persecution, except such as relates to the moral character of a minister, and to the examination of candidates for the ministerial office. Cases of this kind, if deemed necessary and expedient, may be attended to in a private session of Synod.

ARTICLE IV. The business of this Synod shall be to employ the proper means for the promulgation of the Gospel of Jesus Christ, to impart its advice in matters of Christian faith and life, to detect and expose erroneous doctrines and false teachers, and to investigate charges of false doctrines, wrong practice, and immoralities of life, preferred against any of its ministers, and finding them guilty, to expel and depose from the Synod and holy office of the ministry, such as refuse after due admonition to repent of their wrong.

It shall be the duty of Synod, as soon as the wants of the church shall demand, and its resources will justify, to engage in the work of Missions, both domestic and foreign; and also in the work of Beneficiary Education, for the purpose of preparing indigent young men of talents and piety for the work of the ministry in connection with the Lutheran Church, according to such regulations as it may adopt, and consider best calculated to promote these great objects.

Upon application to examine candidates for the ministry, this Synod shall make the necessary provisions to attend to such application, and after due approval by a majority of two-thirds of the members voting, appointing one or more Pastors to consecrate such candidate to the office of the ministry at some suitable time and place by the laying on of hands and prayer.

Synod shall require a probationary period of not less than one year, during which time all candidates for the ministerial office shall be taken on trial.

Upon application, this Synod may receive congregations who may desire to be connected with it, provided they subscribe this Constitution.

ARTICLE V. The officers of this Synod shall be a President, Secretary, Corresponding Secretary, and Treasurer. A majority of all votes cast will be required to constitute an election to any office. The duties of these officers shall be such as usually devolves upon the same in other public bodies, or as may be made obligatory upon them from time to time, by Synod. They shall be elected by ballot, at the regular session, annually, and hold their offices until their successors are elected.

ARTICLE VI. Synod shall meet from time to time upon its own adjournments. Extra sessions may be called by the President, when requested for good and sufficient reasons, to do so, by two ministers and two laymen in its connection.

ARTICLE VII. Synod may at any regular meeting, by a concurrence of two-thirds of all the members present, make such regulations and by-laws as may be deemed necessary, not inconsistent with this Constitution.

ARTICLE VIII. If anything contained in these articles should hereafter be deemed contrary to the Confessional Basis of this Synod, oppressive, or inexpedient, it may be altered or amended. But nothing contained in this Constitution shall be altered or amended unless a proposition for alteration or amendment shall have been laid before one of the sessions of Synod, in writing, and agreed to by two-thirds of all the members voting. The proposition thus agreed to, shall then be laid, in due form, by the Synod in its Minutes before the congregations in its connection, for ratification or rejection by them; and the ministers or vestries of these congregations shall, at some suitable time, before the next succeeding session of Synod, take the vote of these congregations, on the Constitution as amended, allowing the members to vote for its ratification or rejection and send a statement of the vote to that session of Synod. If, then, it shall be ascertained by Synod that a majority of these congregations have voted in favor of ratification, the amendment shall become and be declared by Synod on the face of its Minutes a valid part of said Constitution, and the parts thereof repugnant to such alteration, void.

Thus, it seems, this Synod, after accepting and adopting the true Scriptural basis, as set forth in the Confessions and authorized writings of the Church, adhered to it, and maintained it, in all its transactions and operations; whilst a large number of those who bore the Lutheran name, assumed rather a loose, vacillating, indefinite, compromising policy, ignoring, to a greater or less degree, some of the more important doctrines and teachings of the Church, and rather conniving at the loose, unsettled, unionistic sentiments, which prevailed to such an alarming extent, at that time.

This sound, Scriptural position gave this Synod decided advantages, having something fixed and positive, on which to build, and on which the mind could rely with certainty. The mind really requires something fixed, definite, and positive, on which it may rely and build up. No institution or society can be successfully built up, and long maintained, and perpetuated, on mere negatives and indefinite, unsettled principles. Even, in the structure of a material edifice, a good, solid, settled foundation is required, if the building is to stand properly, and be perpetuated. It was positiveness and definiteness, that gave Luther so much force and success in the days of the Reformation of the sixteenth century. One of the greatest evils of the present age, in regard to the Church, the Family, and the State, is the ignoring of the grand, fundamental principles, on which these divine institutions are really founded and constructed, and the loose, látitudinarian sentiments which now prevail, regardless of fixed, definite principles which underlie our ecclesiastic, civil, and social institutions.

The more this Synod was assailed, abused, and persecuted on account of its doctrinal position, to which it so closely adhered, and which it so fearlessly maintained, the closer it was driven to it, and the more necessary it became for it to investigate, promulgate, proclaim, maintain, and perpetuate the sound, Scriptural doctrines of the Church, from the pulpit, in the family, and through the printing press, assured, that, if these fundamental, Scriptural principles had power and vitality enough in them, to effect the grand and glorious Reformation in the Church, in the beginning of the sixteenth century, they might have a similar effect in the Church in this century.

The printing establishment, founded in 1806, at New Market, Shenandoah County, Virginia,—the fourth, if not the third, one established in that State, was brought into requisition. In speaking of this establishment, Rev. G. D.

Bernheim, D. D., says, in his History of the German Settlements and the Lutheran Church in the Carolinas: "The Lutheran Church in America has had its publication boards and societies in abundance, which have doubtless accomplished a good work; but the oldest establishment of the kind is the one in New Market, Virginia, which dates its existence as far back, at least, as 1810; for the minutes of the North Carolina Synod were printed there, at that time. It was established by the Henkel family, and has continued under their management to this day; at the time of the division in the Lutheran Church in North Carolina, it came at once into the service of the Tennessee Synod, and has issued more truly Lutheran theological works in an English dress than any similar institution in the world. 'We may well say, What hath God wrought? How imperceptible have been his purposes! How brightly they shine forth now.'" Pages 445, 446. In regard to this same matter the *Herold und Zeitschrift*, of January, 1888, a German Lutheran paper, published in Allentown, Pa., says, relative to this family, "For sixty or seventy years, it has done more than any other to arouse its brethren in the faith, in America, to a Lutheran consciousness."

Numerous publications of a doctrinal, devotional, and admonitory character began to issue from that printing establishment, among which were the Unaltered Augsburg Confession, both in a German and in an English dress. At a later date, the Christian Book of Concord, or Symbolical Books of the Evangelical Lutheran Church, first edition in 1851, second, revised edition in 1854; Luther's Small and Large Catechisms, together with an Historical Introduction, to which are added Hymns and Prayers, adapted to Catechetical Instruction and to Family Devotion, translated from the German, in 1852; Luther on the Sacraments, or the Distinctive Doctrines of the Evangelical Lutheran Church, respecting Baptism and the Lord's Supper, &c., in 1853; and Luther's Church-Postil, Sermons on the Epistles for the Different Sundays and Festivals in the Year, translated from the German, in 1869, made their appearance in the English. Thus, this little, determined, positive move, though puny and insignificant in the eyes of men, called more and more attention to the importance of restoring the Church to her normal condition in doctrine, practice, and churchliness. Men, learned, and honest in their relations to the Church, and having her true interest at heart, began to take position in the right direction, and other good, solid, churchly works were issued from other presses, in other sections. The result is before us. It is not extravagant, to say, that three-fourths of those, bearing the name Lutheran, now recognize and accept the Confessional Basis of the Church.

The great Head of the Church often brings into use or action, weak and simple means or instrumentalities, to accomplish great and important results, so that the world may see, that the moving power is from God, and not of man.

The Gospel "is the power of God unto salvation," Rom. 1, 16. "Not many wise men after the flesh, not many mighty, not many noble, are called: But God hath chosen the foolish things of the world to confound the wise; and God hath chosen the weak things of the world to confound the things which are mighty."—1 Cor. 1, 26, 27.

CHAPTER IV.

THE OBJECT OF ITS ORGANIZATION.

THE chief object of the organization of this Synod, was the restoration of the Church to its normal condition, in regard to doctrine, practice, and churchliness. This is evident from the position it took, the basis it adopted, and the course it pursued in promulgating, circulating, and maintaining the pure, Scriptural doctrines of the Evangelical Lutheran Church, according to her Confessional Writings, in the family, in the catechetical class, from the pulpit, and through the printing press, from the time of its organization to the present period.

There was need for such a movement. This appears from the condition of the Church at that time, in respect to doctrine and practice. In the language of Rev. G. D. Bernheim, D. D., in his History of the German Settlements and the Lutheran Church in the Carolinas, so gradual and yet so sure were the departures from the confessed faith of the Church, as well as the assimilation to the teachings and practices of the various denominations, that for a long time it awakened no alarm, and but a learned few had any idea of what the faith of the Lutheran Church was; admirers of Luther there were in abundance, even among the different denominations, but very few knew anything of the secret which made Luther the conscientious, fearless, and zealous man that he was. Multitudes admired Luther's energy and labors, but they knew little of the faith which actuated his efforts, and of the doctrines upon which that faith was based. Had they known it, and experienced it themselves, more would have been accomplished at that time in the Lutheran Church in America, and divisions would not have occurred; then, also, there would have been less manifest desire to unite all denominations into one Church, but a stronger desire to advance the interests of that Church, to which God has given a peculiar field of labor. Pp. 444, 445.

God made use of this division in the Church, in accomplishing a special purpose for the welfare of the Lutheran Church in America. P. 444.

By means of this division the Symbols of the Lutheran Church were translated into the English language. This was a want that had long been felt, but before that time no one possessed the patience and energy to apply himself to the task. There was an abundance of anxious desire manifested by some to make the Lutheran Church in America an English as well as a German Church, but no anxiety manifested itself to anglicize the faith of the Lutheran Church; that is, to translate its Confessions and theology into the English language. All honor then to the Tennessee Synod for undertaking this work, which has accomplished more in preserving the faith of our fathers in this country than any similar undertaking in the English language. Page 445. But as the sad and deplorable condition of the Church at that time, in these respects, has been already fully presented in the first chapter of this work, there is no necessity for a fuller description of it in this connection.

With a view to the accomplishment of this desirable and much needed object, every minister and teacher was required to take an obligation not to teach anything that is in conflict with the confessed doctrines and practices of the Church, and all the books used in the Church were required to conform to these doctrines and practices. And, for its further promotion, quite a number of pamphlets and books, as well as articles in connection with the Minutes of the proceedings of the Synod, of a doctrinal, admonitory, and devotional character, were printed and circulated.

This firm, positive course attracted attention, revived investigation, and thus exerted a healthful, effective influence in the accomplishment of this much needed and important end.

Notwithstanding the conflicts it had to encounter, the obstacles it had to surmount, the taunts it had to hear, and the abuse and persecution it had to endure, on account of its position in regard to doctrine and practice, it still persevered and went forward with a zeal, an earnestness, energy, and fidelity worthy of the cause it had espoused. The leaven had been infused, and the true Lutheran spirit revived. Its work soon prospered, and extended into North Carolina, then to Virginia, Kentucky, Indiana, and Missouri, and afterwards to South Carolina, thence to Alabama, &c. Dormant energies were aroused, the number of ministers was increased, provision was made to supply the wants of many long-neglected congregations, ministers and laymen became more zealous, energetic, and faithful in the discharge of their respective duties, and the Church was thus increased, strengthened, and edified. The evils and disasters which were predicted and deplored by many who preferred to connive at deviations from the pure doctrines and usages, rather than contend for the faith once delivered to the saints, were over-ruled by the great Head of the Church for good, in the promotion of His Kingdom.

CHAPTER V.

ITS WORK AND DEVELOPMENT.

FIRST DECADE.

The most natural, easy, and simple way to present the work and development of this Synod, is, perhaps, to bring into requisition the proceedings as they appear in its Minutes from its organization down to the present period.

Second Session.

Having already stated the more important work of its first meeting, we proceed to call attention to its second convention which took place in Zion's Church, Sullivan County, Tennessee, October 22, 1821, Rev. Adam Miller, pastor.

On Saturday previous, October 20, services, preparatory to the celebration of the Lord's Supper, were held, Rev. David Henkel preaching in the German language from Mark 16, 15, 16.

On Sunday, October 21, a large audience having assembled, Rev. Adam Miller delivered a short sermon in the German language, from Matt. 22, 14. He was followed by Rev. David Henkel, in the English language, on Col. 2, 14. Rev. Philip Henkel then preached in the German, on Luke 22, 15–20. The Lord's Supper was then administered to more than one hundred communicants. Deep solemnity pervaded the whole congregation.

The following are the names of the members who constituted this meeting of Synod: Revs. Paul Henkel, of Shenandoah County, Virginia, Adam Miller, of Sullivan County, Philip Henkel, of Green County, Tennessee, and David Henkel, of Lincoln County, North Carolina. Rev. Jacob Zink was absent. Deacon George Easterly, of Green County, Tennessee, and Mr. Joseph Harr, of Sullivan County, Tennessee, were present; the latter as an applicant for the ministry.

The lay-delegates were Mr. John Smith and Daniel Lutz, Esq., of Lincoln County, and Mr. Peter Boger, of Cabarrus County, North Carolina; Messrs. Nicholas Uely, Martin Lintz, Jacob Leinbach, Frederick Schaeffer, Jacob Heyl (Hoyle), Philip Easterly, of Green County, Michael Brenner, of Sevier County, John Santer, Jacob Deck, H. Herchelroth, of Sullivan County, and Conrad Keicher, of Washington County, Tennessee; and Ambrose Henkel, of Shenandoah County, Virginia.

In the Minutes of this meeting, the following described letters and petitions appear:

1. A letter from Rev. Jacob Larros, of Ohio, in which he vindicates the doctrine of Holy Baptism, according to the Augsburg Confession of Faith, supported by passages from the Holy Scriptures. In it he also speaks of the Kingdom of Antichrist, and presents his objections to the plan or position of the General Synod.

2. A letter from Rev. Antonius Weyer, a member of the Lutheran Synod of Ohio and adjacent States, in which he freely presents his views in regard to the General Synod's system, and the general union of all sects and parties.

3. A letter from Rev. Jacob Grieson, of Guilford County, North Carolina, in which he manifests his regret, that he voted in favor of the General Synod, indicating, that he did not properly understand the matter; and that the result is not what he expected it would be.

4. Is a letter from Rev. Henry A. Kurtz, of Kentucky, in which he states that he had been a member of the Evangelical Lutheran Synod of Pennsylvania, but had tendered his resignation, and asks for assistance to aid him in the formation of a synod, on the plan of the Tennessee Synod, deploring the innovations which prevail in some synods.

5. A letter from Messrs. John Beck, Charles Greim, Henry Conrad, George Greim, Daniel Conrad, Philip Hedrich, and Jacob Conrad, elders and members of several Lutheran congregations in Rowan County, North Carolina, in which they manifest their steadfastness in our Evangel-

ical doctrines, and petition for a minister to serve them, as they are not satisfied with the one they had. In regard to this, it was resolved that Rev. David Henkel visit them.

6. A letter from Rev. Daniel Moser, of Lincoln County, North Carolina, in which he expresses his regret that he cannot attend this meeting of Synod, but hopes to be able to be present at some other time, indicating that he cannot continue in connection with the North Carolina Synod unless it take a better position.

Then follow petitions from seven congregations in North Carolina and Tennessee, asking for ministerial services, advice, &c. The petitions were answered as far as it was possible to do at that time. One of these congregations, Philadelphia, Lincoln County, North Carolina, petitioned for the examination and ordination of Mr. Jacob Cassner (Costner,) to the office of Deacon, but as Mr. Cassner was not present, the matter was deferred till the next meeting of Synod.

Rev. Adam Miller was then appointed to visit, during the synodical year, the different petitioners and congregations in North Carolina and Virginia, and all other congregations belonging to the Synod, and report to the next meeting.

Under the head, "General Transactions of the Synod," appear resolutions, the substance of which we present here:

1. That the objections to the General Synod be compiled and printed. The committee, appointed to attend to this matter, consisted of Adam Miller, David Henkel, Conrad Keicher, Ambrose Henkel, Daniel Lutz, John Smith, and Peter Boger.

2. That a circular letter be addressed to the brethren, of Ohio, to inform them of the intentions of Synod.

3. On motion of Rev. Adam Miller, it was resolved, that a Liturgy be arranged according to the Scriptures and the Augsburg Confession, that Rev. Paul Henkel be appointed to attend to this matter, for the use of Synod, as soon as practicable, that between two and three hundred

copies be printed, and that the expenses be defrayed by the several treasuries.

4. On the request of some of the brethren in North Carolina, it was resolved, that an English session be annually held in North Carolina or an adjacent State.

5. On motion of Rev. Philip Henkel, it was resolved, that it shall be the duty of every pastor and deacon, to register the names of all the baptized in his charge, and to admonish them to continue faithful in their baptismal covenant, and to urge them to attend the catechetical instructions.

6. On motion of Peter Boger, it was resolved, that a copy of the Augsburg Confession, as well as of the Minutes of Synod, be deposited in every church.

7. On motion of Rev. David Henkel, a suggestion was made, that every person applying for ordination to the office of Pastor, shall be required to understand the Greek language well enough to be able to translate the Greek New Testament into the English. This suggestion was deferred till next meeting of Synod.

8. A petition from St. Paul's School at St. James' Church, Green County, Tennessee, was presented, asking Synod to make regulations for its conduct and government. Conrad Keicher, Paul Henkel, and Philip Easterly, were appointed a committee to give that matter attention, and report to the next meeting of Synod.

9. It was resolved, that the next meeting of Synod shall be held fourteen miles south of Green Courthouse, Tennessee, commencing on the third Sunday of October, 1822.

10. On petition of fifteen members of St. James' Church, it was resolved, that next Maundy-Thursday be set apart as a day of prayer and humiliation, to implore Almighty God, to have mercy upon his Church, in these perilous times.

11. Revs. Paul Henkel and Adam Miller were appointed to examine Mr. Joseph Harr. Having sustained the examination, he was ordained to the office of Deacon, by the imposition of hands and with prayer.

The Synod was then dismissed with singing and prayer.

The following is the Parochial Report:

Since 1819, Rev. Adam Miller baptized 188 infants and 24 adults, and confirmed 32; Rev. Philip Henkel, since January, 1821, 119 infants and 10 adults, and confirmed 27; Rev. David Henkel, since July, 1819, 444 infants and 56 adults, and confirmed 69 slaves and 156 white persons; Rev. Paul Henkel, since 1820, 50 infants and 2 adults, and confirmed 20. Revs. George Easterly and Jacob Zink made no reports.

In conclusion follows a long report of the committee appointed to compile the objections against the General Synod, covering 23 pages. It is able, plain, and critical.

Third Session.

This Synod met, in its third session, in St. James' Church, Green County, Tennessee, October 21, 1822.

On Saturday previous, the congregation having assembled, Rev. Paul Henkel preached the preparatory sermon. He was followed by Rev. David Henkel, on Gal. 3, 15–24.

On Sunday, Rev. Adam Miller preached on the Gospel for that day. He was followed by Rev. Paul Henkel, on Matt. 6, 33. The Lord's Supper was then administered to about 140 communicants. After a short recess, Rev. David Henkel preached an English sermon from Titus 3, 4–7. During these services the house was filled to overflowing with attentive hearers.

Monday, the 21st, the Synod was opened with singing and prayer. The following members were present:

Pastors—Revs. Paul Henkel, New Market, Shenandoah County, Virginia, Adam Miller, Sullivan County, Tennessee, Philip Henkel, *pastor loci*, David Henkel, Lincoln County, North Carolina. Jacob Zink was absent.

Deacons—George Easterly, Green County, Tennessee, and Joseph Harr, Sullivan County, Tennessee, were absent, on account of indisposition.

Applicants—Christian Moretz, Cape Girardeau County, Missouri, Richard Blalock, Burke County, and Jacob Cassner (Costner), Lincoln County, North Carolina.

Lay-delegates—Michael Brenner, St. Jacob's Church, Sevier County, Jacob Hatzepiller, Union Church, Washington County, Conrad Keicher, Emmanuel Church, same County, John Froschauer, Solomon's Church, Green County, Abraham Bock, St. Paul's, Monroe County, George Nehs, from the same County, Henry Herchelroth, Bueler's Church, Sullivan County, John Santer and Jacob Deck, Zion's Church, Sullivan County, Tennessee; Ambrose Henkel, from three congregations in Virginia; Peter C. Boger, Rocky River Church, Cabarrus County, Jacob Best, Philadelphia Church, Lincoln County, North Carolina; Joseph Hauf, Golden Spring Church, and John Olinger, Lick Creek Church, Green County, Tennessee; Peter Greim, three congregations, Rowan County, Conrad Kramm, Rocky Spring Church, Burke County, North Carolina.

Rev. Philip Henkel called attention to the ministrations of Mr. Moretz, asking whether they should be recognized, and placed on record in the Minutes. The response was in the affirmative.

The following are, in substance, the petitions presented to the Synod:

1. A petition from Cape Girardeau, Wayne, and Perry Counties, Missouri, signed by seventy petitioners, asking for a minister, certifying to the good moral character of Mr. Christian Moretz, and requesting his ordination. In regard to this petition, it was resolved that said Moretz be examined.

2. A petition from Rocky Spring Church, Burke County, North Carolina, commending the character of Rev. Richard Blalock, formerly a minister of the Separate Baptist Order, requesting Synod to receive him as a minister. In regard to this, it was resolved that Revs. Paul Henkel and David Henkel, as individual ministers, ordain him as a Lutheran minister, if found qualified, and that as soon as he acquires a better knowledge of the Ger-

man language, he be received into connection with the Synod.

3. A petition from three congregations, Pilgrim's, Beck's, and Emmanuel's, Rowan County, North Carolina, expressing their disapproval of the General Synod, presenting their withdrawal, signed by 142 persons, and requesting ministerial services from this Synod. With respect to this petition, it was resolved, that Rev. Paul Henkel visit them during the fall, and that either Rev. Adam Miller or Rev. George Easterly visit them in the spring, and that in the event the congregations can agree with one or the other of the two latter, he shall become their pastor.

4. A communication from Mr. Jacob Aderhold, Lincoln County, North Carolina, suggesting the appointment of a suitable person in each congregation to attend to funeral services, in the absence of the pastor or deacon, and that some change be made in regard to the rules relative to sponsors in baptism.

Relative to this, it was resolved that each congregation use its Christian liberty in respect to these matters, keeping within the teachings of the Augsburg Confession.

5. A petition from Mr. George Risch, now living in Tennessee Valley, Haywood County, North Carolina, in which he indicates his constant adherence to our Church, and solicits a visit from one of our ministers in his community. It was resolved that Christian Moretz visit that section.

6. A petition from fourteen lay-delegates and one minister, representing congregations in Indiana and Kentucky, who had met in Harrison's Church, Nelson County, Kentucky, September 28, 1822, in which they solicit Synod to hold a session in their community, and to transact such business as might promote the interests of the Church, and in which they appointed Rev. Philip Henkel, who had visited them during the summer, to represent their interests in reference to this matter.

In regard to these petitioners, it was resolved, that Rev. Philip Henkel be recognized as their representative in reference to their requests; that Revs. Paul Henkel and David Henkel, and Captain John Bible, as a lay-delegate, visit the petitioners, to render the services desired; that such session be held in Brunnerstown Church, Jefferson County, Kentucky, commencing on the third Sunday in June, 1823; that all congregations interested in that meeting have the privilege of sending delegates; that Rev. David Henkel inform the petitioners of this action of Synod; and that, during the absence of Rev. David Henkel and that of Rev. Paul Henkel, on that mission, Rev. Adam Miller shall visit the congregations of the former, and Rev. Philip Henkel those of the latter.

7. A petition from the congregation at Coldwater, Cabarrus County, North Carolina, signed by fifteen persons, asking to be served by a minister of this Synod, and stating that they do not wish to stand in connection with the General Synod, nor to be served by any of its ministers.

In regard to this, it was resolved, that Rev. Adam Miller visit them during his next journey to North Carolina, and that Rev. David Henkel visit them as often as possible, till Synod shall be able to make better arrangements to supply them.

8. A petition for the examination of Mr. Jacob Costner for the office of Deacon. It was resolved, that Revs. Paul Henkel and Adam Miller examine him and report to Synod.

Letters and Communications Received.

The following is the substance of letters and communications received, read, and acted on:

1. A letter from Rev. Daniel Moser, in which he states his inability to be present, his desire that the next session of Synod be held in North Carolina, giving assurance that it would prove satisfactory to the people, that it might tend to healing the breach hitherto existing, and that Rev. Philip Henkel be requested to visit the congregations.

With respect to this letter, it was resolved, that if Rev. Mr. Moser had given some positive information as to whether he has absented himself from the General Synod, Synod could give him a more satisfactory answer, but in view of the present aspect of things, it can make no definite reply, further than that it desires him to come to some decisive conclusion as soon as possible.

2. A communication, signed by three elders and eight church members, from St. Peter's Church, Rockingham County, Virginia, in which they indicate their adherence to this Synod, and certify the election of Mr. Ambrose Henkel as their delegate.

3. A letter from Rev. Jacob Zink, in which he states that he baptized twenty-eight adults and sixty-nine infants in the State of Louisiana, but many more in the State of Indiana,—the exact number of which he cannot give at this time; that the congregations are all united in opposition to the General Synod; that the General Synod is not Lutheran; that the most of the people in Kentucky,—Lutherans and German Reformed,—are opposed to the General Synod, and that he heartily desires to be present at the meeting of Synod, but is deprived of this privilege. Rev. Zink's absence was excused.

4. A letter from Mr. George Goodman, Cabarrus County, North Carolina, stating, that he much desired to be in attendance at the meeting of Synod, but was prevented by important circumstances from so doing, and that he wished to have a statement inserted in the Minutes in what respects Synod is governed by a majority.

In reply, the following is the gist of the answer: Resolved, that, as the Bible is the only rule and standard of doctrine and church discipline, and as the Augsburg Confession is a clear and correct presentation of the more important doctrines and principles of the Bible, a majority have no right to decide in these matters, in opposition to these teachings, but in other matters, such as deciding the time and place for meetings, and matters that do not come in conflict with the aforenamed standard, the majority have a right to decide.

On the report of the examining committee, it was resolved, that Mr. Jacob Costner be ordained to the office of Deacon in his congregation, by Revs. Paul Henkel and David Henkel, or by one or the other of them,—which was done.

It was also unanimously resolved that examinations of candidates for the office of Pastor, shall be publicly before the Synod.

According to the petition from Missouri, Mr. Christian Moretz was publicly examined, and sustained a favorable examination. He was then ordained as a Deacon.

Mr. Conrad Keicher asked the question: Is slavery to be considered as an evil? In reply, the Synod unanimously resolved, that it is to be regarded as a great evil in our land, and it desires the government, if it be possible, to devise some way by which this evil can be removed. Synod also advised every minister to admonish every master to treat his slaves properly, and to exercise his Christian duties towards them. This probably was the first move in that direction in the South.

Deacon George Easterly was publicly examined as to his qualifications for the office of Pastor, and having sustained a favorable examination, was ordained to that office, Rev. David Henkel preaching a suitable ordination sermon on the occasion.

It was resolved, that Rev. Adam Miller's journal of his last summer's travels, be appended to the Minutes.

Synod approved the objections compiled by the committee, appointed at the last year's session, in opposition to the constitution of the General Synod.

In regard to the suggestion made at the previous session, that every applicant for the office of Pastor must be acquainted with the Greek language, it was resolved, that, as the opportunities for acquiring such knowledge, are not always accessible, the Synod, whilst it regards such knowledge as highly useful, cannot, at this time, demand such requirement.

It was resolved, that Synod meet in Sinking Spring Church, eleven miles west of Greenville, Tennessee, on the third Sunday in October, 1823.

In regard to the action taken at the last session relative to St. Paul's School, Tennessee, the matter was referred to a society to be soon organized for that purpose.

Synod agreed to patronize the printing of Dr. Luther's Sermon Book.

The following is the Parochial Report:

Rev. Jacob Zink baptized 69 infants and 28 adults; Rev. David Henkel, 182 infants and 16 adults, and confirmed 32 slaves and 47 white persons; Rev. Philip Henkel, 107 infants and 14 adults and 1 slave, and confirmed 74; Rev. Paul Henkel, 66 infants and 5 adults, and confirmed 36; Deacon C. Moretz, 29 infants; Deacon George Easterly, 7 infants and 1 adult; Rev. Adam Miller, 89 infants and 8 adults. Rev. Joseph Harr, no report.

Fourth Session.

In its fourth convention, this Synod met in Sinking Spring Church, Green County, Tennessee, October, 1823.

On Saturday, Rev. George Easterly preached from Acts 2, 38–40, and Rev. Philip Henkel from Eph. 2, 8. The services were well attended.

On Sunday, Rev. David Henkel based his sermon on 1 Cor. 11, 23–29. The Lord's Supper was then administered to 81 communicants; after which Rev. David Henkel preached again, on the text John 1, 14. During these services the audiences were large and appreciative.

Monday, October 20, the members of Synod having assembled, the Synod was opened with singing and prayer, followed by a kind, brotherly address, indicating the chief object of the meeting.

The ministers present were, Revs. Philip Henkel, Green County, Tennessee, George Easterly, *pastor loci*,

David Henkel, Lincoln County, North Carolina; Rev. Paul Henkel rendered an excuse for absence, on account of indisposition,—he was excused,—Rev. Adam Miller sent a letter showing his desire to be present, but indicating the cause of his absence, as resulting from the extent of his visitations, which prevented him from being able to reach the place of Synod, in time. He was excused. Rev. Zink was also absent.

Deacons—Christian Moretz, of Missouri, and Jacob Costner, of Lincoln County, North Carolina. Joseph Harr departed this life since the last meeting. We have been unable to find any obituary notice in regard to him.

Lay-delegates—Messrs. Frederick Schaeffer, place of meeting, Henry Meyer, Golden Spring Church, Green County, Henry Long, St. Paul's Church, Knox County, George Schaeffer, Zion's Church, Sullivan County, John Maurer, St. Paul's Church, Monroe County, John Keicher, Emmanuel Church, Adam Herrmann, Union Church, Washington County, Daniel Olinger, Bethesda Church, Green County, Tennessee; George Goodman, of North Carolina; Ambrose Henkel, Shenandoah County, Virginia; Emanuel Permann, Solomon's Church, Green County, Conrad Easterly, St. Jacob's Church, Green County, Jacob Wiszler, Washington County, and Michael Brenner, St. Jacob's Church, Sevier County, Tennessee.

1. The proceedings of the last year's session were read. Rev. David Henkel stated, that, up to this time, he had not, on account of certain circumstances, ordained Richard Blalock to the office of the ministry, according to the resolution passed at the previous session.

2. In regard to the meeting held, last summer, in Nelson County, Kentucky, a printed paper was read. The Synod expressed its entire approbation with the result, and recognized the members of Harrison's Church, Nelson County, Kentucky, and those who met with them in that meeting, as brethren, giving assurance, that, as far as possible,

it will care for them, and indicating regret, that Rev. Paul Henkel, on account of sickness, could not be at that conference.

3. It was resolved, that all who applied for ministerial services from this Synod, be supplied as far as possible. It was also stated, that Rev. Paul Henkel visited the three congregations, which had applied for services, and preached for them, baptized their children, instructed their catechumens, and administered them the Lord's Supper, last fall.

4. In regard to the resolution passed at the last year's session, relative to the circulation of Luther's Writings, as fast as possible, it was stated, that three of Luther's Sermons were already printed, and can be obtained at Dr. Solomon Henkel's printing establishment, New Market, Shenandoah County, Virginia.

The Parochial Report presented is as follows:

Rev. Philip Henkel baptized 87 infants and 12 adults, and confirmed 50 white persons; Rev. George Easterly, 52 infants and 5 adults, and confirmed 13 white persons; Rev. David Henkel, 159 infants and 2 adults, and confirmed 7 slaves and 57 white persons; Rev. Christian Moretz, 87 infants and 9 adults; Rev. Adam Miller, 100 infants and 12 adults, and confirmed 6 slaves and 12 white persons.

The following petitions were received and read:

1. A petition from Keinadt's (Koiner's) Church, Augusta County, Virginia, in which they state, that they have no regular minister at this time, in consequence of the fact that they do not desire a minister from the General Synod, that they do not regard that Synod as Scriptural, and hence they cannot consistently call a minister from it, and that as they regard our Synod as adhering to the Augsburg Confession, they turn their attention to it for the purpose of obtaining a teacher.

2. A petition from the Hawksbill Church, Shenandoah County, now Page County, Virginia, in which they say, that, as Rev. Paul Henkel cannot serve them now, in consequence of ill health, they might secure the services of a

minister in connection with the General Synod, but in view of its doctrinal position, they do not desire to do so, and hence they petition for the promotion of Mr. Ambrose Henkel to the office of the ministry, vouching for his moral character.

3. A petition from Pine Church, Shenandoah County, Virginia, now St. Mary's, of similar import to that of the former.

4. A petition from Cape Girardeau, Perry, Wayne, and Madison Counties, Missouri, requesting the ordination of Deacon Christian Moretz to the office of Pastor, and giving evidence of his good character.

5. A petition from Valley Church, Wythe County, Virginia, in which the petitioners indicate, that they do not wish any longer to co-operate with the North Carolina Synod, that they have withdrawn from it, and desire to be received into our Synod, and also that their preacher, Rev. Andrew Sechrist, acquiesces in this move.

6. A petition from the Church in the Fork, Washington County, Virginia, asking for the promotion of Rev. Andrew Sechrist in the ministerial office.

7. A petition from Zion's congregation, Sullivan County, Tennessee, in which they express a desire, that, if Rev. Adam Miller cannot serve them more frequently, Andrew Sechrist serve them.

8. A petition from Rader's Church, Rockingham County, Virginia, signed by the church council, in which they state, that, as they have no opportunity to be served by a minister, unless it be by one from the General Synod, and seeing that our Synod still adheres to the Augsburg Confession, they desire our Synod to supply them with a minister. They further state, that Rev. Philip Henkel preached for them once last summer, and that they have such confidence in him as induces them to desire him to serve them.

9. A petition from Emmanuel Church, Washington County, Tennessee, in which the petitioners desire the next

meeting of Synod to be held in their church; whereupon Ambrose Henkel also presented a verbal petition from four congregations in Virginia to the same effect.

10. A petition from three congregations in Davidson County, formerly Rowan County, North Carolina, in which the petitioners express their heartfelt thanks for the services received from our Synod, and pray for a continuance of the same.

11. A petition from the congregation in Jeffersontown, Jefferson County, Kentucky, petitioning for a minister belonging to our Synod; especially for David Henkel.

12. A petition from a congregation in Clark County, on Fourteen-mile Creek, Indiana, asking our Synod to provide them with a minister.

13. A petition, verbally stated by Rev. David Henkel, on behalf of Mr. George Risch, in Tennessee Valley, for a minister.

The following action was taken in regard to these petitions:

1. With respect to petitions 5, 6, and 7, in regard to the reception of Mr. Sechrist, it was resolved, that, as he indicates in writing that he accepts and holds our position, he be received and examined, and, if he sustain a proper examination, he be ordained.

2. Relative to petition 4, concerning the pastoral ordination of Deacon C. Moretz, it was resolved, that, as he has faithfully served for two years in his present office, and sustained an irreproachable character, if he sustain a favorable examination, he be ordained to the office of Pastor.

3. In reference to 2 and 3, as to the reception of Mr. Ambrose Henkel as a deacon, it was resolved, that he be received and examined, and, if found qualified, he be ordained to the office of Deacon.

Hereupon, the examination of these three applicants took place, and they stood a favorable examination. After the examination, Rev. David Henkel preached an ordination sermon from Eph. 4, 3–14; after which the applicants were ordained with prayer and with the imposition of hands.

4. In reference to petitions, numbers 1, 8, 10, 11, 12, and 13, relative to services from this Synod, it was resolved, that every preacher present agree to visit a certain district in the bounds of the petitioners desiring services. It was further resolved, that, in the future, when a minister cannot be at Synod, he shall, when necessary, attend to such district as may be assigned to him.

It was also resolved, that Rev. George Easterly visit the congregations in Davidson County, North Carolina, this fall; that, in the spring, Rev. Sechrist visit them again, in case Rev. Adam Miller cannot visit them; and that Rev. Adam Miller visit the petitioners in Augusta, Rockingham, and Shenandoah Counties, Virginia, next spring or in the beginning of summer.

Rev. George Easterly was requested to visit Mr. Risch, in Haywood, North Carolina, this fall.

In the event Mr. Sechrist does not visit Davidson County till spring, thus making it possible for Rev. Miller to make both visits, he shall serve Rev. Miller's congregations, during his absence.

Rev. Moretz was appointed to visit the petitioners in Kentucky and Indiana, this fall, and in the spring or the early part of the summer, either Rev. Philip Henkel or David Henkel is to visit them again.*

Relative to the verbal petition, number 9, it was resolved, that the next meeting of Synod be held in Keinadt's (Koiner's) Church, Augusta County, Virginia, twelve miles east of Staunton, and begin on the first Sunday in September, 1824.

In this connection appears a paper, in which it is stated, that a German periodical, published in Baltimore, Maryland, bearing date, June 25, 1823, was received, in which, it is learned, that, during its last session, in the town of Lebanon,

*It seems to have been the object of Synod, to serve all congregations, that petitioned for services, as far as it was possible for it to do.

Pennsylvania, the Lutheran Synod of Pennsylvania withdrew its connection with the General Synod, by resolving not to send any more delegates to it, and that this resolution shall continue in force, in the future, until the congregations themselves shall revoke it. For this move, certain reasons were assigned, which indicate dissatisfaction on the part of many with the plan of the General Synod.

In view of this fact, in order to obtain desired information, this Synod deemed it not improper to submit the following inquiries to the Pennsylvania Synod, asking a reply:

1. "Do you believe, that Holy Baptism, administered with natural water, in the name of the Father, and of the Son, and of the Holy Ghost, effects the forgiveness of sins, delivers from death and the devil, and confers everlasting salvation upon all who believe it, as the words and promises of God declare?

2. "Do you believe, that the true body and blood of Christ, under the form of bread and wine in the Holy Supper, are present, administered, and received? Do you also believe, that the unbelieving communicants receive in this Supper the body and blood of Christ, under the form of bread and wine?

"We do not ask whether the unbelievers obtain the forgiveness of their sins thereby, but whether they also receive the body and blood of Jesus in this Sacrament.

3. "Do you believe, that Jesus Christ, as true God and man in one person, should be worshiped?

4. "Is it right for the Evangelical Lutheran Church to unite with any religious organization that seeks to deny the doctrines of the Augsburg Confession and Luther's Catechism? Or is it right for Lutherans to go to the Holy Supper with such?

5. "Is your Synod to be henceforth ruled by a majority of the voters?

6. "Does your Synod intend still to adhere to the declaration, that Jesus Christ, the Great Head of his Church, has given no special direction or order for the establishment

of Church Government, as it is declared in the Constitution of the General Synod?

"Your answers to these questions in writing, addressed to our Secretary, Rev. David Henkel, Lincolnton, Lincoln County, North Carolina, will be duly appreciated."

Fifth Session.

This Synod met, in its fifth session, in Keinadt's (Koiner's) Church, Augusta County, Virginia, September 6, 1824.

On Saturday, Rev. George Easterly preached on Heb. 11, 6. On Sunday, Rev. Daniel Moser preached on Tit. 3, 4-7. He was followed by Rev. David Henkel in the English. Then Rev. Philip Henkel preached on 1 Cor. 11, 26. The Lord's Supper was administered. The house was filled with devout worshipers.

On Monday, the members of Synod assembled. The pastors present were: Revs. Paul Henkel, New Market, Virginia; Adam Miller, Sullivan County, Tennessee; Philip Henkel, Green County, Tennessee; George Easterly, of the same County as the latter; David Henkel, Lincoln County, North Carolina. Revs. Jacob Zink and Christian Moretz were absent.

Deacons—Ambrose Henkel, New Market, Virginia. Andrew Sechrist and Jacob Costner were absent.

Delegates—Messrs. George Goodman, Cabarrus County, North Carolina, representing nine congregations; Ludwig Stein, Sullivan County, John Renner, Green County, Tennessee; Daniel Tussing, Pine Church, Shenandoah County, Virginia; Joseph Nehs, Green County, Tennessee; Martin Meyer and John Printz, Hawksbill Church, Shenandoah, now Page County, Virginia; Peter Schaeffer and John Bauman, Rader's Church, Rockingham County, Virginia; Henry Miller, Philip Church, Rockingham County, Virginia; Casper Keinadt and Jacob Keinadt (Koiner), of the place of meeting.

1. Rev. George Henry Riemenschneider, of Pendleton

County, Virginia, having applied for reception into Synod, having given, in writing, satisfactory evidence of his acquiescence with the doctrines and position of Synod, and that more than a year ago he had withdrawn from the Maryland Synod, and a paper, signed by nineteen leading church members, having been presented, vouching for his irreproachable, Christian character, he was received as a regular member of Synod, by the extension of the right hand of fellowship.

2. Rev. Daniel Moser, Lincoln County, North Carolina, having expressed a desire to be received into connection with this Synod, and a petition, number six, signed by members of three of his congregations, testifying to his good moral conduct, and certifying that since 1820 neither they nor their minister belonged to any synod, and asking to be received into Synod; and Rev. Moser, in writing over his own signature, stating that he regarded the doctrines maintained by the Tennessee Synod as in accord with the Augsburg Confession, it was resolved, that he and his congregations be received, and that he be recognized by Synod as one of its pastors.

At 12 M., Rev. Riemenschneider preached on 1 Cor. 10, 15.

3. Rev. David Henkel having stated that during his travels he met Rev. Zink, who informed him that for certain reasons over which he had no control, he could not be present; he was excused, and Rev. Riemenschneider moved that a letter be sent him in the name of the Synod, expressing its appreciation of his labors and encouraging him to continue steadfast in his office.

The following petitions were then read:

1. A petition from Messrs. Andrew Bastian, Peter Allbrecht, and John Setzer, signed by the Sewitzen Church, Rowan County, North Carolina, praying that one of our ministers might visit them, as they desired a minister who teaches according to the fundamental doctrines and regulations of the Lutheran Church.

2. A petition from a congregation in Nelson County, Kentucky, expressing their gratification on account of services already rendered by Synod, and a desire for a continuation of such services.

3. A petition from a church in Jefferson County, Kentucky, expressing gratitude for the inestimable services rendered them by Rev. David Henkel, speaking of him in most favorable terms, and praying for further services.

In connection with this, it should be observed, that Rev. David Henkel was most cordially received and liberally remunerated by these two congregations in Kentucky for his services, and that he received similar treatment from the brethren in Indiana.

4. A petition, signed by the councils of four congregations in Davidson County, North Carolina, in which they express their sincere thanks for services already received, and petition for a preacher.

5. A petition, signed by the elders and deacons of Philadelphia congregation, Lincoln County, North Carolina, in which they pray that a committee be elected, and that the North Carolina Synod be requested to appoint a similar one, and that these two committees meet, and show and state publicly the differences in doctrine between the two synods.

6. A petition from Rev. Daniel Moser's congregation of similar import.

7. A petition from St. John's Church, Lincoln County, North Carolina, of same import.

8. A petition from St. Jacob's Church, Tennessee, in which the petitioners request that less labor be imposed on Rev. Philip Henkel, in traveling, and if this cannot be done, that some other minister serve them during his absence.

9. A petition from Hawksbill Church, Virginia, and a verbal petition from three other churches, praying for the ordination of Mr. Ambrose Henkel to the office of Pastor.

10. A petition from Rader's Church, Virginia, stating

that they have had no minister for a long time, that their young people are being neglected, and that hence they desire that Rev. Adam Miller serve them. In connection with this, there is a petition from old Pine Church of similar import. It also asks for the services of Ambrose Henkel.

11. A petition from a congregation in Harrison County, Indiana, asking for ministerial services.

In regard to petitions numbers 1, 2, 3, 4, 8, 10, and 11, asking for services, it was resolved that the following ministers spend two months each before the next meeting of Synod, in visiting and serving these petitioners: Revs. Adam Miller, George Easterly, Philip Henkel, David Henkel, Daniel Moser, and Ambrose Henkel, and that they arrange the sections which each one is to visit to suit themselves.

Relative to this, it was observed that as this Synod has no treasury, out of which to remunerate traveling ministers, the petitioners are expected to defray such expenses, as they have, to their praise, heretofore done. The laborer is worthy of his reward.

Letters were then read from Revs. C. Moretz and Andrew Sechrist, and Peter Heyl (Hoyle), Esq., delegates elect from congregations in Lincoln County, North Carolina, and Deacon Jacob Costner, rendering excuses for their absence, &c. They were excused.

And also a letter from Mr. Carl Gock, of Pennsylvania, in which he expresses himself as dissatisfied with the General Synod, and states that he had reprinted the report of the committee, appointed during the second session of our Synod, to compile the objections to the constitution of the General Synod, and circulated 1,200 copies, &c.

The petitions numbered 5, 6, and 7 received attention, and among other actions taken in relation to them, it was resolved, inasmuch as there are a number of persons who do not understand the difference between the doctrines held by the Tennessee Synod and those held by the North Carolina Synod, and to establish peace and harmony as far as possible, that a committee, consisting of Messrs. Casper Keinadt, Jacob Keinadt (Koiner), and Adam Leonard, be appointed, with the privilege of selecting a secretary. It shall be their duty to collect, from the writings of the two parties, the conflicting doctrines held by each, and place them opposite to each other, so that every one may see the difference; and if those who have deviated from the teachings of the Augsburg Confession and the Lutheran order shall publicly renounce, in print, such deviations, further steps for a re-union may be instituted.

Rev. Nehemiah Bonham, an English Lutheran preacher of Tazwell County, having appeared since the opening of this session, and expressed a desire to be received into Synod; and presenting a petition from his congregations, in which they testify to the Christian walk and conduct of said Bonham, and ask to be received into Synod, besides other evidence of his good character, after examination he was received into Synod by the extension of the right hand of brotherly fellowship, and his congregations were also received.

Relative to petition number 9, it was resolved, that Ambrose Henkel be examined in regard to his qualifications for the office of Pastor, and, if he sustain the required examination, that he be ordained to that office. The examination proved satisfactory, and he was ordained to that office, by Revs. Riemenschneider, Miller, and Easterly.

It was now resolved, that the next meeting of this Synod be held in St. John's Church, twenty miles northeast of Lincolnton, North Carolina, commencing on the first Sunday in September, 1825.

A young man, Adam Miller, Jr., nephew of Rev. Adam Miller, was introduced to Synod as an applicant for the office of the Ministry. He was placed under the supervision of his uncle.

The following is the Parochial Report:

Rev. George Easterly baptized 72 infants, 8 adults,

and 2 slaves, and confirmed 12; Rev. Daniel Moser, since 1820, 350 infants and 1 adult, and confirmed 121; Rev. Philip Henkel, 171 infants, 9 adults, and 7 slaves, and confirmed 17; Rev. Adam Miller, 118 infants and 22 adults, and confirmed 51; Rev. Christian Moretz, 23 infants; Rev. Paul Henkel, 16 infants; Rev. Jacob Zink, no report; Rev. Nehemiah Bonham, no report; Rev. G. H. Riemenschneider, since 1822, 68 infants and 2 adults, and confirmed 44; Rev. Ambrose Henkel, 42 infants; Rev. David Henkel, 133 infants, 15 adults, and 9 slaves, and confirmed 60.

Synod then adjourned to meet at the time and place designated.

As Appendixes, follow the report of the committee to present in print the differences in doctrine between the two Synods, and a memorial addressed, by Rev. David Henkel, to the Synod of Maryland and Virginia.

Sixth Session.

Synod met in its sixth session, in St. John's Church, Lincoln County, now Catawba County, North Carolina, September 5, 1825.

On Saturday previous, two sermons were preached,—one by Rev. Christian Moretz, and the other by Rev. Ambrose Henkel. On Sunday, two discourses were delivered, and the Lord's Supper administered to 206 communicants.

Ministers present—Revs. Philip Henkel, Geo. Easterly, N. Bonham, Ambrose Henkel, C. Moretz, D. Moser, and David Henkel, and Deacon J. Costner.

Applicant—Mr. Adam Miller, Jr.

Delegates—Messrs. Adam Cloninger, Jacob Pleyler, Andrew Taylor, G. Burkhart, G. Nehs, G. Bible, A. Siegel, Peter Heyl, J. Efird, P. Allbright, G. Goodman, Jonathan Hertzel, Daniel Sechrist, J. Beck, Michael Rudisill, John Ramsauer, David Hahn, C. Kramm, Adam Lingel, John Moretz, H. Rudisill, Elias Bast, and the church council of St. John's.

Eight letters were received and read, assigning reasons

for absence, asking to be excused, and petitioning for ministerial services. The requests were granted.

Action was now taken relative to doctrinal questions which had been propounded, two years ago, to the Pennsylvania Synod, and which had not been as yet answered, nor any reason given for such delay.

In respect to this, Revs. Daniel Moser and Ambrose Henkel, and Messrs. John Ramsauer and Peter Heyl, were appointed a committee to renew the questions.

A memorial was presented, signed by nine persons, requesting Synod to make another effort to effect a union with the ministers of the North Carolina Synod, but in such a manner as not to compromise the genuine Lutheran doctrines.

In reference to this memorial, it was resolved, that, as the ministers of the North Carolina Synod failed to respond to our former proposal for negotiations with a view to adjust the differences, according to the standard of the Church, the same proposition and questions be repeated, and if their answers prove satisfactory, all necessary steps shall be taken to effect peace and harmony; but if the answers should fail to be satisfactory, we further propose to them, that a time and place may be selected, and that each party appoint a speaker to present the disputed doctrines, in such a manner that the audience that may assemble at the time and place, may form their views relative to the differences, and that the arguments on both sides may be afterward published.

The committee, appointed to prepare a paper, containing certain questions to be submitted to the Pennsylvania Synod for its consideration and answers, submitted their report. The questions are similar to those prepared in 1823.

The Secretary was ordered to address a friendly letter to the Rev. Muhlenberg, a member of that Synod, to obtain counsel relative to the present condition of the Church.

Here two petitions from Tennessee follow, asking for the ordination of Mr. Adam Miller, Jr. He was examined and ordained.

Eight petitions from North Carolina, Virginia, and Tennessee, were received, asking for ministerial services. Arrangements were made to supply them.

All the congregations in connection with Synod were advised more generally to introduce Luther's Catechism.

The time and place for the next meeting of Synod were the first Sunday in September, 1826, and Buehler's Church, near Papersville, Sullivan County, Tennessee. The parochial report is favorable.

The following is the Parochial Report:

Rev. George Easterly baptized 40 infants and 6 adults, and confirmed 12; Rev. Nehemiah Bonham, 32 infants and 12 adults; Rev. Ambrose Henkel, 60 infants and 1 adult; Rev. Daniel Moser, 130 infants, 6 adults, and 11 slaves, and confirmed 39; Rev. Christian Moretz, 105 infants, 7 adults, and confirmed 20; Rev. Philip Henkel, 110 infants, 7 adults, and 4 slaves, and confirmed 45; Rev. David Henkel, 135 infants, 6 adults, and 4 slaves, and confirmed 41; Rev. Paul Henkel, 20 infants, 5 adults, and confirmed 10.

Obituary of Rev. Paul Henkel.—Rev. Paul Henkel was a son of Jacob Henkel who was a son of Justus Henkel who was a son of Rev. Gerhard Henkel who was a German Court preacher, and came to America about 1718, and located at Germantown, near Philadelphia, Pennsylvania. Rev. Gerhard Henkel was a descendant of Count Henkel, of Poeltzig, who was instrumental in sending Rev. Muhlenberg to America. Count Henkel was a descendant of Johann Henkel, D. D., LL. D., born in Leutschau, Hungary, and was Father Confessor to Queen Maria about 1530. He sympathized with Protestantism, and maintained friendly relations with Melanchthon, Erasmus, Spalatin, and others who were engaged in the Reformation of the sixteenth century.

Rev. Paul Henkel was born on the Yadkin River, Rowan County, North Carolina, December 15, 1754. Whilst he was a youth, his parents, with their family, moved to Western Virginia. About the year 1776, Paul Henkel determined to prepare himself for the Gospel Ministry, placing himself under the instruction of Rev. Kruch, pastor of the Evangelical Lutheran Church at Fredericktown, Maryland. After having taken a course in the German, Latin, and Greek languages, and other studies necessary to the ministerial office, he applied to the Evangelical Lutheran Synod of Pennsylvania and adjacent States,—

the only Lutheran Synod then in existence in this country. He was examined and licensed to preach. Having received a call from congregations in the Shenandoah Valley of Virginia, at and near New Market, Shenandoah County, he accepted, and located at New Market, Virginia, and extended his labors into other sections, as Augusta, Madison, Pendleton, Wythe, &c., where he laid the foundations of a large number of congregations. On the 6th of June, 1792, he was solemnly set apart to the office of Pastor, in the city of Philadelphia, Pennsylvania. His ordination was performed by Rev. John Frederick Schmidt, pastor of a church in that city. He afterward located in Staunton, Augusta County, Virginia, and labored in that section about three years. He then returned to New Market, Virginia, and resumed his labors among his former congregations. In 1800, he received a call to congregations in Rowan (his native County), North Carolina. He accepted it, but even there, as in Virginia, he did not confine his labors simply to those congregations, but extended them to other places in the surrounding counties. But finding that section unhealthy, on account of chills and fever, he returned in 1805 to New Market, Shenandoah County, Virginia, and became an independent missionary. Not depending for a support on any special missionary fund, but on the promises of his Master and the good will of those to whom he ministered, he made several tours through Western Virginia, Tennessee, Kentucky, Indiana, and Ohio, gathering the scattered members of the Church, administering to them the Word and Sacraments, instructing and confirming the youth, and, as far as practicable, organizing new congregations. During the War of 1812–1815, he took up his residence at Point Pleasant, Mason County, Virginia, and organized several congregations in that section, but at the close of the war, he returned to his old residence at New Market, Virginia, and resumed his missionary labors.

In 1803, whilst he resided in North Carolina, he, with several other ministers, formerly belonging to the Pennsylvania Synod, organized the North Carolina Synod. In October, 1812, while he resided at Point Pleasant, about ten of the brethren of the Pennsylvania Synod held their first special conference west of the Alleghany Mountains, in Washington County, Pennsylvania. To this conference he was invited, but for certain reasons was unable to attend. But at the conference which was held the next year at Clear Creek, Fairfield County, Ohio, he was present, and was recognized as one of their body, although he still belonged to the Synod of North Carolina. In 1818, he took part in the organization of the Ohio Synod, and in 1820, in that of the Tennessee Synod.

In 1809, he published a small work in the German language, on Christian Baptism and the Lord's Supper. This work was afterwards translated into the English. In 1810, he published a German hymn-book for the benefit of the Church, containing two hundred and forty-six hymns. In 1816, he published another hymn-book in the English language, which was afterwards enlarged and improved, and contains four hundred and seventy-six hymns,—a portion of which are adapted to the Gospels and Epistles of the Ecclesiastical Year. A considerable number of these hymns, both German and English, were composed by him. In 1814, he published his German Catechism, and not long afterwards his English Catechism, for the especial benefit of the young, not changing the substance of Luther's Catechism. To these Catechisms he appended an explanation of all the Fast and Festival Days observed in the Church. Soon after this, his little work, written in rhyme, entitled *Zeitvertreib* (Pastime) made its appearance, to the amusement of some, and the annoyance of others,—it was a satirical rebuke to fanaticism and superstition, vice and folly.

He was well proportioned, large and erect, standing about six feet, with well developed physical organs, full of energy and perseverance. His mind was well balanced. His attainments were liberal. As a citizen, he was kind, affectionate, and forbearing. As a neighbor, he was universally esteemed and beloved. As a preacher, he had few superiors in his day. He was animated and often eloquent. His soul was in his Master's cause. Few ministers performed more arduous, faithful, efficient labor than he did. In all the relations of life, he was true, faithful, pious, reliable, and upright.

On the 20th of November, 1776, he entered into the holy estate of matrimony with Miss Elizabeth Negley, who, with her father's family, had emigrated from New Jersey to Virginia. They became the parents of nine children,—six sons and three daughters. The oldest son entered the medical profession, and the other five, the ministerial, becoming Lutheran ministers.

He preached his first sermon in Pendleton County, Virginia, now West Virginia, in the year 1781, on Phil. 2, 5, and his last one, in New Market, Shenandoah County, Virginia, Oct. 9, 1825, on Luke 2, 34.

After faithfully serving his generation for many years, it pleased the great Head of the Church to call him from his labors here to his reward in the Church triumphant. He died of paralysis, on the 17th day of November, 1825; aged 70 years, 11 months, and 11 days, and was buried at New Market, Shenandoah County, Virginia; Rev. Geo. H. Riemenschneider officiating. The sermon was based on Phil. 1, 21.

In speaking of the Rev. Paul Henkel, John G. Morris, D. D., LL. D., says, in his work, "Fifty Years in the Ministry," he "was, in early life and for many years, a laborious missionary among the scattered Anglo-German population in the South. He may indeed be considered as one of the pioneers of the church in that region, which was in those days truly desolate. His narrative, which was printed, has all the interest of romance, and if he had performed the same self-denying labors in the service of any other church he would have received a greater earthly reward."

Seventh Session.

According to appointment, Synod met in Buehler's Church, Sullivan County, Tennessee, September 8, 1826. The ministers, with the usual delegates, were present. The absentees were excused. It was resolved, that, at the next meeting of Synod, both the German and the English languages may be used in the proceedings of Synod. The parochial report shows progress. Rev. David Henkel was elected secretary, his office to continue through the synodical year. It seems, that heretofore that office terminated with the session of Synod. The name of Rev. Andrew Sechrist was, for good and sufficient reasons, dropped from the clerical roll.

The Synod having made several attempts to meet with ministers of the North Carolina Synod in consultation, discussion, or debate, and all having failed, it authorized Revs. Adam Miller, Daniel Moser, and David Henkel to proclaim or announce a public meeting, to be held at or near Organ Church, Rowan County, North Carolina, commencing on the 4th day of November *proximo*, to take into consideration and discuss the points of doctrine about which there were differences, and invite ministers of the North Carolina Synod to be present and participate, with a view to adjust the conflicts and restore harmony.

At this meeting, it was resolved, that Luther's Small Catechism be translated and printed in an English dress, and that Rev. Ambrose Henkel make arrangements to have the matter receive proper attention.

Seventeen petitions from the following States, Virginia, North Carolina, Tennessee, Indiana, and Ohio, numerously signed, requesting ministerial services, were received.—Arrangements were made to supply the wants of the petitioners.

Several letters from Pennsylvania were read, requesting Rev. David Henkel to visit that State and preach and vindicate the distinctive doctrines of the Lutheran Church. He was advised to go, and he finally agreed so to do.

Mr. Samuel C. Parmer, of Tennessee, applied to be received under the care of Synod, with a view to the ministry. He was received, and placed under the care of Rev. Adam Miller.

Adam Miller, Jr., was examined and ordained as pastor, and David Forester as deacon, and a committee was appointed to ordain J. N. Stirewalt as a deacon some time during the synodical year.

It was resolved, that Synod meet in its next session in Zion's Church, Sullivan County, Tennessee, twenty miles west of Abingdon, Virginia, on the first Sunday in September, 1827.

As the Divinity of Christ was called into question, both from the pulpit and in print, Rev. David Henkel was requested to write a book on that subject. He consented to do so. This gave rise to his work against the Unitarians.

The following is the Parochial Report:

Rev. Ambrose Henkel baptized 54 infants, 1 adult, and 2 slaves, and confirmed 10; Rev. Nehemiah Bonham, 40 infants, 10 adults, and 5 slaves; Rev. Christian Moretz, 83 infants, 1 adult, and 4 slaves, and confirmed 14; Rev. Adam Miller, Jr., 53 infants, 1 adult, and 1 slave; Rev. Adam Miller, Sr., 216 infants and 10 adults, and confirmed 138; Rev. Daniel Moser, 104 infants, 1 adult, and 7 slaves; Rev. George Easterly, 52 infants, 2 adults, and 2 slaves, and confirmed 6; Rev. David Henkel, 205 infants, 14 adults, and 7 slaves, and confirmed 83; Rev. Philip Henkel, 100 infants, 5 adults, and confirmed 30.

Eighth Session.

Synod met, according to previous appointment, in Zion's Church, Sullivan County, Tennessee, September 3, 1827. The ministers were all present except Revs. H.

Riemenschneider, Philip Henkel, Adam Miller, Sr., N. Bonham, J. Zink, and Deacon Costner. These were excused.

Rev. David Henkel was appointed secretary for the synodical year. Both the German and English languages, according to previous resolution, were permitted to be used during the sessions of Synod.

The committee, appointed at the previous session, to call a public meeting for the purpose of discussing the points of doctrine, on which there were differences, and invite ministers of the North Carolina Synod to participate with equal rights, reported, stating, that the meeting was appointed and regular notice given, but none of the North Carolina Synod ministers attended.

By those assembled, the committee were requested to make another similar appointment for the same purpose.—Afterwards the committee were again solicited to do the same thing, try another assembly, in Lincoln County, North Carolina. Hence, another meeting was called to assemble, for the same purpose, in St. Paul's Church, in the aforesaid County, on the day after the rising of the North Carolina Synod, which was held in that Church; so that it might be convenient for the ministers of that Synod to be present.—The committee reported the result of this meeting to Synod, —which was, that none of the ministers of the North Carolina Synod attended the meeting. Revs. Daniel Moser and David Henkel appeared, and after the latter made an address, it was thought there was no use in pursuing the matter any further at that time, as there was no one to discuss with.—The report was received and ordered to be spread on the Minutes. The committee, after the failure of this meeting at St. Paul's, requested Rev. David Henkel to prepare a paper, showing the propriety and reasons for such a meeting and such discussion, under the circumstances. He did so, and it was ordered to be printed in the Minutes of this session. See Minutes of 1827.

As the questions, submitted to the Pennsylvania Synod

and the address to the Rev. Muhlenberg, have not been answered, it was resolved, with a view of obtaining the sentiment of several synods, as well as of individual ministers, in regard to the differences, that Rev. David Henkel prepare a pastoral address, showing the position of this Synod in respect to true, genuine Lutheran doctrine, requesting synods and individual ministers to manifest their approval or disapproval of its position. Rev. David Henkel was requested to prepare this pastoral address for publication, other ministers giving such aid as deemed proper. He agreed to prepare this address as soon as time would admit. This address was to be published in both the German and English.

For the distribution of publications and good books, special agents were appointed, who were to be aided by the ministers, &c.

Rev. Ambrose Henkel, who was appointed at the last session of Synod to procure an accurate translation of Luther's Small Catechism, submitted the manuscript translation to Synod. It was received, and after the Synod spent a day in examining it, and finding it satisfactory, he was requested to have it published, with the preliminary observations. This was probably the first full, direct translation of said work ever published in this country in the English.

Rev. David Henkel, who was appointed at the previous session to write a work on the Person and Incarnation of Christ, reported that he had not as yet completed it, owing to a press of other engagements.

At the request of some of the lay-delegates, Rev. David Henkel was asked to make an English translation of the entire Augsburg Confession of Faith. He agreed to undertake the task, provided sufficient time be allowed.

As the constitution of Synod, at its organization, stands among the proceedings of Synod, unseparated from them, as it were, and as there is no definite distinction between the articles that are unalterable and those which are, a committee was appointed to remodel and improve it. This was done, and after a careful examination, it was ordered to be printed in connection with the Minutes of this session.

A resolution was passed requiring ministers to give a very careful and thorough course of catechetical instruction in the doctrines and practices of the Church, to the young and inexperienced, before admitting them to the ancient rite of confirmation, as there was a growing negligence in that direction.

Another resolution was passed admonishing parents to send their children more regularly to such instructions, and to be more liberal in remunerating ministers for their services, especially those who are able to do so.

It was also resolved, that those having a view to entering the ministry, should take a respectable course in literary training, and be examined in regard to such attainments, as well as to their theological acquirements, before entering the ministry; and where opportunities present, they were advised to study the Greek and Hebrew languages, as well as the German and English.

There being petitions for the ordination of Mr. John N. Stirewalt, a committee was appointed to ordain him at some future time during the year. On the 13th day of October, 1827, he was ordained. A petition, requesting Mr. Abraham Miller of Tennessee, to be taken under the care of Synod, with a view to the ministry, being presented, the request was granted.

Then follows a long list of petitions from three different States, praying for ministerial services. Their requests were granted as far as possible.

Synod adjourned to meet in St. Paul's Church, Lincoln County, North Carolina, September 8, 1828. No parochial report appears for this session.

Ninth Session.

Synod convened in its ninth convention, in St. Paul's Church, Lincoln County, North Carolina, September 8, 1828, and continued till the 13th.

The ministers were all present, except Revs. Riemenschneider, Zink, Adam Miller, Sr., and Moretz, and Deacon J. N. Stirewalt. These having rendered sufficient reasons for their absence, were excused.

Thirty-four delegates were present. Three applicants, preparing for the ministry,—Messrs. George A. Leopold, Ephraim Rudisill, and John Huggins,—after examination, were received under the care of Synod.

Rev. David Henkel was unanimously elected secretary, with Mr. Ephraim Rudisill as his assistant.

It was recommended, that the members of the Church, who are able to do so, read the Christian Book of Concord, or the Symbolical Books of the Evangelical Lutheran Church, and that students of theology study it carefully. This clearly indicates the deep interest which this Synod felt relative to the true, fundamental doctrines of the Church, and how it desired to maintain and perpetuate these sound, Scriptural principles.

As the edition of the English hymn-book, used by the Synod, was about exhausted, it was resolved, that it be revised and improved, and that Rev. Ambrose Henkel provide for another edition, and that he be assisted in this work by Revs. Paul Henkel, N. Bonham, G. Easterly, D. Henkel, and Adam Miller, Sr.

With a view to the edification of the members of the Church, it was resolved, that an article or a treatise on some doctrinal subject be annually printed in connection with the Minutes of the Synod, if the matter meet with sufficient encouragement.

This course, it seems, had an excellent effect. It made the people better acquainted with the more important doctrines of the Church, and caused them to take more interest in its promotion.

The Secretary, Rev. David Henkel, was requested to write a treatise on the subject of Prayer, and that it be printed in connection with the proceedings of Synod. This was done, and it is worthy of re-publication at this time. It covers twenty-three pages. Rev. David Henkel reported that the work which he was requested to prepare on the Person and Incarnation of Christ, was completed.

Twenty-six petitions were received from congregations situated in the following States: Virginia, North Carolina, Georgia, Tennessee, Indiana, and Ohio,—returning thanks for services rendered during the past, and praying for a continuation of such services. Arrangements were made to supply the petitioners. After examination, David Forester was ordained to the office of Pastor. No parochial report appears in these Minutes.

Tenth Session.

The tenth session was held in Salem Church, Lincoln County, North Carolina, from the 7th to the 10th of September, 1829.

The following ministers were absent: Revs. Riemenschneider, Bonham, Miller, Sr., Easterly, and Forester, and Deacon Costner. Twenty-three delegates were present. The absent ministers, having rendered satisfactory reasons for absence, were excused. Only eight of the ministers presented parochial reports. These were for two years, and show that by them 1,198 infants, 87 adults, and 31 slaves were baptized, and 511 persons were confirmed.

Twenty-seven petitions from congregations representing five States were presented, returning thanks for services rendered, and praying for a continuation of similar services.

Deacon John N. Stirewalt was ordained as pastor.

The persons, appointed at the last session, to revise, amend, and publish the Church hymn-book, having declined the undertaking of that work, for various reasons, Rev. David Henkel was appointed to compile a suitable hymn-book, and present the manuscript to some future session of Synod for examination.

Rev. David Henkel was requested to prepare an article on Regeneration, and have it published in connection with the proceedings of Synod.

In view of intervening circumstances which occurred since the session of 1827, it was deemed unnecessary to publish the pastoral letter, ordered to be published, at that session.

The Secretary was requested to send copies of the Minutes of this session to the German Reformed Synod of Pennsylvania, which had sent ten copies of its proceedings to this Synod, and also to East Pennsylvania Synod and the Ohio Synod,—each ten copies.

At his request, Mr. John Huggins, theological student, was placed under the special care of Rev. David Henkel.

On motion of Miles Abernathy, Esq., the sincere thanks of this body were tendered to Dr. Solomon Henkel, of New Market, Virginia, for the kindness and liberality manifested towards this Synod in printing and publishing its Minutes and other matter from time to time.

Revs. John L. Markert and Nehemiah Bonham were appointed to visit all the congregations in connection with Synod, and look after their interests, and report to the next meeting of Synod. This course, it appears, had a good effect on the congregations and ministers.

Synod adjourned to meet in Cove Creek Church, Green County, Tennessee, on the second Sunday of September, 1830.

During the first decade the number of ministers, which was six, who entered it at its organization, was increased to seventeen, and five theological students,—an increase of nearly two hundred per cent. During this time one minister, Rev. Jacob Zink, died, and the name of one, for good and sufficient reasons, was dropped from the clerical roll of the Synod.

The number of baptisms reported,—not more than two-thirds of the ministers reported regularly,—was 5,517 infants, 443 adults, and 205 slaves,—total, 6,165. The number confirmed was 1,902. The number of congregations, though no regular catalogue of them appears in the Minutes, as near as can be approximated from the applications for reception in connection with the Synod, was more than thribbled during that period. The labors of the Synod extended into nine States,—Tennessee, North Carolina, Kentucky, Missouri, Virginia, Indiana, South Carolina, Georgia, and Ohio,—sowing the seeds of sound Gospel doctrine. Perhaps there was no Synod at that time which did as much work, in proportion to the number of laborers, as this Synod did.

SECOND DECADE.

Eleventh Session.

The eleventh session of this Synod was held in Emmanuel Church, Green County, Tennessee, beginning September 13, 1830.

It seems, that only four of the pastors, with seventeen lay-delegates, were present at this session. The others, having rendered satisfactory excuses for their absence, were excused. Rev. Philip Henkel was elected secretary. Very little business was transacted. Six petitions, four of which were from the State of Indiana, were received, praying for ministerial services. Their requests were answered as far as it was possible to do at that time. Mr. Eusebius Henkel was received as a student of theology, and put under the special care of his father Rev. Philip Henkel and Rev. George Easterly. Synod adjourned to meet in Buehler's Church, Sullivan County, Tennessee, on the second Sunday of September, 1831.

Twelfth Session.

The twelfth session of this Synod was held in Buehler's Church, Sullivan County, Tennessee, commencing September 12th, and continued to Friday, the 16th, 1831.

Nine ministers were present, and twenty-five lay-delegates. The absentees were excused. Rev. Ambrose Henkel was elected secretary. The committee on letters and petitions consisted of Revs. Philip Henkel, Ambrose Henkel, and Mr. Irenius N. Henkel. On hearing the sad intelligence of the death of Rev. David Henkel, the following persons were appointed a committee to prepare an obituary on his death: Revs. Daniel Moser and Adam Miller, Jr., and Messrs. Philip Rudisill and Henry Goodman.

The applicants for the ministry were Mr. William C. Rankin, of Green County, Tennessee, and Mr. Henry Goodman, of Rowan County, North Carolina.

Petitions asking, that Mr. W. C. Rankin, formerly a licentiate of the Presbyterian Church, be ordained to the office of Pastor, being submitted, after examination and confirmation, Mr. Rankin was ordained to that office.

Mr. John Huggins, of Lincoln County, North Carolina, an applicant for the ministry, applied for license to preach and baptize, but as he had no call from congregations to that effect, his request was not granted.

At the request of Mr. John Easterly, a former applicant for the ministry, he was placed under the care of Rev. Philip Henkel, as a student of theology.

After examination, Mr. Henry Goodman was ordained to the office of Deacon.

Thirty-three petitions, returning thanks for past services and praying for a continuance of the same, were received, and their requests granted. Among these, there were several new congregations.

Rev. Philip Henkel reported that he had organized five congregations in Indiana,—the first in Clear Creek township, Monroe County; the second in Beanblossom township, Monroe County; the third in Park County; the fourth in Whiteriver township, Morgan County, and the fifth on Whiteriver Bluff, Johnson County, Indiana.

The Synod being informed that Greenville College, Tennessee, was not under the control of any denomination, but a State institution, it was recommended to those who wished to take a regular literary course.

Rev. David Henkel, who had been appointed to compile a hymn-book, having departed this life, Rev. Ambrose Henkel was appointed to attend to that matter, with the privilege of selecting such person as he deemed proper to assist him; and so, too, in regard to securing a translation of the Augsburg Confession, and submit it to Synod for examination.

The Parochial Report,—only six of the ministers reporting,—shows that during this and the past year 876 infants, 65 adults, and 37 slaves were baptized, and 320 persons were confirmed.

It was resolved, that the Synod meet, in its next session, in or near Organ Church, Rowan County, North Carolina, on the second Sunday of September, 1832.

The committee on obituary, submitted the following, which was received, adopted, and ordered to be printed in connection with the Minutes:

Obituary of Rev. David Henkel.—We, the members of the committee, appointed to report the particulars relative to the last illness, death, &c., of our worthy and highly esteemed brother in Christ, the Rev. David Henkel (son of the Rev. Paul Henkel), a member of the Evangelical Lutheran Tennessee Synod, beg leave to submit the following:

This much esteemed and venerable fellow-laborer, having finished the work assigned him by Divine Providence, departed this life, June 15, 1831, at 9 o'clock in the morning, to the great grief of his friends and relatives; aged thirty-six years, one month, and eleven days. He was born in Staunton, Augusta County, Virginia, May 4, 1795. His last illness was Dyspepsia, which disabled him from officiating in a public capacity for the term of nine months. He bore his afflictions with a perfect resignation to the will of his Divine Redeemer. He embarked in the cause of his blessed Savior when a youth (A. D. 1812). And we are happy to say, to the praise of this worthy servant of Christ, that his assiduity and vigilance to study and deep researches into the truth of Divine Revelation have seldom been equaled by any. He remained immovable in the doctrines he promulgated to the end of his life. This venerable servant of the Lord had to endure many trials, crosses, and temptations, but he maintained his integrity through them all, trusting to the promises of his Redeemer; and notwithstanding the difficulties he had to encounter, he left a bright example to succeeding pilgrims. His ardent desire for the promotion of his Redeemer's Kingdom, and his love of truth, caused him to submit cheerfully to the difficulties connected with his official labors. When on his death-bed, being interrogated by his friends, whether he still remained steadfast in the doctrines which he had taught, he confidently answered in the affirmative. Being again asked, whether he feared death, he replied in the negative. The last words which he was heard to utter, were: "*O Lord Jesus, thou Son of God, receive my spirit!*" and in a few moments expired.

He entered into the holy estate of matrimony with Miss Catharine Heyl (Hoyle), daughter of Hon. Peter Heyl (Hoyle), of near Lincolnton, Lincoln County, North Carolina.

The perishable remains of this worthy brother were followed to the grave by his loving companion and seven children, together with a numerous train of mourners, who were left, to lament the loss of a kind father, an affectionate husband, a friend and benefactor. The body is deposited at St. John's Church, Lincoln County, North Carolina. The funeral sermon was delivered by the Rev. Daniel Moser, from Phil. 1, 21—"For to me to live is Christ, and to die is gain."

Lord so teach us to number our days, that we may apply our hearts to wisdom!

The committee, appointed to draught the obituary notice of the Rev. David Henkel, requested the Secretary to add any particulars relative to his ministerial labors and writings which he may be able to obtain.

In conformity with the above request, I am enabled, from notes made by my lamented brother during his life time and other sources of information, to which I have had access, to give the following particulars, viz.:

He commenced his Gospel labors at St. Peter's Church, in South Carolina, where he preached his first sermon, November the 1st, 1812, from which period up to the time he preached his last sermon at Philadelphia Church, Lincoln County, North Carolina, on Sunday, the 12th of August, 1830, where he administered the Lord's Supper,—which concluded upwards of three thousand and two hundred sermons; delivered generally to crowded and attentive congregations. He baptized two thousand nine hundred and ninety-seven infants, and two hundred and forty-three adults, and he confirmed one thousand one hundred and five persons.

During the whole course of his ministry, which was distinguished for industry and perseverance, in the cause of his Divine Master, he traveled in all seasons, even the most inclement, and frequently preached two and three times in a day, in the German and English languages. Besides which he maintained an extensive correspondence with many individuals, distinguished for piety and learning, and wrote the following works:

His first work, containing a sermon, entitled, "The Essence of the Christian Religion, and Reflections on Futurity," was published in 1817.

His second, called "The Carolinian Herald of Liberty, Religious and Political," published in 1821.

His third, "Objections to the Constitution of the General Synod," made its appearance, annexed to the Minutes of the Tennessee Synod, held in 1821.

His fourth, entitled "The Heavenly Flood of Regeneration, or Treatise on Holy Baptism," published in 1822.

His fifth, "An Answer to Joseph Moore," who wrote in opposition to the doctrines contained in his Heavenly Flood, published in 1825.

He then draughted 6thly the Constitution, together with the remarks thereon, of the Evangelical Lutheran Tennessee Synod, in 1828: and annexed to the Minutes of the same year, his Treatise on Prayer appeared.

His seventh, A Translation from the German of Luther's Small Catechism, with Preliminary Observations by the translator, published in 1829.

His eighth, "An Essay on Regeneration," published in 1830.

His ninth, "A Treatise on the Person and Incarnation of Jesus Christ, in which some of the principal arguments of the Unitarians are examined," which has just left the press.

Thirteenth Session.

The thirteenth session of this Synod was held in Phanuel's Church, Rowan County, North Carolina, from the tenth to the fifteenth of September, 1832.

On Saturday and Sunday, the usual services were held. Only four ministers were in attendance, and twenty-four lay-delegates. None of the absentees, except Rev. Philip Henkel and Deacon Costner, having sent in sufficient reasons for their absence, were excused for their non-attendance. Rev. J. N. Stirewalt was appointed secretary.

Charges having been preferred, by Rev. N. Bonham and others, against Rev. W. C. Rankin, of deviation, from the Augsburg Confession of Faith, both in regard to doctrine and practice, Mr. Rankin was notified to attend the next session, and answer the charges.

Twenty-two petitions of the usual import, relative to services, &c., were presented, and received such action as they deserved. Among these, there were petitions for the examination and ordination of Deacon Henry Goodman. Having sustained his examination, he was ordained to the office of Pastor.

The place and time for the next meeting, resulted in favor of St. John's Church, Lincoln County, North Carolina, as the place, and the second Sunday of September, 1833, as the time.

The Parochial Report, only five ministers reporting,—one, however, Rev. Adam Miller, Sr., for three years,—shows 808 infants, 69 adults, and 41 slaves, baptized, and 253 confirmed.

Fourteenth Session.

Pursuant to previous appointment, Synod met in St. John's Church, Lincoln County, North Carolina, Monday, September 9th, and continued till the 12th, 1833.

Saturday and Sunday previous were occupied with services suitable to these days.

The ministers, with applicant Eusebius S. Henkel, and thirty-three lay-delegates, representing forty-three congregations, were all present, except Revs. Forester, Bonham, Adam Miller, Jr., Moretz, Markert, and Deacon Costner.

A president and a secretary were elected,—Secretary, Rev. Ambrose Henkel.

In view of satisfactory reasons rendered for absence, all the absentees, except Rev. C. Moretz, were excused.

Relative to the charges preferred against Rev. W. C. Rankin by Rev. N. Bonham, at the previous session, Rev. Bonham being unable to be present during this meeting, and Rev. Rankin desiring to withdraw from this body, in a friendly manner, the matter was not investigated, and the name of Rev. Rankin was dropped from the clerical roll.

With respect to the translation of the Augsburg Confession, which Rev. Ambrose Henkel was requested, at the session of 1831, to procure, he submitted to Synod a translation, made by his brother Rev. Charles Henkel, of Ohio, with proof-sheets, for examination. But a press of urgent business being before Synod, it could not devote time enough for a careful examination. Hence, each member having a copy in proof-sheet form, was requested to examine it carefully, as soon as possible, and send him such suggestions as each deemed proper.

Twenty-seven petitions from different States were presented, classified, and acted on. They expressed satisfaction with the services they had received from Synod, and a desire for further services. Some of these asked for the publication of a good article or a sermon in connection with the Minutes, and others, for the ordination of Eusebius S. Henkel and Irenius Henkel to the office of Deacon. In regard to the latter, as he was absent, no action could be taken at this meeting. The former, having sustained his examination, was ordained to that office.

A letter having been received from Mr. Ephraim Conrad, of Wayne County, Missouri, asking to be received under the care of Synod, as an applicant for the ministry, his request was granted.

It was ordered, that a sermon on the Lord's Supper, translated from the German of Arndt's Postil, be connected with the Minutes, and that they be printed in the German and English. Frederick Hoke, Esq., of Lincoln County, North Carolina, was appointed to contract for the printing of the Minutes.

Rev. Philip Henkel was appointed to prepare the translation of the aforesaid sermon. It was resolved, that the next session of Synod be held in Rader's Church, Rockingham County, Virginia, commencing on the second Sunday of September, 1834.*

Rev. Philip Henkel was also requested to prepare for publication a Dissertation on the Person of Jesus Christ, as

*NOTE.—It appears, that, in consequence of high waters and other causes, scarcely any ministers were able to reach the place of meeting; and, hence, no regular session of Synod was held there; nor were there any proceedings printed for that year.

extant in the Christian Book of Concord, and submit it to the next session.

During the past year, nine ministers reporting,—one for several years,—801 infants, 56 adults, and 17 slaves, were baptized, and 399 persons confirmed.

The death of Rev. Philip Henkel being announced, before the Minutes had passed through the press, the following obituary, prepared by the Secretary, was appended to the Minutes :

Obituary of Rev. Philip Henkel.—Before these Minutes could be put to press, the sad and heartbreaking news was received, that our much beloved brother and fellow-laborer, in the Lord's vineyard, the Rev. Philip Henkel, departed this life, October 9, 1833.

For the satisfaction of his friends and relatives, we subjoin the following brief account :

The deceased was a son of the Rev. Paul Henkel, and a fellow-member of the Lutheran Tennessee Synod, of which he also was one of the first framers. He was born on the 23d September, 1779, in Pendleton County, Virginia.

In early life he imbibed the principles of the Christian religion, and in a short time became a zealous defender of the same. In 1800, he commenced his Gospel labors in the Lord's vineyard, in whose service he continued with undaunted zeal, for 38 years and 3 months, during which time he preached upwards of four thousand three hundred and fifty sermons, of which one hundred and twenty-five were funeral sermons. He baptized four thousand one hundred and fifteen infants, and three hundred and twenty-five adults ; and confirmed to the Christian Church one thousand six hundred and fifty persons.

At the present session of our Synod, we frequently had the pleasure of hearing him proclaim the Gospel of Jesus Christ. Here he was also, (but alas, for the last time !) nominated President of our Synod. And after the close of the Synod, he proceeded, in good health, to visit the congregations in Guilford and the adjacent counties. After he had arrived in Randolph County, North Carolina, he preached in Richland Church, on September 21st, from Col. 3, 1-5. (His last sermon on this earthly stage !) Being invited by a neighboring friend, he retired to his house, where he was at the same evening attacked with the bilious fever, to which, after a short illness, he fell a victim. He departed this life on Wednesday, the 9th of October, 1833. On the day following, he was buried at Richland Church.

His earthly abode was 54 years and 17 days. A short time before he expired, he said : "If it is the will of the Lord, to take me to rest,

I am willing." And then repeated the following lines (which also were the last words that were heard from his lips):

> "Christ is my life alone,
> To die is gain for me;
> I give myself to be his own:
> O may I ever with him be."

Fifteenth Session.

Synod met in its fifteenth session, in Blue Spring Church, Green County, Tennessee, on September 14th, and continued to the 17th, 1835.

Appropriate services were held on Saturday and Sunday previous, and the Lord's Supper administered to a large number of devout communicants.

About one-half of the ministers, with five applicants for the ministry,—Messrs. Daniel L. Schoolfield, Henry Wetzel, Christian G. Reitzel, Samuel C. Parmer, and Wm. Hancher,—and twenty lay-delegates, representing twenty-nine congregations, were present.

After the election of a president, Rev. Adam Miller was appointed secretary.

The Minutes of 1833 were read, as well as a printed letter from Rev. A. Henkel, in which he informed Synod, that very few members had attended the appointment for the meeting of Synod in Rader's Church, Rockingham County, Virginia, in 1834, and that consequently very little business was transacted, except the reading of the letters addressed to Synod, which letters were left in his care, to be forwarded to the next meeting of Synod. The usual committees were appointed. The absentees, on proper reasons, were excused for their non-attendance.

A letter was received from Rev. Eusebius S. Henkel, of Indiana, that they intend to organize a Synod in that State,—a move which this Synod heartily approved, asking the blessing of God to rest upon their labors.

A large number of petitions, expressing thanks for services received, asking the blessing of God on the work of the Synod, requesting a continuance of services, suggesting that suitable articles be appended to the Minutes, &c., were received, and properly acted upon.

Among these is a petition from Wythe, Smyth, and Washington Counties, Virginia, in which the petitioners state their withdrawal from the North Carolina Synod, together with their pastor, Rev. Andrew Sechrist, whose name, for sufficient reasons, had been dropped from the clerical roll of this Synod, and desire to be received with their pastor into this Synod. Rev. Sechrist, having confessed, that experience had taught him, that, in withdrawing from Synod, he had committed an error, for which he was sorry, and solemnly pledged himself to teach and practice according to the Holy Scriptures and the Augsburg Confession of Faith, he and his congregations were received in connection with Synod.

Rev. Ambrose Henkel submitted sufficient reasons for the delay in regard to the publication of the Church hymn-book.

Messrs. C. G. Reitzel and D. S. Schoolfield were examined with respect to their qualifications.

Rev. A. Henkel was respectfully requested to complete the hymn-book as soon as practicable.

There being a great demand for books, and especially for English Catechisms, the Secretary was requested to write to Dr. Solomon Henkel, New Market, Virginia, relative to that matter, calling for catechisms and other useful books.

Rev. Philip Henkel, who was requested to prepare a translation from the Christian Book of Concord, on the Person of Christ, and submit it to this meeting of Synod for examination and publication, having departed this life, the translation was made by the Secretary, assisted by Mr. J. R. Moser, as it appears in connection with the Minutes of this session.

In regard to publications, the Synod took the following action:

Inasmuch as this body deem it highly important that the writings of the late Rev. David Henkel be printed and bound, so that they may be handed down to future generations, be it resolved, that the Secretary be directed to correspond with Dr. Solomon Henkel relative to this matter, and report the result of his correspondence to the next meeting of Synod.

The following applicants, Messrs. Hancher, Reitzel, Schoolfield, and Parmer, having sustained their examinations, were ordained to the office of Deacon.

Philadelphia Church, Lincoln County, North Carolina, was chosen as the place for the next meeting of Synod, and the second Sunday of September, 1836, as the time.

The Parochial Report shows that 1130 infants, 63 adults, and 41 slaves were baptized, and 515 persons confirmed.

After the close of the Synod, the Secretary received a letter directed to Synod, by Rev. John L. Markert, of Indiana, written by order of and in the name of the Evangelical Lutheran Synod of Indiana, in which he states, that the suffering condition of the Church in the West, pressed upon them from all directions, to adopt some plan to withstand the enemy. For this purpose councils were held and propositions made, and the final result was the organization of a synod. A meeting was held in Johnson County, Indiana, on the third Sunday of August, 1835, and after proper consultation, the Constitution of the Tennessee Synod was received and adopted, and the organization effected. In that letter, they entreat their brethren of the Tennessee Synod not to consider this course as an intention to separate from them, but as a means of strengthening the same cause.

The ministers of the Tennessee Synod who effected that organization, were Revs. J. L. Markert, Christian Moretz, and Eusebius S. Henkel.

Sixteenth Session.

This session was held in Philadelphia Church, Lincoln

County, North Carolina, beginning on the 12th and closing on the 16th of September, 1836.

On Saturday and Sunday previous appropriate services were conducted and suitable sermons preached, both in the German and English languages, and the Lord's Supper administered to 240 communicants.

Only about one-half of the ministers, with four applicants and twenty-seven lay-delegates, were present.

The applicants were Messrs. Henry Wetzel, from Wythe County, Virginia, Abel J. Brown, Jacob Killian, and Jonathan R. Moser, Lincoln County, North Carolina.

After the election of a president, Mr. J. R. Moser was appointed secretary. Very few of the absentees were excused, and a resolution passed urging the ministers to be more faithful and regular in attending the meetings of Synod. Mr. George Wetzel, of Wythe County, Virginia, was admitted to a seat and vote in Synod. The Secretary of the previous session, appointed to correspond with Dr. Solomon Henkel relative to supplying the books desired by Synod for circulation, reported rather favorably. An agent to attend to this matter was appointed. The books mostly in demand just at that time were David Henkel on the Person and Incarnation of Christ, his Answer to Joseph Moore, and the English Catechism.

A letter having been received from Mr. Jonah Hottel, Esq., of Wythe County, Virginia, in which charges were preferred against Rev. Andrew Sechrist, and the latter having received no previous notice of such preferment, so as to enable him to prepare for defending himself against these charges, the matter was deferred, for investigation, till the next meeting, Mr. Sechrist agreeing to cease his ministerial work till the case shall have been adjusted. Notwithstanding this fraternal course on the part of the Synod, it seems, Mr. Sechrist absented himself from further attendance during this session of Synod, without leave. For this course of conduct he was censured by the Synod.

Mr. Solomon S. Miles, of Lancaster District, South

Carolina, having appeared in the presence of Synod, and stated his intention of re-publishing Luther's Commentary on Galatians, in the English language, the Synod recommended the work and encouraged Mr. Miles in this enterprise.

The usual petitions received proper attention. The petition for the examination and ordination of deacons S. C. Parmer and William Hancher to the office of Pastor, and applicants Abel J. Brown, Jacob Killian, and Jonathan R. Moser to the office of Deacon, were taken into consideration. These candidates for the ministry having sustained favorable examinations, were regularly ordained to the offices indicated in the petitions, except Mr. Parmer who was absent, and consequently could not submit to the requirements necessary for ordination. Mr. H. Wetzel was continued as a student of theology.

It was resolved, that the Minutes be printed in German and English, and that a sermon of Luther's be appended. The agent was requested to send copies of the Minutes to the recent Indiana Synod. Only four ministers reporting, the Parochial Report shows 490 infants, 20 adults, and 14 slaves baptized, and 113 confirmed. The death of Rev. John N. Stirewalt being announced, it was resolved, that a suitable obituary notice be prepared and appended to the Minutes. But it appears that for the want of proper information relative to Mr. Stirewalt, the publication of the obituary was delayed till the next session.

Synod adjourned to meet in Koiner's Church, Augusta County, Virginia, on the second Sunday in September, 1837.

Seventeenth Session.

According to adjournment, Synod convened in Koiner's Church, Augusta County, Virginia, on Monday, the 11th of September, and continued its sessions to the 15th, 1837.

Saturday and Sunday were devoted to religious services, preaching, confession and absolution, and the dispensation of the Lord's Supper.

On Monday, the Synod was organized, by the election of a president and Rev. J. R. Moser as secretary.

Rev. John J. Riemenschneider, a member of the Ohio Synod, being present, was received as an advisory member of Synod. Mr. Peter Wetzel was taken under the care of Synod as a student of theology. A part of the absentees were excused.

A letter having been received from Rev. Andrew Sechrist, assigning reasons for his absence, but making no reference to the charges preferred against him, at the previous session, it was deemed proper to appoint a committee to take into consideration his case and report to Synod. The committee consisted of Revs. William Hancher and D. S. Schoolfield, and Mr. Jacob Stirewalt.

After due consideration, this committee submitted the following report: Whereas, at the last session of this Synod, serious charges were preferred against Rev. Andrew Sechrist, and whereas he was notified by Synod to appear at this meeting and defend himself against these charges, and whereas he has failed to appear in person, or to write anything in justification of his course, and whereas the charges are of such a nature as to disparage the ministerial office, we, your committee, recommend, that he be no longer regarded as a minister in connection with this Synod. This report was received and adopted.

The petitions, numbering thirty-four, of the usual character, received proper attention. Among these, there was a petition from Probst Church, Pendleton County, Virginia, now West Virginia, asking to be received by Synod, and recommending Mr. A. S. Link as a suitable person for the ministry; and other petitions asking for the examination and ordination of candidates for the ministry.

Rev. Ambrose Henkel, who had been appointed, by Synod, to compile and prepare matter for an English hymn-book, and submit the manuscript to Synod for examination, presented the copy. A committee, consisting of Revs. H. Goodman and Wm. Hancher, and Messrs. Wm. Wolford,

E. Leineberger, and Peter Wetzel, were appointed for that purpose. After careful examination, the committee submitted a favorable report, suggesting, that if any of the members of Synod desired to examine the work more thoroughly, they might do so, and report any desirable changes to the compiler. The report was adopted.

Relative to a letter received from Rev. Adam Miller, Jr., in regard to the Augsburg Confession, it was resolved, that Dr. Solomon Henkel correspond with Rev. Miller with respect to that matter.

According to resolution, the proceedings of this meeting were to be printed both in German and English, and a copy sent to each of the ministers of the Evangelical Lutheran Indiana Synod.

Having sustained a favorable examination, deacons D. S. Schoolfield, Abel J. Brown, Jacob Killian, and Jonathan R. Moser were ordained as pastors, and applicants Henry Wetzel, A. S. Link, Jacob Stirewalt, and Alfred J. Fox as deacons.

During this session, as far as reported, 817 infants, 24 adults, and 13 slaves were baptized, and 291 were confirmed.

As the obituary notice of the death of Rev. John N. Stirewalt was not received in time to be inserted in the proceedings of the session of 1836, it was ordered to be printed in connection with the Minutes of this session.

Salem Church, Lincoln County, North Carolina, was agreed upon as the place for the next meeting of Synod, and the second Sunday in September, 1838, as the time.

Obituary of Rev. John N. Stirewalt.—It is with feelings of deep sorrow that we record the death of our worthy and beloved co-laborer, Rev. John N. Stirewalt, a member of the Evangelical Lutheran Tennessee Synod. He departed this life, August 13, 1836, in Rowan County, North Carolina; aged 34 years and 6 days. He died of lung disease, with which he was afflicted a number of years.

The Lord, in whose hands stand the death and life of man, saw fit to remove this useful laborer in his Vineyard from time into eternity.

At an early age, he was instructed, by his parents, in the rudiments of the Christian religion, and after he had completed his literary and classical course of study, he entered the ministry, in the year 1827, and was ordained to the office of Pastor, August 10, 1829, during the Synod held in Salem Church, Lincoln County, North Carolina.

He was an earnest and zealous teacher of the principles of religion, fearlessly proclaiming the everlasting Gospel eight years and ten months, with great joy and zeal. During this period he dispensed the bread of life; and, notwithstanding his sickness, he made known the saving Gospel of the crucified Savior, with efficiency, to many who had been deprived of it, both in his native State and in adjoining States.

In view of his fidelity to the end of his days, we trust, in yonder, glorious day, he is crowned with an unchangeable crown, and clothed with immortality. During his sickness he frequently admonished his friends and visitors to continue steadfast in the doctrines he had taught them, and shortly before his departure he said: I hope that God the Father, through Christ, may be merciful to me and all others, saying I hope and trust to die in the same faith I taught others, exclaiming, God help us all. Amen.

After the cold hand of death had closed his eyes, his body was placed in the silent grave at Sewitzen Church, Rowan County, North Carolina, to await the resurrection morning. Rev. Daniel Moser rendered the funeral services, and preached a sermon from Phil. 1, 21-23.

As the deceased had intended to move to Virginia, his family, consisting of his wife and four children, soon after his death took their departure, and located on a farm which he had previously purchased, adjoining the corporate limits of the town of New Market, Shenandoah County, Virginia.—JONATHAN R. MOSER, *Secretary of the Evangelical Lutheran Tennessee Synod.*

Eighteenth Session.

In pursuance of previous appointment, Synod assembled in Salem Church, Lincoln County, North Carolina, September 8, 1838.

Saturday and Sunday were spent in worship, preaching, and communion services.

About two-thirds of the ministers, with thirty-three lay-delegates and two applicants, Mr. Peter Wetzel and Mr. Banks McRee, were present.

After the election of a president, Rev. Abel J. Brown was appointed secretary.

After the usual routine business relative to petitions,

returning thanks for services rendered, asking for services and ordinations, making suggestions, &c., had received proper attention, deacons Alfred J. Fox and Jacob Stirewalt were examined with respect to their qualifications for the ministry, and proving themselves worthy and qualified to bear that office, they were solemnly ordained as pastors.

The Secretary submitted the following preamble and resolutions:

"Whereas, repeated, unfair measures have recently been taken by the Synod of South Carolina, for the purpose of bringing into disrepute the Evangelical Lutheran Tennessee Synod; and more especially by the remarks contained in a sermon delivered during her last session by Rev. John Bachman, D. D.; which was published by her sanction and under her immediate patronage; which sermon (if its pernicious influence be not counteracted) is well calculated to make a wrong and an unfavorable impression on the minds of persons otherwise honestly disposed, and to render our Synod, her doctrines, and her ministers the objects of contempt, of ridicule, and of incessant and unmitigating persecution; and believing as we do, that we stand on the primitive basis of the Lutheran Church, and that the doctrines of the glorious and ever memorable Reformation, effected through the special instrumentality of the illustrious Saxon Reformer, Dr. Martin Luther, and his immortal coadjutors, are perfectly compatible with the Word of God, which we acknowledge to be the only infallible rule of faith and practice; be it therefore resolved,

1. That we consider the proceedings of the South Carolina Synod toward us as uncourteous, ungenerous, unfair, and uncharitable;

2. That we regard the allegations contained in Dr. Bachman's sermon as being without the least shadow of foundation or slightest approximation to truth, and nothing but base calumny, and calculated to disparage our Synod."

Resolved, that the foregoing preamble and resolutions be adopted.

On motion, it was unanimously resolved, that the Secretary and Rev. A. Miller, Jr., be requested to write and publish a vindication of the Evangelical Lutheran Tennessee Synod, in reply to Dr. Bachman's sermon.

"Inasmuch as this body has been informed that the Synod of Virginia, during her last session, entered a resolution in the Minutes of her proceedings, stating that she did 'not recognize the members of the Tennessee Conference as Evangelical Lutheran ministers,' be it

Resolved, that the Secretary correspond with the president of the Virginia Synod, to ascertain what are the reasons why she does not recognize the members of our Synod as Evangelical Lutheran ministers."

The Synod recommended the Treatise on the Person and Incarnation of Christ, written by Rev. David Henkel, and informed the brethren that the Church hymn-book, prepared by Rev. Ambrose Henkel, by order of Synod, is now published, and may be obtained any time by applying to the publisher, Dr. Solomon Henkel, New Market, Shenandoah County, Virginia.

Revs. Ambrose Henkel, Jacob Killian, and Jacob Stirewalt were requested to prepare a liturgy for the use of the Church, and lay it before Synod at its next session for examination.

The number of baptisms and confirmations, as far as reported, is 480 infants, 7 adults, 42 slaves, and 93 confirmed.

Synod adjourned to meet in Emmanuel's Church, Sullivan County, Tennessee, on the second Sunday of September, 1839.

After the close of Synod, the Secretary received a letter from Rev. Ephraim R. Conrad, a member of the Indiana Synod, calling attention to the condition of the Church in Missouri, the State in which he resided, and praying Synod to send to their assistance Rev. J. R. Moser, or Rev. A. J. Brown, or some other minister of our Synod. The Secretary recommended special attention to be given to that request.

Nineteenth Session.

Pursuant to resolution of the last session, Synod convened in Emmanuel Church, Sullivan County, Tennessee, September, 1839. Saturday and Sunday were devoted to the services usual on such occasions.

After the appointment of a president, Rev. A. J. Brown was elected secretary. The usual committees were appointed. The ordinary business received proper attention.

In regard to Rev. Adam S. Link, it was resolved, that inasmuch as he has failed to write to Synod, absented himself from it, and united with the Ohio Synod, he be no longer regarded as a member of this Synod, and that his name be dropped from the clerical roll.

Rev. Christian Moretz, a member of the Indiana Synod, being present, was invited to a seat in the Synod, with all the rights and privileges of a member. He responded in a most happy and affectionate manner, giving a brief statement of what was being done in the Synod he represented, for the cause of the Church, and asking the blessing of God on the labors of the brethren of the Tennessee Synod, of which he had been a member, and from which he so much regretted that duty required him to take his leave.

With respect to the appointment of a committee, at the previous session, consisting of Revs. A. J. Brown and A. Miller, Jr., to write a reply to statements which appeared in a sermon delivered by Rev. Dr. Bachman, of Charleston, South Carolina, in opposition to this Synod, and have it printed, it appeared that the committee had complied with the request, and that a large number of copies of the work had been circulated. The Synod approved of the manner in which the charges were refuted, and tendered its thanks to the committee for their prompt and able defence of Synod against the declarations made in that sermon.

Rev. A. J. Brown, having been appointed, at the previous session, to write to the Virginia Synod, to show cause why it could not recognize the members of the Tennessee

Synod as Evangelical Lutherans, stated, that he had written a kind, brotherly, Christian letter to the President of that Synod, Rev. J. B. Davis, asking the reasons why his Synod could not recognize the members of the Tennessee Synod as Evangelical Lutherans, but had received no reply, for reasons he knew not. In view of this fact, he asked, that a copy of the letter he wrote be appended to the Minutes, so that the unprejudiced public might have all the necessary light in regard to the matter. His request was granted.

Rev. Jacob Killian then presented a copy of the proceedings of the last meeting of that Synod to this Synod, which shows the action of that Synod towards this Synod, in justification of its previous resolution, and the reasons why the President of the former did not reply to the Secretary of the latter.

A committee of four, Revs. Hancher, Killian, Wetzel, and Brown, were appointed to prepare a reply to this action of the Virginia Synod, and submit it to Synod. At the proper time the reply, which was clear, forcible, and convincing, was submitted and adopted.

The committee, which had been appointed at the previous session, to prepare a liturgy for the use of the Church, submitted the manuscript copy for examination. A committee, consisting of Revs. A. Miller, Jr., H. Goodman, and G. Easterly, Messrs. A. W. Abernathy, D. Siegle, and G. Burkhart, were appointed to examine the manuscript. After a careful examination, they submitted a very favorable report, approving the work. The report was received.

The death of Rev. Daniel Moser being announced, the Synod passed the following resolutions:

1. That we deeply sympathize with the family in their sad and irreparable loss of an affectionate husband and a kind father.

2. That Rev. Adam Miller prepare a brief obituary notice of the life and labors of the said Moser, and publish it in connection with the Minutes of this Synod.

The number of baptisms and confirmations this synodical year, according to the report, which is not full, is 672 infants, 74 adults, 25 slaves, and 348 confirmed.

The time and place agreed upon for the next meeting, were Pilgrims' Church, Davidson County, North Carolina, and the second Sunday of September, 1840.

Obituary of Rev. Daniel Moser.—On the 11th day of July, 1839, our worthy and highly esteemed friend and co-laborer in the vineyard of our Lord and Savior, Jesus Christ, Rev. Daniel Moser departed this life, in Lincoln, now Catawba, County, North Carolina; aged 49 years, 2 months, and 3 days.

On the 8th day of May, 1790, he was born of Christian parents, in Orange County, North Carolina, and, in his infancy, was baptized by Rev. Henry Barnhardt. On the 3d day of October, 1808, he was confirmed, by Revs. John L. Markert and Philip Henkel to the Evangelical Lutheran Church, in Lauen Church, Guilford County, North Carolina. He entered the ministry in the year 1812, and was ordained to the office of Pastor in the year 1820, during the Synod which met, in that year, in the Evangelical Lutheran Church, in Lincolnton, North Carolina.

In this office, he maintained honor, dignity, and firmness, adhering closely to the Gospel of our Divine Redeemer, and gave diligence in serving God, and leading an upright life and irreproachable conduct, in his labors, rightly dividing the word of truth.

As a preacher, it may be said with truth, that he was firm in the faith, and worthy of his vocation; as a husband, he was kind and affectionate; as a father, pleasant and instructive; as a citizen, he was friendly and liberal; and, in a word, his whole life was irreproachable, as far as it is possible for that of man to be. Well may it be said, that in his death the community, in which he lived, was deprived of one of its best members, and sustained an irreparable loss. Yet we must bow to the will of our heavenly Father, and exclaim: He is the Lord; he doth what seemeth good in his sight.

Brother Moser labored in the gospel ministry about twenty-seven years. During this period he preached 1,943 sermons, baptized 2,450 persons, and confirmed 821. He preached his last sermon in St. Peter's Church, Lincoln County, North Carolina, on the 30th day of June, 1839, on Matt. 28, 20: "Teaching them to observe all things whatsoever I have commanded you," &c.

His last sickness was paralysis. He was found about a mile and a-half from his residence, sitting at the road. His right side was entirely paralyzed. When he was found he was speechless, and remained so till his end, which took place on the seventh day of the attack. Consequently, he was deprived of the power to speak to his relatives and neighbors, which they so much regretted. Yet, we have reason to believe that, in view of his well grounded hope, he was fully assured of his gracious acceptance. His earthly remains were interred in the grave-yard at St. John's Church, Lincoln County, North Carolina. His funeral services were rendered and a sermon was preached on the occasion by the writer of this notice, from 2 Tim. 4, 7, 8: "I have fought a good fight," &c. Rev. A. J. Brown then followed with impressive and pertinent remarks, suited to the sad and solemn occasion. In conclusion we add, "Blessed are the dead which die in the Lord from henceforth; yea, saith the Spirit, that they may rest from their labors, and their works do follow them."—ADAM MILLER.

Twentieth Session.

This session was held in Pilgrims' Church, Davidson County, North Carolina, from Monday the 14th to Wednesday the 16th of September, 1840.

During this session thirty-one petitions, of the usual import, were submitted to Synod, and received proper attention.

Among these is a petition from a number of Lutherans of South Carolina, in which they state, that they formerly belonged to the South Carolina Synod, but as that Synod had deviated from the doctrines and usages of the Church, and introduced innovations, run into fanaticism, &c.; and that, from what they had heard and read, they were satisfied that the Tennessee Synod adhered to the true doctrines and usages of the Church; hence, as their pastor, Rev. Godfrey Dreher, had more labor to perform than he could endure, they entreated Synod to send some suitable minister to assist him in his arduous labors. Synod resolved that Rev. A. J. Brown visit these petitioners.

Applicants Messrs. J. Rhodes and J. W. Hull, having declined to submit to an examination with a view to ordination to the office of Deacon, were continued under the care of the Synod.

Rev. Jacob Stirewalt, one of the committee to compile and publish a suitable liturgy, reported, that the work is now passing through the press, and will soon be ready for circulation.

The practicability and expediency of publishing a religious periodical within the bounds of Synod, were considered. The matter met with favor, but it was deferred for future consideration.

Revs. Miller, Brown, and Moser were appointed to select or prepare a suitable article to be printed in connection with the Minutes. A few remarks on the Instruction of Youth, together with Luther's Preface to his Large Catechism, were selected and prepared by the committee.

During this synodical year, as far as reported, 616 infants, 3 adults, and 20 slaves were baptized, and 240 confirmed.

Synod adjourned to meet in Rader's Church, Rockingham County, Virginia, on the second Sunday of September, 1841.

During this decade, there were 12 applicants for the ministry, 17 ordinations, including those to the office of Deacon, and 2 deaths of ministers, and 6,690 infants, 408 adults, and 250 slaves baptized, and 2,569 persons confirmed. Unfortunately, the parochial reports are not full. Probably not more than three-fourths of the ministers presented reports.

THIRD DECADE.

Twenty-first Session.

This session of Synod convened in Rader's Church, Rockingham County, Virginia, September 13, 1841.

Saturday and Sunday previous were occupied, as usual on such occasions, with devotional services, preaching, and communion.

After the appointment of a president, Rev. A. J. Brown was elected secretary. The usual committees were appointed. The petitions and papers designed for Synod, were received, and placed in the hands of the committees, whose reports received proper attention.

With respect to a petition from Mill Creek Church, Hardy County, Virginia, now West Virginia, asking to be received in connection with the Synod, and to be supplied with the ministrations of the Gospel, the request of the petitioners was granted.

Relative to a petition from New Market, Virginia, and one from Koiner's Church, Virginia, the committee reported as follows:

"No. 21 is a petition from members of our church in New Market, Virginia, in which the petitioners request our Synod to give an expression of its sentiments in reference to 'New Measures;'—the union of all the different denominations into one great body as recommended in the "Fraternal Appeal to the American Churches;"—the celebration of the Centenary of Lutheranism, as recommended by the General Synod at its last session;—also, that we do something in reference to the denunciation of our Synod, by the General Synod in 1839, and its recent proceedings in reference to our Synod;—and that we again express our opinion of the General Synod.

No. 22 is a petition from Koiner's Church, Augusta County, Virginia, of nearly the same import."

In regard to this matter, the following action was taken:

"The subject of 'New Measures' was now taken up, and, after considerable discussion, it was unanimously

Resolved, That we decidedly disapprove the *new measures* which have been introduced into the Lutheran Church by modern enthusiasts, believing that they are contrary to the Word of God, the doctrine of the Augsburg Confession of Faith, the Symbolical Books of the Lutheran Church, and her usages in her purest and best ages, and calculated to sow the seed of discord among her members."

"The subject of a *general union of all the different denominations into one great body*, was then taken up, and, after considerable discussion, it was

Resolved, That inasmuch as the Church of Christ is a collection of all true believers, and is not now, nor never was divided, and as it is impossible for different and conflicting doctrines all to be in accordance with the Word of God, and a Christian union of the different denominations to be effected without a unanimity of sentiments, and as professors greatly differ in their religious sentiments and modes of church government, the union of all the different denominations into one great body, is impracticable and inexpedient; and if effected, instead of promoting, would prove detrimental to the true interest of the Redeemer's Kingdom, and endanger the civil and religious liberties of our happy country.

In reference to the General Synod and its proceedings towards our Synod, it was

Resolved, That whereas the General Synod has frequently denounced the Tennessee Synod as an anti-Lutheran and an anti-Christian body, both in its doctrines and practices, and some of its members have recently made systematic efforts to have our Synod recognized as an Evangelical Lutheran body, and have expressed a desire to bring it into connection and co-operation with the General Synod, and have been violently opposed in this by others of its members; be it therefore

1. *Resolved*, That with us it is a matter of but little importance whether that body recognizes our Synod as an Evangelical Lutheran Synod or not, inasmuch as our orthodoxy and existence as a Lutheran body, in no wise, depend on its decisions.

2. *Resolved*, That we cannot recognize the General Synod as an Evangelical Lutheran body, inasmuch as it has departed from the primitive doctrines and usages of the Lutheran Church.

3. *Resolved*, That under existing circumstances we feel no disposition to unite with the General Synod, and never can unite with it, unless it return to the primitive doctrines and usages of the Lutheran Church.

4. *Resolved*, That Rev. A. J. Brown be appointed to draw up our objections to the General Synod, and show

from its own publications wherein that body has departed from the doctrines and usages of the Lutheran Church; and submit his manuscript to our Synod at its next session for examination, and if approved, it be printed.

The celebration of the Centenary of Lutheranism in the United States, as recommended by the General Synod, at its last session, was then taken up, and, after a short discussion, it was unanimously

Resolved, That whereas the General Synod, at its last session, recommended the celebration of the Centenary of Lutheranism in the United States, and have not only called upon those Synods connected with it, but all other Lutheran Synods, to unite with and aid them in this celebration by their contributions to raise $150,000 to endow their literary and other institutions; and whereas our Synod has been asked to express its opinion in reference to this subject, be it

Resolved, That we decidedly disapprove the proposed centenary celebration, and will discountenance it by refusing to unite in it, and by withholding our contributions to raise the proposed sum."

In reference to the petitions, requesting the examination and ordination of Messrs. J. Rhodes and J. W. Hull to the office of Deacon, it was resolved, that, in the absence of these persons, the request cannot be complied with at this time.

With regard to the petitions, requesting the examination of Deacons C. G. Reitzel and H. Wetzel, relative to their qualifications for the office of Pastor, the request was granted, and the ordinations conferred.

On application, Mr. Denis D. Swaney, of New Market, Virginia, was received under the care of Synod, as a student of theology.

In reference to the action of Synod, during its previous session, concerning the establishment of a religious journal, the following action was taken :

"*Resolved*, That we have no doubt that the publication of a religious periodical, within the bounds of our Synod, if devoted principally to the publication of correct translations from the writings of Luther, and conducted by some one of our pastors, who would take upon himself the responsibility of the task, would be of lasting utility in the Church; but, that the Synod does not feel willing to take upon itself the responsibility of such a publication. We have reason to believe, that such a publication, as long as conducted according to the acknowledged Symbols of the Lutheran Church, would meet with general encouragement among our brethren; but whether such a work could be sustained, could not well be ascertained before the next Synod; therefore,

Resolved, That we recommend subscriptions to be taken up in our congregations, to ascertain what number of subscribers can be procured."

According to the Parochial Report, 461 infants and 15 adults were baptized, and 155 were confirmed.

Concerning the action of Synod at its session, taken relative to reports circulated about Rev. D. S. Schoolfield, the committee reported the following: "In reference to the case of the Rev. D. S. Schoolfield, we are happy to state, for the satisfaction of our brethren, that we have received a letter from the Rev. Wm. Hancher, in which he informs us, that the charges against Mr. Schoolfield were legally investigated by the congregation in which it was said they had occurred, and that he was honorably acquitted."

Synod adjourned to meet in Trinity Church, Lincoln County, North Carolina, on the second Sunday of September, 1842.

Twenty-second Session.

The twenty-second session of Synod was held in Trinity Church, Lincoln County, North Carolina, commencing on the 12th and closing on the 16th of September, 1842.

Saturday and Sunday previous were occupied as usual on such occasions.

This meeting was well represented, there being present 13 ministers, 4 applicants, and 37 lay-delegates, representing

42 congregations. After the appointment of a president, Rev. A. J. Brown was elected as secretary. The routine business was transacted in the regular manner.

St. John's Church, Augusta County, Virginia, on application, was received into Synod.

Rev. A. J. Brown, who was appointed to prepare for publication the Objections to the General Synod of the United States, and submit his work to Synod for examination, stated, that, on account of intervening circumstances, he had not been able to complete the work, but that he would be able soon so to do. He then submitted the manuscript as far as he had finished it. A committee was appointed to examine it. The report of the committee was quite favorable. Another committee was appointed to examine the other portion of the work as soon as it could be finished, and if the work be approved, it should be published.

Three applicants, Messrs. Polycarp C. Henkel, Jesse R. Peterson, and Jacob M. Shaver (Schaeffer), were received under the care of Synod.

Revs. J. R. Moser and C. G. Reitzel and Mr. P. C. Henkel were appointed to select and prepare a suitable article to be printed in connection with the Minutes. They selected an article on Good Works, from the Christian Book of Concord. It appears in connection with the Minutes.

Mr. Denis D. Swaney was ordained to the office of Deacon.

At a called session, held in St. Paul's Church, Lincoln County, North Carolina, December 13, 1841, it seems, applicants John Rhodes and Joel W. Hull were ordained to the office of Deacon.

The death of Deacon John Rhodes having been announced, it was resolved, that Rev. A. Miller prepare a suitable obituary, and have it appended to the Minutes.

During this synodical year, 739 infants, 49 adults, and 1 slave were baptized, and 505 persons were confirmed. Synod adjourned to meet in St. James' Church, Green

County, Tennessee, on the first Sunday in October, 1843.

Obituary of Rev. John Rhodes.—Departed this mortal life, on the 3d of September, 1842, the Rev. John Rhodes; aged 22 years and 14 days.

This amiable and interesting young man was a member of the Evangelical Lutheran Tennessee Synod. He was ordained and set apart to the gospel ministry, on the 13th day of December, 1841. He manifested great zeal in the cause of his divine Redeemer, and bade fair for great usefulness to society, as an "able minister of the New Testament." About three months previous to his death, he visited the churches under the pastoral care of Parson Dreher, in South Carolina; and, sometime during the month of August, he returned to his native State, (North Carolina, Lincoln County,) to visit his affectionate mother and family, and to attend the ensuing session of the Evangelical Lutheran Tennessee Synod; when and where, in all probability, he would have been promoted to the office of Pastor. He returned home in the enjoyment of excellent health, to enjoy (for a few days) the society of relatives and friends. But, alas! in the midst of those scenes of social enjoyment, so agreeable and interesting to kindred spirits, he was attacked with fever, which, in a short time, terminated his earthly existence. He bore his afflictions with much Christian fortitude and resignation to the will of his Heavenly Father. He said, "that if it was the will of God to take him into Eternity, he did not crave his life." A short time before his death, he called his mother and family to his bedside, where he united with them in prayer to God, to aid them in the trying moments of their separation. He then proceeded, though laboring under great bodily debility, to give them an expression of his faith, upon which he was about to leave this world; he solemnly warned them to guard against false doctrine and teachers; admonishing them to continue in the true doctrine, "as once delivered to the saints." He solemnly assured his affectionate mother, that she should be entitled to an interest in his prayer, to his last moments. He yielded up his soul to God, his Heavenly Father, without a murmur, about five minutes after 7 o'clock, A. M. In the person of the deceased, the mother has been deprived of a dutiful son; the family of an affectionate brother; and society of an invaluable member. The body of the deceased was deposited in a family graveyard, near Vestal's Ford; his funeral sermon was preached in Philadelphia Church, on the same day, by the writer of this notice, from Phil. 3, 20–21: "For our conversation is in heaven; from whence we also look for the Savior, the Lord Jesus Christ, who shall change our vile body, that it may be fashioned like unto his glorious body, according to the working, whereby he is able even to subdue all things unto himself."

Twenty-third Session.

This session convened in St. James' Church, Green County, Tennessee, on September 30, 1843.

Besides the regular routine business, the more important transactions of Synod consisted in the reception of five applicants for the ministry,—Messrs. James M. Wagner, Henry Mumpower, Timothy Moser, John Conly, and Moses Roberts, and the ordination to the office of Deacon of Messrs. Jesse R. Peterson, P. C. Henkel, and I. M. Shaver.

The Parochial Report shows 444 infants, 29 adults, and 2 slaves baptized, and 190 confirmed, during the year; only six ministers, however, reported. Rev. A. J. Fox was elected secretary of this session.

It was resolved, that Synod adjourn to meet in Zion's Church, Catawba County, North Carolina, on the first Sunday of October, 1844.

Twenty-fourth Session.

Pursuant to previous arrangement, Synod met in Zion's Church, Catawba County, North Carolina, on Saturday, the 5th day of October, 1844. After the appointment of a president, Rev. A. J. Fox was elected secretary.

During this session, the name of Deacon S. C. Palmer was, for sufficient reason, stricken from the clerical roll.

On petition, St. Paul's Church, Page County, Zion's Church, and St. Jacob's Church, Shenandoah County, and St. Jacob's Church, Rockingham County, Virginia, were received into connection with Synod. Messrs. James K. Hancher, Thomas Crouse, and Jacob D. Emmett were taken under the care of Synod.

Revs. A. Henkel and J. Stirewalt were appointed to prepare a paper on the Duties of Church Officers, and submit it to the next session of Synod.

Applicants T. Moser and James M. Wagner were ordained to the office of Deacon.

Rev. Adam Miller, Sr., having departed this life, Revs. G. Easterly and A. J. Fox were appointed to prepare a suitable obituary notice on him and append it to the Minutes.

The Parochial Report, several of the ministers reporting for two years, presents the baptism of 1135 infants, 99 adults, and 14 slaves, and 441 confirmations.

Synod adjourned to meet in Zion's Church, Shenandoah County, Virginia, on Saturday before the first Sunday in October, 1845.

Obituary of Rev. Adam Miller, Sr.—Departed this mortal life, Rev. Adam Miller, Sr., our venerable, esteemed, and most worthy brother, and fellow-laborer in the vineyard of our benign Redeemer, Jesus Christ, on the 6th day of July, A. D., 1844; aged 84 years, 2 months, and 18 days.

Mr. Miller was born in York County, Pennsylvania, on the 18th day of April, 1760, of Christian parents, who, in his infancy, dedicated him to the Lord, by observing his own appointed means, the ordinance of Holy Baptism. He was brought up and instructed in the nature and observance of this sacred vow, made by his parents, until matured by age and discretion; and upon being convinced, by the solemn and divine truths of the everlasting Gospel, he publicly confessed his Lord and Savior, Jesus Christ, by being confirmed, according to the custom of the Evangelical Lutheran Church, a member of the same, in which he continued to occupy a respectable station, as a private member, until the 53d year of his age, having previously migrated to Sullivan County, Tennessee. That part of the country being quite destitute of ministers, who were members of the Lutheran Church, the calls for ministers were many. These things, with the very many pressing solicitations of his friends and brethren in the church, so wrought upon his philanthropic mind, that he was ultimately induced to embark in the ministry of the Gospel. He delivered his first sermon in the year 1813, and was ordained to the office of Pastor of the Evangelical Lutheran Church in the year 1820, by the members composing the first regular session of the Tennessee Synod, convened at Solomon's Church, Green County, Tennessee, in which capacity he continued successfully to act until his death.

He served in the gospel ministry about thirty years, during which time he labored much, preached a great many sermons, and broke the bread of life to many immortal souls. And, indeed, his labors everywhere appeared to be owned, blessed, and crowned with abundant success, by the great Head of the Church. He preached his last sermon in the Poor Valley Church, Washington County, Virginia, from Luke, 4th chapter and 18th verse, six days before he breathed his last.

Notwithstanding the simplicity of his style, and the plainness of his manner of delivering his sermons, he, as far as acquainted, was universally distinguished and admired for his candor, zeal, faithfulness, and untiring diligence in the performance of the duty assigned him by his Divine Master. In a word, his character, as a minister, may truly be said to have been highly exemplary and interesting. As a husband, he was kind and endearing; as a father, he was gentle and indulgent; and as a citizen and member of society, he was affable and inoffensive. Hence, it may truly be said, that, by his death, the church has been deprived of a useful minister; his relatives of a valuable friend; and society of a worthy and exemplary member. Nevertheless, we would feel a disposition to bow with due deference to every event directed by heaven, and say, Thy will be done, O Lord!

His last illness appears to have been a violent attack of the Scarlet Fever. His sufferings were truly great, though he bore them with great fortitude and submission, until the 5th day after his attack; when, feeling that he was fast sinking, he requested the 71st Psalm to be read in his hearing, which having been done, he declared the contents to be his own sentiments, and then added, "Cast me not off in the time of old age; forsake me not when my strength fails me." He then requested the 573d hymn in the Lutheran Church Hymn-book to be sung. On the next day the violence of the disease grew too powerful for his age and weak frame, and he closed his eyes in the sleep of death. His perishable remains were committed to the narrow confines of the grave, in a family graveyard, near the place where he expired. His funeral sermon was preached by the Rev. A. J. Brown, from Hebrews, the 11th chapter and 4th verse, at Poor Valley Church, and was followed by the Rev. William Hancher, with appropriate and interesting remarks.

We add, in conclusion, that we trust that while his perishable body reclines in the cold mansions of the dead, his disembodied and never-dying spirit is reaping the rich reward of all his earthly toils, in the world of never-ending bliss and glory.

Twenty-fifth Session.

This convention of Synod assembled in Zion's Church, Shenandoah County, Virginia, October 6th, and continued till the 9th, 1845.

It was organized by electing a president and Rev. H. Wetzel as secretary.

Synod learned, with regret, of the death of applicant John Conly.

Inasmuch as Rev. Daniel S. Schoolfield had failed to appear before Synod in person, to justify his course of procedure, as well as to write, to explain the causes of his conduct, as requested, it was resolved, that his name be erased from the clerical roll of Synod, and he be no longer recognized as a member of it.

Revs. A. Henkel and J. Stirewalt, who were appointed at the previous session to prepare a paper on the Duties of Church Officers, reported that they had not as yet completed that work, but would continue their efforts.

"On motion of Dr. S. G. Henkel, seconded by the Secretary, it was

Resolved, That two copies of the Minutes of the present session of Synod be sent to each of the Old School Evangelical Lutheran Synods in the United States, not connected with the General Synod, as a token of respect.

Inasmuch as we have no newspaper published under our auspices, and as the *Lutheran Standard*, of Ohio, and the *Lutherische Kirchenzeitung*, of Pennsylvania, are published by Old School Lutheran Synods, and have taken a stand against 'new measures,' a motion was made by Dr. S. G. Henkel, that we recommend said papers to our church members, and that a copy of our Minutes be sent to each of the editors of said papers.

After some discussion, the above motion was laid over until tomorrow morning, and Synod closed with singing and prayer."

"Synod met, and was opened with singing and prayer.

Dr. Henkel's motion was now again called up. After some further discussion on the subject, it was

Resolved, That inasmuch as this body is not sufficiently acquainted with the *Lutheran Standard* and *Kirchenzeitung*, we defer an expression until the next session of Synod.

The committee, Ambrose Henkel, Jacob Killian, Jacob Stirewalt, J. K. Hancher, Samuel G. Henkel, and Marcus H. Rudisill, on Documents No. 4, reported as follows:

1. Whereas a charge of a serious nature is alleged against the Rev. Adam Miller, and as this Synod is not a judiciary, but an advisory body, and simply claims the

right of imparting her useful advice, and employing the proper means for the purpose of promulgating the Gospel of Jesus Christ; and inasmuch as a majority of his elders have held a meeting, and have investigated the charge alleged against him; and said meeting of elders, after an investigation of the charge, unanimously declared him innocent; and they see no cause why he should not resume his official labors; and as a respectable number of the members of his congregations concur with the decision of the elders; however, as there still seems to be a dissatisfaction existing in the matter, it is

Resolved, That the Revs. H. Goodman and J. Killian be appointed to take the voice of his congregations in a clear and distinct manner, as soon as possible, and if the voice of the congregations wish him to continue his official duties, that we, in that case, concur with them, provided they honorably acquit him.

2. And whereas a charge has also been alleged against the Rev. J. W. Hull, we, in reference to this matter, would recommend the following, viz.: That inasmuch as Mr. Hull has been acquitted by his elders, and as there yet seems to be some dissatisfaction in his congregations, and Mr. Hull manifests a desire to have a reconsideration, we would therefore recommend his congregations to re-examine the matter, and see if things cannot be amicably adjusted, and that the Rev. J. Killian attend to this matter; and, in case the congregations succeed in deciding the matter, that we concur with them.

Resolved, unanimously, That this report be accepted and adopted."

With respect to preparing the Christian Book of Concord, or the Symbolical Books of the Evangelical Lutheran Church, to appear in an English dress, the following action was taken:

"Inasmuch as the book, entitled the Christian Concordia, contains the acknowledged Symbols of the Evangelical Lutheran Church, and is extant only in the German and

Latin languages, Dr. S. G. Henkel requested this body to express their views as to the expediency of translating and publishing said work in the English language; and if deemed expedient, he proposed to procure a correct translation of it, and publish it in the English language, as soon as practicable. Whereupon it was

Resolved, unanimously, That we consider it expedient that the Concordia be translated and published in the English language, and that the proposal of Dr. S. G. Henkel meets our entire approbation, and that we encourage him in his undertaking."

Applicants James K. Hancher and Thomas Crouse, after sustaining satisfactory examinations, were ordained to the office of Deacon.

Messrs. Jonathan Easterly and Socrates Henkel were taken under the care of Synod, as students of theology.

The Parochial Report shows that 642 infants, 32 adults, and 11 slaves were baptized, and 169 persons confirmed, during the year.

Synod adjourned to meet in St. Daniel's Church, Catawba County, North Carolina, on the third Sunday of October, 1846.

Twenty-sixth Session.

Synod convened, in its twenty-sixth session, in St. Daniel's Church, Catawba County, North Carolina, October 17, 1846. It was organized by the election of a president and Rev. J. R. Moser secretary.

As the time of the Synod was taken up by a matter of the greatest importance, it was resolved, that the action of the last session relative to the *Lutheran Standard* and *Kirchenzeitung*, cannot receive much attention.

The Adam Miller case, as it was called, was the all-absorbing subject. The case was brought up by the committee, appointed to report on the charge against Rev. Adam Miller, which was a very grave and serious one. It was resolved, that Mr. W. W. McGinnas be appointed to give a relation of all the circumstances connected with that case. After a short recess, Mr. McGinnas proceeded to present the facts in the case, and the circumstances connected with it. After a thorough investigation, the Synod resolved, that the requirements of the action taken by Synod the previous year in regard to that case had not been complied with on the part of the said Miller. Whereupon Mr. Miller withdrew himself from the Synod. In view of this fact, Synod deemed it unnecessary to take further action relative to the matter at that time.

Mr. Michael Rudisill, an elder of St. Paul's Church, Catawba County, North Carolina, and also Messrs. Ephraim Shell, Daniel Rader, and John Hass withdrew themselves and the congregations they represented.

In reference to the case of Rev. J. W. Hull, he voluntarily asked a suspension from the exercise of the ministerial functions, until his difficulties be properly adjusted. His request was granted.

Concerning the drafting of regulations on the Duties of Church Officers, Revs. A. Henkel and J. Stirewalt were continued as the committee.

After sustaining a satisfactory examination, Deacons Jesse R. Peterson, Polycarp C. Henkel, and J. M. Shaver, were ordained to the office of Pastor. Mr. Adam Efird was received as a student of theology.

The report shows that, during the year, 528 infants and 26 adults were baptized, and 235 persons confirmed.

Synod adjourned to meet in Buehler's Church, Sullivan County, Tennessee, on Saturday before the first Sunday in October, 1847.

Twenty-seventh Session.

This session convened in Buehler's Church, Sullivan County, Tennessee, October 2, 1847.

The organization was effected by appointing a president, and electing Rev. Abel J. Brown, secretary.

Besides the ordinary routine business, the following are the more important transactions of this meeting :

A committee, consisting of Revs. Forester and Easterly, was appointed to prepare an obituary on the death of Rev. Nehemiah Bonham.

"The committee appointed to examine and report on the papers pertaining to the case of the Rev. J. W. Hull, submitted the following:

Papers, Class 1st, Nos. 1, 2, 3, 4, 5, and 6, are petitions from Bethany Stand, St. Martin's, Mt. Moriah, Goose Creek, Morning Star, and Rocky River Churches, North Carolina, signed by 73 persons, members of the Lutheran Church, in which most of the petitioners state that they have been supplied with preaching, during the past year, by brother Hull; and that after the limit assigned him by the action of the last Synod, had expired, he preached at their request, and upon their responsibility. They further state, that they believe he has been acquitted of the charge alleged against him, according to the Constitution of our Synod and the Holy Scriptures: and that further action upon the subject would be contrary to both. They also pray that he may be continued amongst them as their minister.

Papers, Class 2d, are certificates of the good general character of Mr. Hull, as a Christian and Christian minister, signed by 202 persons belonging to the Lutheran, Presbyterian, Methodist, Baptist, and Seceder Churches, and persons in connection with no church.

Papers, Class 3d, is a certificate by Mr. Setzer, known to one of the committee as a man of intelligence and high standing in society, stating that Mr. Hull has made efforts to reconcile his wife and induce her to live with him, but without success.

From all the light the committee have been able to obtain upon this difficult and painful subject, they are of opinion that Mr. Hull is censurable in some respects; and especially for having, as they think, in violation of his agreement with the Synod, at its last session, preached before the difficulties between him and his wife were settled; but that in this there is a mitigating circumstance, as will appear from papers, Class 1st.

The committee recommend,

1. That Mr. Hull preach for those churches which have petitioned for his services.

2. That the Synod advise Mr. Hull, as he is not wholly free from censure, that he be very careful as to his walk and conversation, and that he make all possible, reasonable efforts, to adjust the difficulties existing between him and his wife, and live with her in peace and harmony, as the Scriptures require man and wife to live together.

Adopted by vote of the Synod."

"The committee, composed of A. J. Brown, J. Stirewalt, J. Killian, John Moser, A. W. Abernathy, and Daniel Seagle, on letters and petitions addressed to Synod in reference to the Rev. Adam Miller, formerly a member of the Tennessee Synod, but who, while under heavy charges of immorality, withdrew his membership from our connection, at the last session of our Synod, submitted the following:

In the papers committed to our hands, we find three different classes:

1. There are several petitions, signed by members of churches which have, through their delegates to Synod, withdrawn from our connection, and persons not belonging to our church, which, your committee are of opinion, require no action from Synod.

2. There are two petitions, one from St. James' Church, Greene, and the other from Salem Church, Cocke County, Tennessee, in connection with our Synod, and some petitions from individual members belonging to different churches in connection with the Synod; also a letter from the Rev. G. Easterly, in which the petitioners and the writer of the letter charge our Synod with having dealt with Mr. Miller contrary to our Constitution and the Scriptures, and call upon Synod to reconsider and revoke its former proceedings in reference to the said Miller; and, at the same time, declaring their intention of withdrawing from

our connection, in case we do not comply with their request.

3. There is another class of petitions from churches in connection with our Synod, formerly under the pastoral charge of Mr. Miller; and also two letters from the Rev. Ambrose Henkel and the other from the Rev. Polycarp C. Henkel, in which the petitioners and writers of the letters express it as their opinion that Synod has acted, in reference to Mr. Miller, in strict accordance with our Constitution and the Holy Scriptures, and protest against its revoking any of its former proceedings in his case; some of the petitioners moreover declare that it would be subversive of the best interests, if not ruinous to the Synod, to receive the said Miller again into its connection; and that if it does, they, in that case, will withdraw their connection from our Synod.

After a full investigation of the whole matter, and the most serious and prayerful reflection upon this difficult and painful subject, your committee, under a deep sense of their responsibility, would recommend the following resolution for the adoption of Synod:

Resolved, That in the opinion of this Synod, the Synod has not, in its former proceedings, in reference to the charges against the Rev. Adam Miller, violated either its Constitution or the Holy Scriptures, and cannot therefore disannul its proceedings.

The balance of the forenoon session was spent in the discussion of this matter. A recess being given, Rev. Goodman preached from John 5, 39.

After sermon, the discussion was resumed, and after a thorough consideration, the report was adopted with but two dissenting voices.

After a satisfactory examination, Deacons Timothy Moser, James M. Wagner, and James K. Hancher were ordained to the office of Pastor, and Mr. Adam Efird to that of Deacon.

Rev. Ambrose Henkel was requested to prepare a translation of Luther's Sermon on the Sin Against the Holy Ghost, and have it appended to the Minutes.

During this synodical year, 738 infants and 51 adults were baptized, and 315 persons confirmed.

Synod adjourned to meet in Solomon's Church, Shenandoah County, Virginia, on Saturday before the first Sunday in October, 1848.

Twenty-eighth Session.

This convention assembled in Solomon's Church, Shenandoah County, Virginia, September 30, 1848.

It was organized by electing a president, and Rev. J. R. Moser, secretary, with Rev. H. Wetzel as assistant.

In relation to Rev. Joseph W. Hull, it was resolved, that Synod rejoices to learn that his difficulties have been satisfactorily adjusted.

With respect to the obituary ordered at the previous meeting, to be prepared on Rev. N. Bonham, and appended to the Minutes of that session, it was ordered that, as it did not reach the printer in time to appear in that number of the Minutes, it be appended to this number.

"Dr. S. G. Henkel laid before this body copies of several works published by Mr. Ludwig, of New York; and Revs. Stirewalt, J. R. Moser, Wetzel, Swaney, and Mr. D. M. Henkel, were appointed a committee to examine and report on the same. The report was favorable.

Dr. Henkel also informed Synod that the translation of the Book of Concord has been in progress for some time, and is now gone through with for the first time; but before it will be ready for the press, the whole will have to receive some further revision. He expects to be able to have it ready for delivery some time next summer. The object in deferring the publication is to give time to have the translation as correct as possible.

Dr. Henkel also stated, that inasmuch as the distinctive doctrines of the Lutheran Church on the Sacraments, are not generally understood by the English community, owing to the fact, that the most of Luther's works are extant only in the German and Latin languages, he therefore announces to our body that he contemplates publishing a volume containing a translation into English of Luther's letter on Anabaptism, and his sermon on the subject of Baptism, in which he gives a full explanation of the whole subject of Baptism; and also his larger confession on the Lord's Supper, which treats that subject in full. He proposes, if deemed expedient by Synod, to make arrangements to have the work correctly translated, and published as soon as practicable.

Resolved, That the proposition of Dr. Henkel meets with the entire approbation of Synod; and that we most cheerfully recommend the work to our churches.

Whereas, in a work published by Dr. Hazelius, of Lexington, South Carolina, entitled 'The History of the American Lutheran Church,' we find erroneous statements in regard to our body; and whereas said work has been recommended to the public by various ecclesiastical bodies and religious publications; and whereas those statements, under such circumstances, are well calculated to mislead the mind of the public and prejudice it against our body, and operate very injuriously to the cause of truth, be it therefore

Resolved, That the Rev. A. Henkel, J. Stirewalt, J. Killian, Dr. S. G. Henkel, and Mr. Socrates Henkel, be appointed a committee to examine the statements referred to, and correct such errors as they may notice therein; and that they request the editors of the *Lutheran Standard*, *Lutheran Observer*, and such other papers as may be deemed expedient, to publish such corrections in connection with this preamble and resolution.

The committee, composed of J. R. Moser, H. Wetzel, S. G. Henkel, and T. Moser, appointed to report on the subject of entering into a friendly correspondence with the Western Virginia Synod, handed in the following report.''

'We, the committee appointed to report on the subject

of entering into a friendly correspondence with the Western Virginia Synod, submit the following.

We find the following papers having reference to the subject:

No. 1 is a letter to Synod, by Rev. A. J. Brown, in which he states that he received a letter from the Rev. E. Hawkins, a member of the Western Virginia Synod, on this subject, which he refers, together with his answer to the same, to our Synod, for their action.

No. 2 is the above-named letter of Rev. E. Hawkins to brother Brown, the object of which is the establishment of a friendly correspondence between our Synod and the Western Virginia Synod, by a reciprocal interchange of delegates between the two Synods.

No. 3 is brother Brown's answer to Rev. Hawkins' letter, in which he gives his views on this subject.

No. 4 is a petition from St. Paul's Church, Augusta County, Virginia, stating that the petitioners 'are opposed to any union of energies and resources between us and the New Lutherans, except on the condition that they first renounce all their Anti-Lutheran doctrines, measures, &c.'

After mature deliberation on this subject, your committee would recommend the following resolution for the adoption of Synod:

Resolved, That, although it would afford us the highest gratification, and we most sincerely desire to see those who are one with us in name, also united in doctrine and practice; and in that case, would most cheerfully unite and co-operate with them in such measures as are calculated to advance and promote the cause of truth; yet, we wish it to be distinctly understood, that however much a union is desired, it can only be effected upon the assurance of a strict adherence to the doctrines and usages of our Church, as set forth in its Symbols; and until we can have this assurance, we, on our part, can consent to no such union.

Unanimously adopted.

Resolved, That we rejoice to learn that some of our

German Lutheran brethren in the West, have formed themselves into a Synod, called "The German Evangelical Lutheran Synod of Missouri, Ohio, and other States," and that they are publishing a German paper, styled "*Der Lutheraner*," which is devoted to the promulgation and defence of the primitive doctrines and usages of the Lutheran Church; to which paper we would call the attention of our German brethren."

Deacon Denis D. Swaney was ordained to the pastoral office, and applicant David M. Henkel to that of Deacon. Mr. Daniel Efird was received as a theological student.

The number of baptisms, as reported, is 430 infants, 26 adults, and 5 slaves, and that of confirmation, 252.

Synod adjourned to meet in Beck's Church, Davidson County, North Carolina, October 20, 1849.

Obituary of Rev. Nehemiah Bonham.—"The following is an abstract of the facts collected by the Rev. George Easterly and D. Forester, in relation to our departed brother in Christ, the Rev. N. Bonham:

The Rev. N. Bonham was born on the 1st day of November, 1765. He studied theology under the care of the Rev. Paul Henkel, and received license to preach in the year 1790, being 25 years of age; and in the year 1791 he was ordained pastor by the Rev. John George Butler, a member of the Maryland and Virginia Synod. In the year 1824, he attached himself to the Tennessee Synod, and continued an active member of the same until the year 1844, when he was thrown from his carriage and severely wounded, by which he was disabled from rendering further services to the church, as he never recovered from the injuries he received by the fall.

He departed this life on the 5th of November, 1846; aged 81 years and 4 days, of which about 54 years had been devoted to the ministry. His death was lamented by an affectionate wife and eight children, and also by the little flock which he had gathered at Morning Star Church, Haywood County, North Carolina, at which place his remains were solemnly deposited."

Twenty-ninth Session.

This meeting convened in Beck's Church, Davidson County, North Carolina, October 20, 1849.

Rev. J. R. Peterson was elected secretary, with Rev. P. C. Henkel as assistant.

The following will present, in brief, the more special proceedings of this convention:

Christian Moretz, Jr., was received as a student of theology.

"Whereas the Rev. George Easterly has withdrawn himself from this body since the last session of our Synod, by forming a body in Tennessee, which styles itself 'The Reorganized Evangelical Lutheran Tennessee Synod;' and whereas the said body, in its proceedings, has charged our Synod with violating its constitution, according to 'their opinion;' be it therefore

Resolved 1. That the name of the Rev. G. Easterly be no longer retained in our clerical catalogue; and

2. That so soon as the said body shall have clearly pointed out in what respect our Synod has violated its constitution, we shall proceed to meet the charge."

On petition, St. Paul's Church, Gaston County, North Carolina, was received into connection with this Synod.

At a called session of a portion of the ministers of Synod, held in Emmanuel's Church, New Market, Virginia, September 11, 1849, Deacon David M. Henkel was ordained to the office of Pastor.

As far as reported, 631 infants and 44 adults were baptized, and 295 persons confirmed.

Synod adjourned to meet in Solomon's Church, Cove Creek, Green County, Tennessee, on Saturday before the third Sunday of September, 1850.

Thirtieth Session.

This session met in Solomon's Church, Green County, Tennessee, September 14, 1850.

After the election of a president, Rev. J. R. Peterson was appointed secretary.

Union Church, Washington County, Tennessee, and

Winkler's Church, Burk County, North Carolina, were received into Synod.

On petition, St. Paul's Church, Catawba County, North Carolina, which had been withdrawn from Synod, contrary to its will, by its delegate, at the time Rev. Adam Miller, in October, 1846, withdrew from Synod, was received back into Synod again. St. John's Church, in the same county, which had been withdrawn from Synod, in a similar manner, at the same time, was also received back into Synod.

Rev. D. Forester not considering himself properly a member of Synod, it was ordered that his name be no longer continued in its clerical catalogue.

It was also resolved, that, in the future, the number of the congregations and of the communicants be also included in the parochial report.

After submitting to the usual examinations, Deacons Adam Efird and Thomas Crouse were ordained as Pastors, and applicants Daniel Efird, James Fleenor, and J. B. Emmert as Deacons.

With respect to the case of the Rev. Adam Miller, who withdrew from the Synod in October, 1846, which resulted in an effort to form what was erroneously called the "Reorganized Evangelical Lutheran Tennessee Synod," the Committee on Letters, among other things, reported the following:

"No. 5 are the proceedings of the third meeting of the 'Associate Council' of the Lutheran churches of Catawba, Lincoln, and Gaston Counties, North Carolina, which assembled at Salem Church, Lincoln, North Carolina, on Friday, the 2d of August, 1850, in which they state that every honorable effort was made to acquit the Rev. A. Miller of the charge of adultery preferred against him, but that all resulted in an entire failure, and did not render his innocence even probable. They also show, to some extent, the futility of the proceedings of the pretended 'Reorganized Evangelical Lutheran Tennessee Synod,' and the falsity of its allegations preferred against our Synod. They also recommend Synod to reply to the charges made by the said 'Reorganized Evangelical Lutheran Tennessee Synod' against us."

Concerning this same case, it was also ascertained that the committee, appointed to reply to and refute these charges, had done so in a very able and satisfactory manner. The reply is appended to the Minutes of this session, and covers nineteen closely printed pages. It is clear and exhaustive, and leaves no room for escape; and in confirmation of the same position, it is followed by an appendix, signed by twelve elders who formerly belonged to the said Miller's charge. It is regretted that the reply is too long for insertion in this connection.

At a called session of a part of the ministers of Synod, held in Koiner's Church, Augusta County, Virginia, April 7, 1850, applicant Socrates Henkel was examined, and ordained to the office of Deacon, by Revs. Jacob Killian and Henry Wetzel.

According to the report, during this year, 530 infants and 44 adults were baptized, and 212 confirmed.

The time and place fixed for the next meeting were, Saturday before the first Sunday in October, 1851, and Koiner's Church, Augusta County, Virginia.

During this decade, there were sixteen applicants for the ministry; sixteen were ordained to the office of Deacon, and fourteen to that of Pastor; one minister withdrew from Synod, the names of two ministers were discontinued from the clerical catalogue, and two died; 6,576 infants, 442 adults, and 28 slaves were baptized, and 2,828 persons were confirmed. It should be kept in view that the reports were not generally full.

FOURTH DECADE.

Thirty-first Session.

Synod met in its thirty-first convention in Koiner's Church, Augusta County, Virginia, October 4–10, 1851.

Rev. Jacob Killian was elected president, and Rev. H. Wetzel, secretary.

Rev. Andrew Henkel of the Evangelical Lutheran Joint Synod of Ohio, being present as a delegate from that Synod, was received as an advisory member.

Among the proceedings of this meeting, the following is of general interest:

Rev. Denis D. Swaney was granted an honorable discharge from this Synod to the Evangelical Lutheran Synod of Ohio.

The Rev. John F. Campbell appeared and presented credentials as a delegate from the "Lutheran Synod of Virginia," to this convention of our Synod. But inasmuch as the Synod of Virginia, at her sessions in 1838 and 1839, passed resolutions, denouncing the ministers of the Evangelical Lutheran Tennessee Synod, and misrepresenting her doctrines, and warned the vacant churches in Virginia against them; and inasmuch as these resolutions were calculated to excite the public mind against our ministers and the doctrines of the Lutheran Church, where they are not known; it was therefore

Resolved, That we cannot consistently with a sense of duty to ourselves, as an Evangelical Lutheran Synod, receive delegates from the Virginia Synod, until they render us justice by rescinding the aforenamed resolutions, and give us evidence of their strict adherence to the doctrines contained in the Symbols of the Evangelical Lutheran Church.

After the Rev. Mr. Campbell could not be received as a delegate, he was invited by the President to a seat as an honorary member, which he cordially accepted.

The Committee on Letters submitted the following, which was received and adopted:

Number five is a letter from Prof. Reynolds, directed to Rev. Andrew Henkel, delegate to this Synod from the Joint Synod of Ohio, with the request that he present this Synod with its contents,—in which he expresses a desire to see a closer and more efficient union between the Tennessee and Ohio Synods, which have the same doctrinal basis, than that which now exists, or can be effected by simply adopting a system of an interchange of delegates, and suggests several methods by which he thinks this union can be effected. He also expresses a desire that this Synod should increase her efforts to extend the circulation of the *Lutheran Standard* and *Evangelical Review*, among her members.

Your committee are gratified to learn, through the interesting and fraternal communication of Prof. Reynolds, that our brethren in Ohio wish to approach us in a closer connection in reference to energies and resources, to promote the cause and welfare of the Church in general.

Your committee beg leave, therefore, to submit the following resolutions:

Resolved 1. That in reference to a closer and more efficient connection between the Joint Synod of Ohio and this Synod, it is deemed inexpedient for Synod at present to propose any plan further than that of sending delegates.

2. That Synod repeat her former recommendation of the *Lutheran Standard*, and that our ministers use their influence with their members to increase its circulation.

3. That inasmuch as the *Evangelical Review* calls forth some of the ablest expositions of the doctrines of our Church, and also exposes contrary doctrines, Synod recommends it to the clergy particularly, and the public in general, who wish to become acquainted with the controverted points of doctrine.

Melanchthon Church, Randolph County, North Carolina, was received into Synod.

Dr. S. G. Henkel, one of the publishers of the "Book of Concord" in the English language, now informed Synod that that work is completed and ready for delivery.

A committee was appointed to report, at some future stage of this meeting, on the above publication of the Book of Concord.

Committee—Rev. Messrs. Wm. Hancher, J. Killian,

A. Henkel, of Ohio, H. Goodman, A. Efird, and Col. Hedick.

At the proper time, the committee submitted the following report:

"The committee to whom the duty was assigned to report on the Book of Concord, lately published by Solomon D. Henkel and Brothers, beg leave to report:

That the short space of time allotted them, together with a sense of their inadequacy to judge upon a work so important as the one assigned, would induce them to suspend their judgment in regard to the correctness of the translation; but that the work is otherwise well executed, and its contents such, as to be of inestimable value to all who desire a thorough acquaintance with the doctrines and usages of the Evangelical Lutheran Church. And, although the committee beg leave, for the reasons above assigned, to suspend their individual judgment upon the translation, yet, from the knowledge they have of the literary attainments and abilities of the translators, and the reviser of the translation, they would not hesitate a moment to say, that they believe it fully expresses the sense of the original in which it was written. And the committee beg leave further to state,—That, considering the peculiarly critical condition in which the Lutheran community is placed at this time, and also the great importance of the undertaking, together with the unavoidable expense it incurred, they are constrained to say, that the Church should feel herself under deep obligations to the individuals engaged in the above.

We, the committee, beg leave to recommend the following resolutions:

Resolved 1. That this Synod owe a deep sense of gratitude to the brethren who were engaged in the above arduous work; and that her thanks be herewith tendered to them.

Resolved 2. That she earnestly recommend this work to all her ministers in particular, and their members in general.

Resolved 3. That these recommendations be extended

to all who call themselves Lutheran ministers, throughout the Lutheran Church, and the community in general.

Resolved 4. That the above report and resolutions be published in the *Lutheran Standard*, and that the Secretary forward a copy of the same to the Rev. C. Spielmann for that purpose."

Received and adopted unanimously.

Dr. S. G. Henkel informed Synod that the work, "Luther on the Sacraments," which he announced to Synod in 1848, (see Minutes of 1848, page 7,) is now in progress of publication, and will be out by next meeting of this Synod. He also informed Synod that Luther's Large and Small Catechisms, in one 12mo. volume, are in course of publication, and will be ready for delivery in a few months.

Resolved, That Synod learns with much pleasure, and feelings of gratitude to the publisher, the nearness of completion of the above named works.

The firm of Solomon D. Henkel & Brothers, New Market, Virginia, consisted of four brothers, namely, Dr. Samuel Godfrey, Mr. Siram P., Mr. Solomon D., and Dr. Solon P. C. Henkel. They were sons of Dr. Solomon Henkel, who was a son of Rev. Paul Henkel.

Of this firm, Dr. Samuel Godfrey Henkel made all the necessary arrangements to secure correct translations of these works, as well as to assure their publication in an English dress. The best authenticated copies of the original works had to be obtained for use in the translations. He had the general supervision and management of the translations during their progress and completion, and superintended the matter as it passed through the press. The undivided gratitude of the Church is due this firm in view of such untiring efforts and labors in presenting these works to the public in the English language.

Whilst, as a physician and surgeon, he had few superiors in the State, he was a zealous Christian, of respectable attainments in English, German, and Latin, as well as a good practical printer, well up in Lutheran theology and general literature, always taking a deep interest in the Church,—a man of sound judgment, with indomitable energy and untiring zeal. He was very familiar with the German language, and spoke it fluently.

The following is what he says relative to this matter, in the prefaces to the first and second editions of the Christian Book of Concord:

"The Book of Concord, comprising the Symbols of the Evangelical Lutheran Church, has as yet enjoyed but a limited circulation in the United States. Wrapped in the obscurities of its original languages,—the Latin and German,—that venerable production of the Reformation has been left to slumber almost entirely in silence and neglect. Numerous causes have contributed to prolong this neglect. The descendants of German emigrants in America, have never cultivated the language and literature of their fathers with due interest; many of them are unable to read German; while many, able to read, and occupying elevated stations, have never manifested a laudable zeal for the doctrines of the Church. The most obvious cause, however, seems to be, that the larger portion of Lutherans in America, are accustomed to read the English language only, and consequently have never had an opportunity to appreciate the value of their Symbols.

Yet, we cherish the anticipation of a brighter day in the Lutheran Church. In a land of freedom, of science, and art, where the generous spirit of political wisdom encourages the exercise of reason, and guards the decisions of conscience; where industry, energy, and enterprise, though daily attaining fresh prospects of future improvement, are continually unburying the sacred treasures of the past, we believe that the doctrines of our Church will ultimately be reclaimed, and that men of our western clime will enter into the investigation of these doctrines with all the avidity natural to a love for the truth. That these doctrines and these principles of immutable truth, are congenial with the tastes and feelings of the American mind, we may fearlessly deduce from recent facts. Within the last few years, the Book of Concord and Luther's House-Sermons have been reprinted in this country; and several of Luther's works have lately been translated into the English language, and circulated extensively.

It was, therefore, reasonable to presume, that a faithful translation of the Book of Concord into the English language, was demanded by the necessities of the times, and would effectually co-operate with these laudable exertions. Partial translations indeed of the Augsburg Confession had been made at different times; but it had never been fully rendered into English until 1831, when a translation was completed by the Rev. Charles Henkel, assisted by Professor Schmidt, of Columbus Seminary, Ohio; and several small fragments from the Book of Concord, were subsequently translated by others.

At the urgent solicitation of many zealous members of the Church, we announced, October 9th, 1845, our resolution to procure a correct English version of the entire work, and publish it as soon as practicable. Since that period no time or labor has been spared to fulfill our promise.

We have had to engage the talents not only of men familiar with the Lutheran doctrine, as well as with the German and English languages, but, in consequence of the obsolete style in which the German copy of this work was originally written, we have constantly had recourse to men who were able to consult the Latin copy whenever it was requisite. And here we feel bound in justice to the industry and valuable abilities of those who contributed their friendly aid, to specify the several portions furnished by each.

The Augsburg Confession, the Apology, the Smalcald Articles, the Appendix, and the Articles of Visitation, in a version purely literal, were furnished by the Rev. Ambrose and Socrates Henkel. The Large Catechism was translated, in the same manner, by the Rev. J. Stirewalt; the Epitome by the Rev. H. Wetzel; and the Declaration by the Rev. J. R. Moser. The Small Catechism was copied mainly from the translation by the Rev. David Henkel, published in 1827. Much assistance in reviewing the proof-sheets throughout the publication of the work, was rendered by Joseph Salyards, Principal of the New Market Academy, who has long cultivated the study of science and general literature; and he likewise furnished translations of all the Prefaces, from the Latin, and of the Historical Introduction, from the German.

All these translations when collected, were carefully compared with the original by the Rev. Ambrose Henkel, and afterwards, with the exception of the Historical Introduction and the Prefaces, were revised, transcribed, and prepared for the press by the Rev. Socrates Henkel. We have derived considerable assistance, too, in the progress of the work, from the Rev. L. Eichelberger.

The principal translations were made from the German edition of 1790, published at Leipsic; and, being favored by the Rev. C. P. Krauth, with a copy of the original German Dresden edition of 1580, we were enabled to compare them with that also. The Latin copy, to which uniform reference was made in comparing the translations, was that published by Hase in 1846; and from this the Prefaces were all translated. Whenever the German copy presented insuperable obscurities, recourse was also had to this edition in numerous passages. The Appendix was taken from the German and Latin edition published by Muller, printed at Stuttgard, 1848, from which the Historical Introduction was also translated.

Deeming it most compatible with the nature of the work,—the subjects being chiefly of a didactic and doctrinal character,—we have endeavored throughout to preserve as just and uniform a medium as possible, between a translation purely literal, and one which admits all the freedom and elegance of English composition. We have labored to be faithful, and yet not to offend the fastidious ear. We have been anxious to preserve the serious tone and spirit of the pious original. But, as imperfection is the fate of all human efforts, the candid reader will no doubt discover many inaccuracies. Any friendly suggestion, therefore, pointing out such defects, will be received with gratitude, and enable us to render a second edition more worthy of an intelligent public.

May our labors be the instrument, in the hands of Providence, for promoting an acquaintance with the Book of Concord, the *norm* of all genuine Lutherans since 1580, and for extending the doctrines taught by the illustrious Reformer!

In presenting the second edition of the Book of Concord in the English language, the publishers take pleasure in announcing that the whole work has again been carefully revised and compared with the original text. The first edition, though containing many imperfections, met nevertheless with a kind reception in the church; which induced the publishers to use every effort that seemed necessary to bring the work to greater perfection. Accordingly, before publishing a second edition, the talents of individuals, known as literary men and prominent theologians in the Church, were engaged, who were requested to revise the work, comparing it with the original, not changing however the language of the first edition more than would be found necessary to render it a good translation; and to these gentlemen sincere acknowledgments are due for a vast number of valuable suggestions.

The Augsburg Confession was revised by Rev. C. P. Krauth, D. D., Professor in the Theological Seminary, Gettysburg, Pa.; the Apology, by Rev. W. F. Lehmann, Professor of Theology, Columbus, Ohio; the Smalcald Articles, by Rev. Wm. M. Reynolds, D. D., President of Capital University, Ohio; Luther's Small and Large Catechisms, by Rev. J. G. Morris, D. D., Baltimore, Md.; and the Formula of Concord and Catalogue of Testimonies, by Rev. C. F. Schaeffer, D. D., Easton, Pa. The Historical Introduction was also carefully compared and revised by the original translator; and every attention was given by the publishers to have the corrections faithfully attended to; thus they feel confident, that the English translation of the Book of Concord will meet that encouragement from the Church, which her Symbols originally received."

After sustaining a satisfactory examination, Deacon Socrates Henkel was ordained to the office of Pastor.

Synod adjourned to meet in Salem Church, Lincoln County, North Carolina, on the first Sunday of October, 1852.

The Parochial Report presents the following: 68 churches, 3,329 communicants, 604 infant baptisms, 5 slaves, and 37 adults, and 250 confirmations.

Thirty-second Session.

Pursuant to adjournment, Synod met in Salem Church, Lincoln County, North Carolina, October 2–7, 1852.

The election of officers resulted in favor of Revs. Jacob Killian, president; A. J. Brown, secretary; and A. Efird, treasurer.

The usual routine business received proper attention.

At the request of petitioners, Salem, St. Peter's (Piny Woods), St. Paul's, Zion's, St. Jacob's, St. John's, St. Peter's, and Bethlehem Churches, South Carolina, and Lingel's, Caldwell County, North Carolina, were received in connection with Synod.

The President gave notice that, at some future time, he would introduce resolutions in regard to ministerial support.

Rev. J. K. Hancher gave notice that he would introduce resolutions in regard to ministerial education..

Rev. A. J. Brown gave notice that, at some future period, he would introduce resolutions relative to the establishment of a Literary Institution and Missionary operations. With respect to this, it was

Resolved 1. That the Synod devise some plan for the establishment of a Literary Institution, which will not conflict with our present Constitution.

Resolved 2. That, in reference to Beneficiary Education and Missionary operations, societies for these purposes be formed disconnected with this Synod.

The President, Rev. J. Killian, introduced the following preamble and resolutions, which were unanimously adopted.

Whereas, it not unfrequently occurs that the amount of salary promised and paid to the pastor by his congregations, or charge, is so limited, either by reason of the negligence or inability of his church members, that he is driven by the force of circumstances to devote a considerable portion of his time to other pursuits than those of the ministry, to procure for himself and family the necessaries and comforts of life,—thereby greatly diminishing his usefulness as the spiritual shepherd of Christ's flock;—and whereas we believe that each congregation or charge that possesses the ability to do so, is *morally* bound to make reasonable provisions for the temporal wants of their ministers; for the Holy Scriptures declare that, "If we have sown unto you spiritual things, is it a great matter that we should reap your carnal things?" "The laborer is worthy of his hire." "Even so hath Christ the Lord ordained, that they which preach the Gospel, should live of the Gospel." Therefore, with a view to the expression of the convictions of this Synod, on this subject, we do hereby adopt the following resolutions:

Resolved 1. That we view with feelings of deep regret and mortification, the extremely low views entertained by too many of our church members in reference to the adequate support of the ministry, and the importance of meeting punctually their engagements to its maintenance.

Resolved 2. That, as a Synod, we entertain the belief that those congregations which withhold from their minister his just dues, have no Scriptural grounds to hope for, much less to expect the blessings of a righteous and just God to descend upon them, whilst keeping back "the wages of him that is hired," as their spiritual shepherd.

Resolved 3. That the congregations which entertain enlightened views upon this subject, and manifest by their practice a disposition to conform to justice, the demands of Christian liberality and correct moral principle, are entitled to our praise and gratitude as a Synod; and we do most devoutly pray that God may bless them abundantly in all their efforts to elevate the standard of piety and Christian obligation.

After sustaining a regular examination, Deacon Daniel Efird was ordained to the pastoral office, and applicants James E. Seneker, John Seneker, Christian Moretz, Jr., and Adam Fleenor, were ordained to the office of Deacon.

After a long and interesting discussion in reference to the establishment of a Literary Institution within the bounds of our Synod, it was

Resolved 1. That the ministers of this Synod be requested to take the sense of the members of their respective congregations as to the propriety and practicability or impracticability of establishing a Literary Institution within the bounds of our Synod, disconnected with the Synod, and that they report to the next session of our Synod.

Resolved 2. Further, that this Synod appoint an Educational Convention, to meet at the time and place of the next meeting of the Synod, and that the congregations in connection with this Synod be advised to appoint their delegates to Synod, delegates also to the Convention, and that a committee be appointed to devise a plan for the establishment of a Literary Institution, and also to prepare a Constitution for its government.

The President appointed Revs. P. C. Henkel, A. J. Fox, J. R. Peterson, and D. M. Henkel, as the committee.

During this year, the Parochial Report shows 97 congregations, 4,131 communicants, 637 infants, 26 adults, and 30 slaves were baptized, and 179 persons confirmed.

Synod adjourned to meet in Emmanuel's Church, Sullivan County, Tennessee, on Friday before the third Sunday in October, 1853.

Thirty-third Session.

This session assembled in Emmanuel's Church, Sullivan County, Tennessee, on Friday before the third Sunday of October, 1853.

Revs. Ambrose Henkel was chosen president, J. R. Peterson, secretary, and J. Stirewalt, treasurer.

The usual business was transacted.

The committee, Revs. J. Stirewalt, J. M. Wagner, A. J. Brown, and Ambrose Henkel, to whom were referred the resolutions of the Pennsylvania Synod, in reference to union with the General Synod, together with the accompanying letter of the committee appointed to transmit them to the Evangelical Lutheran Tennessee Synod, suggesting to our Synod the propriety of uniting with them, in the "General Synod of the Evangelical Lutheran Church of the United States," examined the said papers carefully, and respectfully submitted the following:

Whereas, we regard the Unaltered Augsburg Confession as the authorized and universally acknowledged Symbol of the Evangelical Lutheran Church, and consequently the belief and acknowledgment of it, in its entireness, as essential to the existence of Lutheranism in its integrity; and whereas we profess, in our Synodical Constitution, to believe the doctrines of the Christian system, as exhibited in this Symbol, and have pledged ourselves to teach according to it; and, whereas the doctrinal position of the General Synod, as we understand it, is only a qualified acknowledgment of the Augsburg Confession, as we think is evident:

a) From the Constitution of this body, in which there is no clause binding its members to teach according to the Unaltered Augsburg Confession, and not even a distinct mention of this instrument.

b) From the Constitution recommended by the General Synod to the District Synods connected with it.

c) From the form of oath required of Professors in its Theological Seminary, when inducted into office.

d) From the construction placed upon its Constitution by the framer of that instrument, and other prominent members of it.

e) From the various publications made by distinguished members of the General Synod, in which distinctive doctrines of our Church Confessions are openly assailed, and for doing which, they have never been called to account. Be it therefore

Resolved 1. That we cannot, under existing circumstances, take any steps towards a union with the General Synod.

Resolved 2. That we duly appreciate the motives which prompted the Pennsylvania Synod to invite us to unite with them in the General Synod, and shall ever be thankful to this body for any advice which it may see proper to give, or any suggestions which it may make to us, and will calmly and prayerfully consider them, but at all times act according to the dictates of our own judgment.

Resolved 3. That we have witnessed, with heartfelt gratitude to the Great Head of the Church, the revival of increased attachment to our excellent doctrinal standards, and particularly the Unaltered Augsburg Confession, and the open and decided stand taken in favor and support of them by distinguished sons of the Church, and even by prominent members of the General Synod.

Resolved 4. That we are encouraged to hope that the time may yet come, when all in this country, professing Lutheranism, and having departed from the doctrines of the Church, will return to her confessional standards, and that we will continue to labor and pray with increased energy and faith and zeal, for the accomplishment of this great and desirable object.

Resolved 5. That our Secretary send a copy of these resolutions to the Pennsylvania Synod.

Relative to the petitions from Illinois, Indiana, Missouri, and Arkansas, it was *Resolved*, That, inasmuch as Rev. J. B. Emmert has it in contemplation to perform a visit to the West, and Rev. J. K. Hancher has conditionally promised to visit some of the petitioners, these brethren be requested to give them proper attention.

In the report of the committee on letters we notice the following:

No. 10 is a letter from Rev. A. Biewend, a member of the Missouri Synod, in which he informs us that he was appointed a delegate to this body, but that, owing to intervening circumstances, he was prevented attending. He also expresses the hope and desire that a more intimate acquaintance may be formed between these two bodies.

Your committee would recommend the following for adoption:

Resolved 1. That we duly appreciate the kind regard of the Missouri Synod, and that we also desire a more intimate acquaintance with them, and that we appoint Rev. J. R. Moser a delegate to the next session of that Synod.

2. In reference to all papers addressed to this Synod, relative to the establishment of a Literary Institution within the bounds and under the patronage of this Synod, we recommend the following:

Whereas, this subject was, by the last session of Synod, referred to a convention, to be held for the purpose of considering the propriety and practicability of such a move, be it, therefore,

Resolved, That this subject requires no further action from this body, and that the committee appointed to devise a plan for the establishment of a Literary Institution, and to prepare a Constitution for its government, be discharged.

After the usual examination, Deacons James Fleenor and J. B. Emmert were ordained as pastors.

The Parochial Report shows 75 congregations, 5,049 communicants, 782 infants, 78 adults, and 16 slaves baptized, and 588 confirmed.

St. Peter's (Piny Woods) Church, Lexington District, South Carolina, was agreed upon as the place, and Saturday before the first Sunday in November, 1854, as the time for the next meeting.

The following Appendix to the Minutes of the Tennessee Synod is of interest to the Church:

"As Secretary of the Evangelical Lutheran Tennessee Synod, for the last Synodical year, I have received the following communications for the Synod, since the adjournment of its last session.

1. A letter from Rev. R. A. Fink, Secretary of the 'Evangelical Lutheran Synod of Virginia,' communicating certain resolutions of rescission, passed by that body, in reference to the Tennessee Synod, which I give entire, together with the preamble.

'Whereas, it is desirable for the good of our Lutheran Zion, and the cause of our Lord Jesus Christ, that unity and fraternal love should characterize all our relations as Lutherans—therefore,

'*Resolved*, That the resolutions of this Synod, passed at its meeting in 1838 and 1839, in regard to the Tennessee Synod, and contained on the Minutes of our Synod, are hereby rescinded.

'*Resolved*, further, That, as far as possible, we will seek to cultivate fraternal relations with our brethren of the Tennessee Synod, and that a delegate be appointed to said body to represent this Synod in its next annual convention in 1854.

'*Resolved*, That our Secretary be instructed to forward a copy of these resolutions to the said Tennessee Synod.'

2. A letter from Rev. Messrs. Theo. Brohm and A. Hoyer, who had been appointed delegates from 'The German Evangelical Lutheran Synod of Missouri, Ohio, and other States,' to the recent session of our Synod. As the letter is both interesting and encouraging, I give it in full.

NEW YORK AND PHILADELPHIA,
OCTOBER 6, 1853.

REVEREND AND DEAR BRETHREN:—

Animated by an ardent desire to cherish the unity in spirit with all true Lutherans wherever, the German Evangelical Lutheran Synod of Missouri, Ohio, and other States, at her last annual meeting at Cleveland, Ohio, had appointed the undersigned as delegates to attend your synodical meeting and to deliver her fraternal greetings. But after having learned the place where your Synod is to meet this year, we regret to be precluded, by the great distance, and other local difficulties, from the great pleasure of carrying out our commission, both honorable and agreeable to us, as a greater sacrifice of time would be required than we can properly answer for to our respective congregations.

In order to compensate this want of personal attendance, we take the liberty, with consent of our president, to address your reverend body by these few lines, assuring you of our fraternal love and sympathy, founded upon the conviction, that it is one and the same faith which dwells in you and in us. We are highly rejoiced in this vast desert and wilderness, to meet a whole Lutheran Synod steadfastly holding to the precious Confessions of our beloved church, and zealously engaged in divulging the unaltered doctrines and principles of the Reformation among the English portion of Lutherans, by translating the standard writings of our Fathers, at the same time firmly resisting the allurements of those who say they are Lutherans, and are not.

Our synod extends, through our instrumentality, the hand of fraternity to you, not fearing to be refused, and ardently desires, however separated from you by different language and local interests, to co-operate with you, hand in hand, in rebuilding the walls of our dilapidated Zion.

We are authorized to beseech your venerable Synod, to delegate as many of your members as you may deem proper, to our synodical meeting, to be held next year at St. Louis, promising hereby a friendly and hospitable reception.—Should your Synod next year assemble at a place easier accessible, and more convenient to us, we, or they whom our synod may appoint, shall not fail to attend.

Praying that the Lord may vouchsafe to replenish your reverend body with the spirit of truth, wisdom, zeal, love, and peace, and bless your deliberations for the glorification of His holy name, we remain, dear brethren, with sincere respect and love, your co-laborers in the vineyard of the Lord.

THEO. BROHM,
A. HOYER, *of Philadelphia.*

3. A copy of the Minutes of the German Evangelical Lutheran Synod of Missouri, Ohio, and other States, for 1853.

A. J. BROWN.

November 3, 1853."

Thirty-fourth Session.

Synod assembled in St. Peter's (Piny Woods) Church, Lexington District, South Carolina, on Saturday before the first Sunday in November, 1854.

The election for officers resulted in favor of Rev. A. J. Brown, president; Rev. J. R. Peterson, secretary; and Rev. J. M. Wagner, treasurer.

The usual business received proper attention.

On regular application, Salem Church, Alexander County, North Carolina, and Emmanuel Church, Lexington District, South Carolina, were received into Synod.

On learning that the Virginia Synod had rescinded the resolutions it had passed against this Synod in 1838 and 1839, it was resolved, that Synod rejoices to learn that the Virginia Synod has at length done our Synod the justice to rescind its former obnoxious resolutions; and that, in view of this fact, we will endeavor to cultivate a feeling of fraternal regard for the Virginia Synod.

Rev. Theodore Brohm, of the Synod of Missouri, Ohio,

and other States, was introduced to Synod, and received as a corresponding member by this body. Rev. G. Dreher and Michael Rauch, of the Lutheran Church, were received as advisory members.

The Rev. Theodore Brohm, of the Missouri Synod, being present, the following preamble and resolutions were unanimously adopted:

Whereas, the Rev. Theodore Brohm, of the city of New York, delegate of the Synod of Missouri, Ohio, and other States, has appeared amongst us, and we are assured from personal interviews with him, as well as from other sources of information, that the Synod which he represents adheres strictly to the doctrines of the Evangelical Lutheran Church, as exhibited in her confessional standards, and are zealously and actively engaged in promoting the interests of the Redeemer's kingdom; be it, therefore,

Resolved 1. That we are highly gratified to see brother Brohm in our midst.

Resolved 2. That we fully and cheerfully reciprocate the kind and fraternal feelings expressed and manifested towards us by the Missouri Synod.

Resolved 3. That we will endeavor to cultivate a more intimate acquaintance and a closer union with the Missouri Synod.

Resolved 4. That, for this purpose, Rev. Socrates Henkel be appointed a delegate from this body to the Eastern division of the Missouri Synod, to be held in Baltimore; and that Rev. J. R. Moser be appointed our delegate to the Western division of said Synod, at its next session.

Mr. Julius L. Stirewalt having been ordained to the office of Deacon by Revs. A. Henkel and H. Wetzel, his name was ordered to be inserted in the clerical roll.

In answer to petitions from time to time addressed to this body, it was

Resolved 1. That a committee be appointed to devise a plan for the division of this Synod into district synods, and report to next meeting of Synod.

Committee—Rev. Messrs. P. C. Henkel, J. R. Peterson, A. Henkel, H. Wetzel, A. J. Brown, and Wm. Hancher.

Resolved 2. That Rev. S. Henkel collect and preserve the archives of this Synod.

According to the Parochial Report, 722 infants, 27 adults, and 15 slaves were baptized, and 251 persons were confirmed during the year.

Synod adjourned to meet in Emmanuel's Church, New Market, Shenandoah County, Virginia, on Friday before the third Sunday in September, 1855.

Thirty-fifth Session.

This convention met in Emmanuel's Church, New Market, Virginia, September 14, 1855.

Revs. A. J. Brown was elected president; J. Killian, secretary; and S. Henkel, treasurer.

Besides the usual transactions of this meeting, the following business deserves notice:

Rev. Spielmann, President of Capital University, Columbus, Ohio, the delegate appointed to this body by the Western District Synod of Ohio, was introduced to Synod, and invited to a seat and vote. Rev. J. P. Cline, of the Virginia Synod, was invited to a seat as an advisory member.

Rev. Martin Sondhaus, having presented an honorable dismission from the Pennsylvania Synod to this body, was received as a member.

The name of Rev. Joel Swartz, (now Rev. Joel Swartz, D. D.,) having been ordained by Rev. Socrates Henkel and Rev. D. M. Henkel, was ordered to be enrolled in the clerical catalogue.

On petition from the Lima charge, in Allen County, Ohio, Rev. Paul J. Stirewalt was ordained to the office of Pastor.

Phanuel's Church, Rockingham County, and Bethlehem Church, Augusta County, Virginia, were received into Synod.

For reasons regarded as sufficient, it was resolved, that

the name of Rev. Joseph W. Hull be erased from the clerical catalogue, and that he be no longer regarded as a minister of this Synod.

In answer to petitions and letters. in reference to districting this Synod, Dr. S. G. Henkel offered the following preamble and resolution, which were unanimously adopted:

Inasmuch as the committee, appointed last year, to report a plan for districting the Synod, failed to report, and as there are letters and petitions now before Synod, in reference to this matter, and which require our notice, therefore, as the best answer we can return for the present, be it

Resolved, That, in order to meet the inconveniences which seem to present themselves for want of some annual meeting of our clergy, where young men may be examined and ordained, and also to give an opportunity to interchange views in reference to the wants of the church, and also to give occasion for united efforts in preaching—we would recommend that the members of this Synod, who reside near enough to each other for that purpose, hold some annual meeting, according to their own appointment, where they may transact such matters as would not seem to call for the united advice of Synod. This meeting might be termed a Special Conference.

Rev. D. M. Henkel asked for a letter of honorable dismission, which was granted.

Dr. S. G. Henkel submitted the following proposition for the consideration of this body:

Inasmuch as the Evangelical Lutheran Tennessee Synod has been instrumental in bringing before the Lutheran Church in the United States her fundamental doctrines, by the translation of her Symbols into the English language, would it not, in order that her doctrines be brought before the Church more fully, be advisable that Luther's Church Postil be translated into the English language?

If it meet the approbation of Synod, I propose, as soon

as practicable, to procure a correct translation of that work, and to publish it in two octavo volumes.

Resolved, That a committee be appointed to report on Dr. S. G. Henkel's proposition to this body—"to publish as soon as practicable a correct English translation of Dr. Luther's Church Postil."

The President appointed Revs. H. Wetzel, C. Spielmann, H. Goodman, and M. Sondhaus, said committee.

The committee, Revs. H. Wetzel, H. Goodman, M. Sonhaus, and C. Spielmann, appointed to report on Dr. S. G. Henkel's proposition to publish a correct English translation of Luther's Church Postil, submitted the following:

We, the committee appointed to report on the proposition of Dr. S. G. Henkel, as to publishing Dr. Luther's Church Postil in the English language, respectfully submit the following:

Being fully convinced of the great value and excellence of Luther's Church Postil, and its importance to our ministers and congregations, and being influenced by a desire that this great work be made accessible also to our English ministers and church members, be it

Resolved 1. That we learn with joy that Dr. S. G. Henkel contemplates publishing Luther's Church Postil in the English language.

Resolved 2. That we will do all that we can to encourage and assist Dr. Henkel in this enterprise.

This report was received and adopted.

Dr. S. G. Henkel now addressed the Synod on the necessity and importance of giving an expression in regard to ministerial support. Whereupon, the following committee was appointed to report in reference to this subject.

Committee—Dr. S. G. Henkel, John Leonard, and I. L. Wagner.

The committee, appointed to report on the subject of Ministerial Support, submitted the following:

Inasmuch as the ministers of the Tennessee Synod have heretofore received from their congregations a very inadequate support, so much so, that many of them have been compelled to resort to some other employment in order to be sustained, thereby, to a great extent, destroying their usefulness in the ministry, we respectfully submit the following resolution for adoption:

Resolved, That we remind our church members, both as individuals and congregations, of the teaching of the Word of God that the laborer is worthy of his hire, and that we appeal to them as to Christians, and with a view to their own best interests and the interests of their congregations, and the perpetuity of the preaching of the Gospel among them, that they see to it that their pastors be not thus neglected, and left to struggle amidst pecuniary embarrassments. We would also assure them, unless they use more diligence in this matter, the time will come when they will be deprived of the services of the faithful minister of the truth, and they will be visited only by wolves in sheep's clothing.

On motion, the above preamble and resolution were unanimously adopted.

For this year, the report shows the baptisms of 513 infants, 46 adults, and 10 slaves, and the confirmation of 244 persons.

Synod adjourned to meet in Melanchthon Church, Randolph County, North Carolina, on Saturday before the fourth Sunday in October, 1856.

Thirty-sixth Session.

This meeting convened in Melanchthon Church, Randolph County, North Carolina, October 25, 1856.

The officers elected were: Revs. J. K. Hancher, president; T. Moser, secretary; and J. M. Wagner, treasurer.

Mr. Eli E. Smyre and Mr. Augustus R. Bennick were received as students of theology.

Notice was then given, that, under certain conditions, petitions would be addressed to the next meeting of this body, for a dismission of the ministers and churches of our

Synod in North and South Carolina, from the Tennessee Synod, with a view to the formation of a new synod.

After considerable discussion, on motion, the subject of said notice was postponed until some future period of this session.

On petitions, Bible's Church or Chapel, Tennessee, Friendship Church, Watauga County, North Carolina, and Zion Church, Hardy County, Virginia (now West Virginia), were received.

Deacons Christian Moretz and A. Fleenor were ordained to the pastoral office, and applicant John M. Smith to that of Deacon.

On motion, by Rev. C. G. Reitzel, the following preamble and resolution were adopted :

Whereas, the destitutions of our beloved Lutheran Zion are alarmingly great, and whereas, from the North and South, East and West, the Macedonian cry is annually coming to us, "Come over and help us," and break the bread of life to us and our children. And whereas, we believe that it is the Christian's duty to make provision for his destitute and perishing brethren, be it, therefore,

Resolved, That this body earnestly recommend the congregations connected with this Synod, to establish congregational treasuries, for the purpose of aiding domestic missionaries, and young men of hopeful piety and promising talents, who are laboring to qualify themselves for the work of the Gospel Ministry in the Lutheran Church, and as a means of encouragement and comfort to our destitute brethren, report the result of such efforts, annually, to Synod.

In answer to petitions praying for a division of this body, be it

Resolved, That it be made the duty of the ministers of this body, to take the vote of their respective congregations, with a view to ascertain their wishes upon this subject, and report the result to the next session of Synod ; our brethren present from Virginia concurring, and willing to form a separate organization in their State, provided the vote should result in favor of such organization.

The following brethren were appointed delegates to sister synods:

Rev. M. Sondhaus, to Joint Synod of Ohio; Rev. J. Stirewalt, Northern District Synod of Ohio; Rev. J. M. Wagner, Western District Synod of Ohio; Rev. J. R. Moser, Missouri Synod; Rev. J. Killian, Pennsylvania Synod; Rev. H. Wetzel, Eastern District Synod of Missouri.

Synod adjourned to meet in Solomon's Church, Green County, Tennessee, September 26, 1857.

During this year, as reported, there were 741 infants, 57 adults, and 24 slaves baptized, and 752 confirmed.

Thirty-seventh Session.

Synod assembled in Solomon's Church, Green County, Tennessee, September 26, 1857.

Revs. A. J. Fox was elected president; J. M. Wagner, secretary; and H. Goodman, treasurer.

In regard to a division of the Synod, it was resolved, that, under existing circumstances, it is deemed inexpedient at this time.

Messrs. M. J. Stirewalt, Dr. H. H. Maxwell, J. C. Barb, and J. Cloninger made application to be received under the care of Synod as students of theology. Rev. H. Wetzel then offered the following preamble and resolutions, which were adopted:

Whereas, it has been customary in this Synod, when applied to, to receive under her care, as students of theology, young men; and whereas, we wish to make this as beneficial to them and as safe to ourselves as possible, therefore,

Resolved, That young men making application to be received under the care of this Synod, as students of theology, be examined as to the motives by which they are prompted in seeking their way into the ministry; and the extent to which they are willing to qualify themselves for this high and holy calling.

Resolved, That, if any young man of good report, suitable talents, and a willingness to qualify himself suitably for the ministry, make application as above, but has not the means to qualify himself, we then exert ourselves to secure to him the needed assistance.

Resolved, That the examination be conducted by a committee of three ministers and four laymen, and that they report to Synod. Whereupon the following committee was appointed, viz.: A. J. Brown, H. Wetzel, A. J. Fox, and Messrs. Jacob Keicher, John Moser, Jacob Stephens, and Ambrose Costner.

We, the committee, who were to hold a Colloquium with Messrs. Maxwell, Cloninger, Barb, and Stirewalt who made application to be taken under the care of Synod as students of theology, have attended to that duty; and would report that we were pleased with the young gentlemen, and recommend that they be received as students of theology. We were gratified to learn that Messrs. Barb and Stirewalt have made respectable progress in literature, the latter having made, in addition to the Sciences and Mathematics, considerable progress in the languages; and that they be advised to prosecute their literary studies still further. We recommend that Mr. Maxwell prosecute his theological studies under the care of some of our older ministers.

Report received and adopted. It was then

Resolved, That Messrs. Stirewalt, Barb, Maxwell, and Cloninger, be received under the care of Synod as students of theology.

The Committee on Minutes reported that the Northern General Synod, at its session in 1857, rescinded the resolution it passed at its session in 1839, against this Synod.

The following committee was appointed to revise the Liturgy of Synod: Revs. S. Henkel, J. Killian, A. Henkel, A. J. Brown, J. M. Wagner, J. K. Hancher, J. R. Peterson, and Dr. S. G. Henkel. Upon motion, the President, Rev. A. J. Fox, was added to the committee.

New Jerusalem Church, Davidson County, North Carolina, was taken into connection with this Synod.

The rules and regulations, prepared by Rev. H. Wetzel, were appended to the Minutes of this session of Synod. It was

Resolved, That the President of Synod furnish Rev. Joel Swartz with a letter of honorable dismission from this Synod, with a view of joining one of the District Synods of Ohio.

The following brethren were appointed delegates to sister synods: Rev. H. Goodman, to the Eastern District Synod of Ohio; Rev. J. Stirewalt, Joint Synod of Ohio; Rev. J. K. Hancher, Western District Synod of Ohio; Rev. A. J. Brown, Pennsylvania Synod; Rev. J. R. Moser, Missouri Synod.

Deacons J. E. Seneker and J. A. Seneker were ordained to the office of Pastor.

The Parochial Report shows 677 infant baptisms, 41 adult, and 21 slave, and 219 confirmed.

Synod adjourned to meet in Zion's Church, Lexington District, South Carolina, on Friday before the third Sunday in October, 1858.

Thirty-eighth Session.

This convention met in Zion's Church, Lexington District, South Carolina, October 15, 1858.

In the clerical catalogue of this meeting appear the names of Rev. George Schmucker and Rev. John H. Hunton. It seems the latter was ordained during a meeting of the Special Virginia Conference of the Evangelical Lutheran Tennessee Synod, and the former was received into said Conference at the same time, and their names ordered to be enrolled in the clerical catalogue of the Synod.

The election of officers resulted in favor of Rev. J. Killian, president; Rev. P. C. Henkel, secretary; and Rev. J. M. Wagner, treasurer.

Rev. Samuel Rothrock, of the North Carolina Synod, and Revs. Prof. W. Berley and N. Aldrich, of the South

Carolina Synod, were received as advisory members, and Rev. Godfrey Dreher.

Whereas, there are petitions before this Synod praying for a revision of the constitution of this Synod, and whereas objections have been laid to this instrument before this meeting, be it therefore

Resolved, That a convention, to be composed of all the clerical members of this body, with a lay-delegate from each congregation, be convened at Mt. Moriah Church, Rowan County, North Carolina, on Friday previous to the second Sunday in February, 1859, for the purpose of taking into consideration the propriety of amending or revising our present Synodical Constitution; and, that if said convention can agree upon such revision or amendment, that then their action be carried by the different ministers to their respective churches, and that the same be placed before them; and that said congregations send up their views thereupon to this session of Synod, to be held in the year 1859, for her action on the same.

The committee, appointed at the previous session on the revision of the Liturgy, having been relieved, Revs. A. Henkel, H. Wetzel, and S. Henkel were appointed to revise said Liturgy:

The following ministers were appointed delegates to sister synods: Rev. J. Killian, to the Joint Synod of Ohio; Rev. H. Wetzel, to the Eastern District Synod of Missouri; Rev. J. R. Moser, to the Western District Synod of Missouri; Rev. H. Goodman, to the Eastern District Synod of Ohio. Rev. H. Wetzel was appointed to preach the opening sermon at the next session of our Synod, on the subject of Pastoral Duty. Rev. P. C. Henkel was appointed his alternate.

There were, according to the report, 640 infants, 56 adults, and 29 slaves baptized, and 453 persons confirmed.

Deacon John M. Smith was ordained Pastor, and M. J. Stirewalt, Deacon.

Rev. J. L. Stirewalt was granted a letter of honorable dismissal.

Synod adjourned to meet in Bethlehem Church, Augusta County, Virginia, on Saturday before the second Sunday in September, 1859.

Thirty-ninth Session.

Saturday, September 10, 1859, Synod assembled in Bethlehem Church, Augusta County, Virginia.

Rev. A. Efird was elected president; Rev. S. Henkel, secretary; and Rev. J. Stirewalt, treasurer.

Rev. C. Beard, of the Virginia Synod, was invited to a seat as an advisory member.

With respect to the revision of the Constitution, the following action was taken:

Whereas, the revision of the Constitution of this Synod, a matter of no little importance to the future prosperity of the congregations, in its connection, should receive mature consideration; and, whereas, it appears from letters addressed to this meeting of Synod, that the arrangement of the revision proposed by the convention appointed at the last session of Synod, is not satisfactory, be it, therefore,

Resolved, That a committee be appointed, consisting of members of this session, present from the different sections of the Synod, to whom shall be referred all the papers addressed to this meeting, bearing upon the subject; and that it be made the duty of said committee to examine the revision prepared by the convention, to make such arrangement of its parts as may be deemed proper, to make such suggestions as may be considered necessary and suitable, and to report to this meeting.

On motion, a committee was appointed in accordance with the resolution, consisting of the following members of Synod: Revs. A. Efird, H. Goodman, H. Wetzel, J. Killian, J. Stirewalt, J. R. Peterson, M. J. Stirewalt, J. C. Barb, S. Henkel, Dr. S. G. Henkel, and A. Koiner, Esq.

The report of this committee was received and adopted, and the revision of the Constitution, as amended by this committee, was taken up, and read section by section, and article by article, and after several slight amendments, it was adopted section by section and article by article. It was then

Resolved, That the revision, as amended, be appended to the Minutes of this meeting, and that it be made the duty of all the ministers in connection with this Synod to lay the same before their respective congregations for their acceptance or rejection, and report the result of the action of the congregations to the next meeting of this Synod, that final action may be taken.

Revs. J. R. Peterson, A. J. Fox, P. C. Henkel, A. Efird, J. Killian, A. J. Brown, and J. M. Wagner, were appointed a committee to draft by-laws and rules of order for this Synod, and report them for adoption at its next convention.

On motion, by A. Koiner, Esq., the following preamble and resolution were passed :

Whereas, Synod has heard with deep regret the inadequacy of the support of our ministers, and the destitution of some of our congregations; therefore, be it

Resolved, That each minister of this Synod is hereby requested to preach at least one sermon to each of his congregations, during the ensuing synodical year, on the duty of the congregations to give their ministers an adequate support, and also one sermon urging the claims of our destitute congregations, and the necessity of encouraging young men to engage in the work of the ministry.

A letter of honorable dismission was granted Rev. M. Sondhaus.

Deacon Miles J. Stirewalt was ordained to the office of Pastor.

Q. S. Stirewalt and John S. Bennick were received as students of theology.

During this synodical year, 669 infants, 38 adults, and 65 slaves were baptized, and 280 persons were confirmed.

The time for the next meeting was Saturday before the

third Sunday of October, 1860, and the place, St. John's Church, Catawba County, North Carolina.

Fortieth Session.

Synod assembled in St. John's Church, Catawba County, North Carolina, on Saturday before the third Sunday of October, 1860.

The officers of this session were: Revs. A. J. Fox, president; J. R. Peterson, secretary; and J. M. Smith, treasurer.

On application, Bethphage Church, Lincoln County, North Carolina, was received into Synod.

The following ministers, belonging to the Synod and residing in the State of Tennessee, viz.: A. J. Brown, J. K. Hancher; J. C. Barb, J. M. Shaffer, J. Cloninger, James Fleenor, and J. B. Emmert, with the congregations under their charge, laid petitions before this meeting, for an honorable dismission from this body for the purpose of forming a new synod in East Tennessee.

The following is a copy of the petitions of congregations praying for dismission, setting forth the reasons by which they are influenced and the principles by which they intend to be guided:

To the Evangelical Lutheran Tennessee Synod, to be convened in St. John's Church, Catawba County, North Carolina, on Saturday before the third Sunday in October, 1860:

DEAR BRETHREN:—We, the members of Buehler's Church, Sullivan County, Tennessee, respectfully ask your reverend body to grant us an honorable dismission from the Evangelical Lutheran Tennessee Synod, for the purpose of uniting with a new Lutheran synod to be formed in Tennessee.

We have not taken this step hastily and rashly, but after long and prayerful reflection. We are satisfied that if a new synod be formed in this State with proper views and feelings, upon the right basis, it will greatly conduce to the interest of the Redeemer's Kingdom in this section of His Moral Vineyard. In taking this important step, it is proper and due as an act of respect to the parent Synod, that we should briefly set forth the considerations by which we have been influenced.

1. Our Synod is scattered over so wide an extent of territory as to render it at all times, when our Synod meets in another State, very inconvenient and expensive for our ministers and delegates to attend its annual meetings ; and, in some instances, utterly impracticable, without neglecting our domestic and private business.

2. The present arrangement in regard to the places at which Synod shall convene from time to time, is such that we cannot have a meeting of it in our own State more than once in four years, thus depriving our congregations for three successive years of whatever advantages may result from a meeting of the Synod in our midst.

3. As our Synod is at present organized, or is likely to be organized under any constitution that has been proposed for our adoption, we can transact among ourselves all the business ordinarily transacted, as well as it can be transacted by the whole Synod. Our principal business is to examine and ordain candidates for the ministry; and this can be done by the ministers and churches in any State connected with the Synod, and has been done by the brethren in Virginia for several years, and by us in Tennessee on one occasion, at our recent conference meeting.

4. The wide extent of territory over which we are scattered, and the great difficulty, if not the impossibility, of having all the different sections of the Church fairly and fully represented in our synodical meetings, renders it a slow process to bring to an issue any important measure in which Synod may engage. Of this we have an illustration in the attempts which have been made to revise our Synodical Constitution.

These, dear brethren, are some of the leading considerations which have influenced us to the pursuance of our present course. Others might be stated, but we deem it unnecessary. It may be proper to add, that we are by no means disaffected towards our brethren with whom we have been so long and pleasantly connected, with whom we have so often met and taken sweet counsel, and contended for the faith once delivered to the saints, and which is so clearly set forth in our venerable Augsburg Confession. Nor do we, in the formation of a new Synod, contemplate any change in the doctrinal basis upon which our Synod was organized, nearly half a century ago, and upon which she has ever since uniformly and firmly stood. Under this banner our Synod has already achieved many a signal and glorious victory, and under this she is destined still to be victorious. With this we are satisfied, and upon this we intend still to stand.

In view of the considerations above stated, we flatter ourselves you will grant us an honorable dismission from your venerable body.

May the unerring spirit of God guide you in all your deliberations, so that they may redound to the glory of God and to the advancement of the Redeemer's Kingdom.

In answer to the above petitions, the following preamble and resolution were adopted by Synod:

Whereas, our ministerial brethren in the State of Tennessee,—A. J. Brown, J. K. Hancher, J. C. Barb, J. M. Shaffer, J. Cloninger, J. Fleenor, and J. B. Emmert, with their congregations, have asked an honorable dismission from this body, with a view to the formation of a new synod in their own State, and whereas they give us the assurance, that, in taking this step, they have no other object in view than the welfare of our beloved Lutheran Zion, and the more extensive dissemination of the time-honored and heaven-blessed doctrines of our Church; therefore, be it

Resolved, That whilst we are sincerely sorry to sever the ties which have bound them to us as a part of our Synod, we feel it to be our duty to grant their request, with the fervent prayer, that the smiles and rich blessings of the Great Head of the Church may rest upon them, and that all their efforts to extend the Redeemer's Kingdom, may be crowned with abundant success.

These ministers and congregations organized the synod, styled the Evangelical Lutheran Holston Synod of Tennessee.

The committee, Revs. J. Killian, A. Efird, and S. Henkel, on revision of the Constitution, reported as follows:

We, the committee, appointed to report on the subject of the Revised Constitution, respectfully submit the following:

Upon examination of the papers coming from congregations and individuals in connection with our Synod, and of the statements of the result of the vote taken in the congregations, in regard to the Revised Constitution, we find that some of them failed to take action in reference to this matter, as required by a resolution passed at the last meeting of our Synod; and that the vote, as far as presented to Synod, resulted in favor of the revision by a very considerable majority. But after careful and mature consideration, your committee are constrained to believe that, in view of the present aspect of things, it is inexpedient at this time to take final action on the Revised Constitution; and,

Whereas, it might leave the impression, that the confessional basis, as set forth in the second article of the Revised Constitution, influenced this action; and, whereas, this might detract from the character of the Synod for orthodoxy, and be construed as a rejection of our confessional basis, your committee would earnestly recommend the passage of the following resolution: be it

Resolved, That this Synod adopts as its basis the following, and that the ministers belonging to this Synod subscribe it:

1. The Holy Scriptures, the inspired writings of the Old and New Testaments, alone, shall be the only rule and standard of doctrine and church discipline.

2. As a true and faithful exhibition of the doctrines of the Holy Scriptures, in regard to faith and practice, this Synod receives the three Ancient Symbols of the Church,—the Apostolic, Nicene, and Athanasian Creeds,—and the Unaltered Augsburg Confession of Faith. It receives also the other Symbolical Books of the Evangelical Lutheran Church, (namely, the Apology, the Smalcald Articles, the Small and Large Catechisms of Luther, and the Formula of Concord) as a true and Scriptural declaration of the doctrines taught in the said Augsburg Confession.

The report was adopted.

A committee, consisting of Rev. Messrs. A. J. Fox, J. M. Smith, and T. Moser, was appointed to examine and ordain brother E. E. Smyre, at Phanuel's Church, Rowan County, North Carolina.

The committee, appointed at the last Synod to prepare a Code of By-Laws and Rules of Order for Synod, was continued, after striking off the names of Rev. Messrs. A. J. Brown and J. M. Wagner. The committee thus consisted of Rev. J. R. Peterson, Rev. A. J. Fox, Rev. P. C. Henkel, Rev. A. Efird, and Rev. J. Killian.

A committee, consisting of Rev. A. Henkel, Rev. S. Henkel, and Dr. S. G. Henkel, was appointed to collect all historical facts relating to the confessional basis of this Synod, and report to the next meeting.

According to the Parochial Report, 649 infants, 39 adults, and 29 slaves were baptized, and 452 persons were confirmed.

Synod adjourned to meet in St. John's Church, Lexington District, South Carolina, November 9, 1861.

During this decade, 19 ministers were ordained, 2 received on letters, the name of 1 was erased from the clerical roll, 3, besides those residing in Tennessee, were dismissed to other synods, 26 churches were received, 6,634 infants were baptized, 445 adults, and 244 slaves, and 3,647 persons were confirmed. These are the numbers of baptisms and confirmations shown by the Parochial Reports, which are by no means full; perhaps, not more than two-thirds were really reported.

FIFTH DECADE.

Forty-first Session.

Synod met in St. John's Church, Lexington District, South Carolina, on Saturday before the second Sunday in November, 1861.

The officers elected were: Revs. A. Efird, president; J. M. Smith, secretary; and M. J. Stirewalt, treasurer.

Revs. J. Moser, Prof. J. P. Smeltzer, Prof. J. M. Schreckhise, D. M. Blackwelder, and Smithdeal, of the South Carolina Synod, were received as advisory members.

Rev. John H. Hunton was granted a dismission to the Pittsburgh Synod.

The Committee on Rules of Order reported. The report was received and adopted, and ordered to be appended to the Minutes.

Messrs. D. E. Fox and L. A. Fox were received as theological students. I. Conder was ordained.

A convention, having been called to meet in Salisbury, North Carolina, May, 1862, composed of delegates from the Southern Synods, the Synod appointed Revs. A. J. Fox, E. E. Smyre, of North Carolina, and Revs. J. Killian and S. Henkel, of Virginia, to represent it in that convention.

The Parochial Report, only eight ministers reporting, shows 346 infant baptisms, 44 adult, and 18 slave, and 358 confirmations.

In regard to the time and place for the next meeting, it was

Resolved, That in consequence of the political troubles of our country, and as Virginia is so near the seat of war, and as we know not when our troubles will end, when Synod adjourns, it adjourn to meet in Grace Church, Catawba County, North Carolina, on Saturday before the first Sunday in October, 1862.

Forty-second Session.

Synod convened in Grace Church, Catawba County, North Carolina, on Saturday before the first Sunday in October, 1862.

The following persons were elected officers of Synod: Revs. T. Moser, president; J. M. Stirewalt, secretary; and Thomas Crouse, treasurer.

In consequence of the political troubles and conflicts and the War between the States, the convention called to meet in Salisbury, North Carolina, failed to convene; and for the same reasons, the members of Virginia, Tennessee, and Missouri, whose presence, under these circumstances, was not expected, were excused for their non-attendance.

The By-Laws and Rules of Order, not meeting the general approbation of the congregations, were rescinded.

Mr. D. E. Fox, after examination by Rev. P. C. Henkel, was licensed to preach.

The Parochial Report, only seven ministers reporting, shows 412 infant baptisms, 39 adult, and 8 slave, and 306 confirmations.

Synod adjourned to meet in St. John's Church, Catawba County, North Carolina, on Saturday before the third Sunday of October, 1863.

After the adjournment of Synod, the Secretary being informed of the death of Deacon Jacob Costner, and an obituary being submitted to him, he ordered it to be appended to the Minutes, as follows:

Obituary of Rev. Jacob Costner.—The Rev. Jacob Costner was born August 27th, 1788, and departed this mortal life March 19th, 1862, at the advanced age of 72 years, 7 months, and 2 days. He intermarried with Mary Ann Rudisill, December 10th, 1810, who bore him ten children, five of whom preceded him to eternity.

Mr. Costner was born of pious parents who dedicated their son to God in infancy, by the Sacrament of Holy Baptism, and at an early age he was admitted to full communion with the Evangelical Lutheran Church by the rite of confirmation. In Mr. Costner's early life, the scarcity of ministers in the Lutheran Church was very great, and he was ordained to the office of Deacon, as it was then established in the

Evangelical Lutheran Tennessee Synod, but from causes not clearly understood by the writer, he never labored in the ministry. Mr. Costner was warmly attached to the Church of his fathers, and was active in the performance of whatever he considered his duty, and so long as strength permitted, his place in the congregation was never vacant; but for a number of years before his death, his strength so far failed as to prevent his regular attendance upon the public ministrations of the Gospel. His concern, however, for the prosperity of the Church continued unabated, and, as he neared the grave, his prospects for heaven grew brighter. The writer visited him during the somewhat protracted and painful sickness which terminated his earthly existence, and had opportunities of hearing from him expressions of a well-grounded hope of acceptance with God.

In all the relations of life, Mr. Costner was exemplary. He was an affectionate husband, a kind and indulgent father, and a useful citizen.

Forty-third Session.

Pursuant to adjournment, Synod assembled in St. John's Church, Catawba County, North Carolina, October 17, 1863.

The election for officers resulted in favor of Revs. J. R. Peterson, president; J. M. Smith, secretary; and M. J. Stirewalt, treasurer.

Rev. H. Goodman gave notice, that, at a suitable time, he would call the attention of Synod to the importance of missionary work in the Confederate Army, during the War between the States, which commenced in the spring of 1861, and ended in the spring of 1865,—four years.

This matter being brought up, a committee of four, consisting of Revs. A. J. Fox, P. C. Henkel, H. Goodman, and Mr. J. F. Plonk, was appointed, to propose a plan for such work. After consideration, this committee submitted the following:

Whereas, this Synod is fully aware of the great necessity of doing something to supply our own soldiers in the Confederate Army with the preaching of the Gospel by our ministers,

Resolved 1. That we establish an Army Mission in the following manner: Let as many ministers in connection with this Synod as will subscribe this resolution, be obligated to perform missionary labors in the Confederate Army, for the period of one month in each year, if our funds and the situation of the army will permit.

Resolved 2. That two ministers go at the same time, and that in rotation, being chosen by lot at each annual meeting of Synod.

Resolved 3. That their expenses, at least, be defrayed by donations obtained from the congregations by solicitation.

Resolved 4. That those ministers, having performed such missionary visits as herein required, shall make a return of their traveling expenses to a treasurer hereinafter provided, who shall pay said expenses out of the funds he may have in hands for said purpose.

Resolved 5. That a treasurer be appointed whose duty it shall be to receive such money as may be collected for the purpose herein stated.

Resolved 6. That it be the duty of the ministers, associated with this enterprise, to take up collections in their several congregations, semi-annually; and that they forward said collections to the treasurer.

This was received and adopted. Moses Harmon, Esq., Newton, Catawba County, North Carolina, was elected treasurer of the mission funds, and Rev. P. C. Henkel as corresponding secretary with the army and ministers, to secure information as to the points and times best suited for such work.

The committee to bring up the Revised Constitution for the consideration of this body, handed in the following:

Whereas, it was made our duty to prepare and submit to Synod a suitable plan for the revision of the Constitution of Synod, we, your committee, beg leave to submit the following:

That a session of Synod convene at Zion Church, on Saturday before the 4th Sunday in March, 1864, at which time it is contemplated to consider the propriety or impropriety of adopting the Constitution submitted to Synod at her session in 1860, with such suitable amendments as may be agreed upon, which shall then be printed and submitted to the different congregations, in connection with the Tennessee Synod, for their approval, amendment, or rejection.

We, the ministers and lay-delegates of the present Synod, unanimously and most earnestly entreat the ministers and congregations, not represented in the present session of Synod, seriously to consider this matter, and such *ministers* to be present, and such *congregations* to be represented, each, by one lay-delegate.

This report was received and adopted.

Messrs. L. A. Fox and D. E. Fox were authorized, in special cases, to exercise the functions of a pastor.

David S. Henkel and David A. Goodman were received as theological students. It was ordered, that 1,500 copies of the Minutes be printed, and that a work, entitled "A Few Fragments on Regeneration," by the late Rev. David Henkel, be printed in connection with the Minutes for circulation in the Confederate Army.

The Parochial Report, only seven reporting, shows 193 infant baptisms, 8 adult, and 14 slave, and 214 confirmed.

Synod adjourned to meet in St. Mark's Church, Gaston County, North Carolina, on Saturday before the second Sunday in October, 1864.

Forty-fourth Session.

This session of Synod was held in St. Mark's Church, Gaston County, North Carolina, commencing October 8, 1864.

The officers elected were: Revs. J. M. Smith, president; A. J. Fox, secretary; and M. J. Stirewalt, treasurer.

Rev. J. R. Peterson introduced the following preamble and resolutions, which, after a free interchange of opinions, were unanimously adopted.

Feeling, as we do, the great want of a religious periodical in the families of our connection, and as the *Southern*

Lutheran is the only paper of Lutheran character now published in the Confederate States, be it, therefore,

Resolved, That this Synod most cheerfully recommend the *Southern Lutheran* to the families composing our congregations, and that the ministers connected with this Synod be encouraged to introduce it into our families.

Resolved, That a collection be taken immediately after the sermon to-day for the purpose of sending the *Lutheran* to the soldiers.

The matter in regard to the adoption of the Revised Constitution being brought up, it was resolved, that final action on that matter be deferred till the next meeting.

Licentiate L. A. Fox was ordained to the office of Pastor, and applicants D. S. Henkel and D. A. Goodman were licensed to perform the functions of the ministry.

The Parochial Report for this year shows 2,187 infant baptisms, 13 adult, and 26 colored, and 261 confirmations. Ten ministers reported, and the presumption is, that some of them reported for several years.

Synod decided to meet in its next convention, in St. Peter's Church, Catawba County, North Carolina, October 21, 1865.

Forty-fifth Session.

This meeting assembled in St. Peter's Church, Catawba County, North Carolina, October 21–24, 1865.

The following officers were elected: Revs. J. R. Peterson, president; C. Moretz, secretary; and J. M. Smith, treasurer.

Philadelphia Church, Caldwell County, and Pizgah Church, Alexander County, North Carolina, were received into Synod.

In regard to the Revised Constitution, final action was deferred till the next annual meeting of Synod.

Rev. A. J. Fox gave notice, that he would, some time during this session of Synod, bring to its notice the subject of publicly licensing young men for the ministry.

When this subject was brought up, a committee, consisting of Revs. A. J. Fox, P. C. Henkel, and T. Moser, was appointed to draft a licensure. The form was submitted in due time, and ordered to be printed in connection with the Minutes.

Previous to the year 1862, Synod did not practice the licensure policy, and it continued that policy for only a few years. The contingencies of the Civil War gave rise to that system, so far as this Synod is concerned.

D. E. Fox was ordained to the office of Pastor, and David S. Henkel and David A. Goodman were licensed for one year.

During the year, according to the report, only eight ministers reporting, 282 infants, 21 adults, and 2 colored, were baptized, and 156 confirmed.

The time and place for the next meeting were, Thursday before the fourth Sunday in October, 1866, and Beck's Church, Davidson County, North Carolina.

Forty-sixth Session.

This session of Synod convened in Beck's Church, Davidson County, North Carolina, October 25, 1866.

Revs. A. Efird was elected president; L. A. Fox, secretary; and J. M. Smith, treasurer.

Rev. A. J. Fox suggested the propriety of organizing conferences in the Synod.

The ministers and congregations in Virginia, in connection with the Tennessee Synod, having already organized a conference in that State, called the Virginia Conference of the Evangelical Lutheran Tennessee Synod, the ministers and congregations in North Carolina were divided into three conferences, designated the Eastern, the Middle, and Southern Conferences, and the ministers and congregations in South Carolina were formed into a conference, called the South Carolina Conference of the Evangelical Lutheran Tennessee Synod. These conferences were not allowed to transact any business which properly belonged to the Synod.

Rev. A. J. Fox offered the following which was adopted:

Commission to the General Synod of North America.

Whereas, The Evangelical Lutheran Church in the Southern States, is, when compared with other branches of the great Christian family, but a very feeble body, and feeble as it is, is divided into nine or ten small synods, embracing in the aggregate not more than 200 ministers and 350 churches with about 35,000 communicant members; and,

Whereas, We firmly believe in union there is strength, but in division there is weakness; and,

Whereas, The central point in the Lutheran Church is her doctrinal standards, to which she must firmly cling or cease to exist, and five of these Southern synods having united themselves in a body known as the General Synod of the Evangelical Lutheran Church in North America, and adopted as her doctrinal basis the Augsburg Confession of Faith; and,

Whereas, We, as a Synod, are anxious to do all we can to promote the interests of true Evangelical Lutheranism, and we think this can be done best by uniting the energies and resources of the Symbolical Lutheran Church in these States; therefore,

Resolved, That one of our most experienced and influential ministers be appointed a *commissioner* to meet the next regular meeting of the "General Synod, &c.," to convene in Staunton, Va., in May, 1867, and to confer with that body upon the practicability and possibility of uniting our Synod with said General Synod, and to report to the next session of this Synod the result of any conferences he may have with the General Synod or any of her authorized committees. Afterward this Synod shall take such steps as she shall determine best. This commissioner shall observe the following instructions in all his intercourse with the General Synod: this Synod proposes a union with the General Synod upon these conditions, viz.: That the General Synod pledge herself that no church journal or book shall be published, or other publications shall ever be made by her order or under her sanction that contains anything contrary to any article of the Unaltered Augsburg Confession of Faith, and that no professor shall be appointed in any Theological Seminary who will not solemnly promise to teach correctly all the doctrines of said Confession, and that no Synod shall ever be received into her connection who does not without any reservation subscribe the said Confession; and further, with this distinct understanding upon her part, that, if at any time in the judgment of the delegates who represent this Synod, the General Synod shall violate the above principles our delegates may withdraw from that session to report to the next session of this Synod whose action alone shall determine the future course of this Synod in relation to the General Synod.

The Synod proceeded to ballot for the commissioner.— Rev. Dr. A. J. Fox was chosen principal and Rev. J. R. Peterson, alternate.

The following action was taken in regard to a church paper, called *Evangelical Lutheran*: Inasmuch as we feel the great necessity of a good Lutheran Church journal circulating among our people, but not feeling ourselves able in the present crippled condition of pecuniary affairs to commence the publication of such a paper now, and as there is a weekly paper purporting to be strictly and symbolically Lutheran (at least in doctrinal features), published in Charlotte, N. C., in which we find some things, it is true, of a practical character which we cannot endorse, yet in view of the above stated facts and some other things we, for the present,

Resolve, To approve the circulation of the *Evangelical Lutheran* among our people.

Rev. Jacob Stirewalt, having sent to Synod a copy of resolutions passed by the Virginia Special Conference, praying for the advice of this Synod in regard to the formation of a new synod in Virginia, based upon the "time-honored and established doctrines and usages of the Lutheran Church;" the following action was taken:

Whereas, The ministers and congregations, in connection with this Synod who are located in the great Valley of Virginia, have expressed a desire to organize themselves into a separate synod, although we regret to separate from those with whom we have been for so many years associated, yet in view of the reasons presented by them, and the great distance that separates us from them and, consequently, the difficulty of meeting as often as the interest of the Church requires; therefore,

Resolved, That we approve, unanimously, the measure proposed by these brethren, and advise them to organize as soon as possible with such constitution and other regulations as may not be inconsistent with the Word of God and the Symbolical Books of the Lutheran Church, and promise them that as soon as the President shall be officially informed that this has been done, he will give them an honorable dismission from this Synod, with a distinct understanding, however, that a regular correspondence be maintained by the interchange of delegates or by the formation of some central organization.

The death of Rev. D. E. Fox having been announced in the President's Report, a committee, consisting of Revs. I. Conder and J. M. Smith, was appointed to prepare suitable resolutions relative to him. The following was submitted:

Memorial of Rev. D. E. Fox,

who departed this life, September 4, 1866; aged 31 years.

Whereas, It has pleased the Great Head of the Church, since our last session of Synod, to remove from our midst our beloved brother, Rev. D. E. Fox; therefore,

Resolved 1. That by this afflicting dispensation we have lost a worthy young brother, who had labored but a short time in his Master's vineyard.

Resolved 2. That, notwithstanding our deep regret for

his removal and the loss to our Church, since it has resulted in his everlasting gain, we bow in humble resignation to the will of God.

Resolved 3. That we deeply sympathize with his afflicted wife in her bereavement, and commend her to Him, who is the husband of the widow, and makes all things work together for good to them that love God.

Resolved 4. That these resolutions be incorporated with the Minutes of this Synod, that a copy be sent to the *Evangelical Lutheran* for publication, and a copy, also, to the bereaved wife of the deceased.

It was adopted by rising and standing in silence.

M. L. Fox, M. D., was received under the care of Synod as an applicant for the ministry.

Spanish Grove Church, Forsythe County, North Carolina, was received.

Relative to the Revised Constitution and the Rules of Order and By-Laws, the following action was taken: Inasmuch as the Revised Constitution, prepared by the Extra Session of this Synod convened in Zion Church, Catawba County, N. C., on the 26th day of March, 1864, upon which final action was postponed by the regular session in 1864, and again in 1865 to the present session, has been approved by a large majority of the congregations of our Synod; be it, therefore,

Resolved, That it is and shall be, until altered, amended, or disapproved by this Synod in the manner provided for in its last article, the organic law of this Synod.

Resolved, That the Rules of Order and By-Laws, which have been read and approved, rule by rule, and section by section, be now adopted as a whole, and, henceforth, until altered or amended as provided for in the last article, be in full force and effect in the Synod.

A delegate was appointed to the next convention of the Holston Synod.

With respect to the Freedmen, the following action was taken:

Whereas, The colored people among us no longer sustain the same relation to the white man they did formerly, and that change has transferred the individual obligations and responsibility of owners to the whole Church; and,

Whereas, Some of them were formerly members of our congregations and still claim membership in them, but owing to the plainly marked distinctions which God has made between us and them, giving different colors, &c., it is felt by us, and them also, that there ought to be separate places of worship, and, also, separate ecclesiastical organizations, so that every one could worship God with the least possible embarrassment; and

Whereas, These colored people are considered firm adherents to our Church, and we feel it our imperative duty to assist them in adopting such measures as will meet best the necessities of their present condition; be it, therefore,

Resolved 1. That whenever any of our colored brethren desire to preach, they may make application to some one of the ministers of our Synod, who shall inform the President, when it shall be the President's duty to appoint two ordained ministers who, in connection with two laymen whom they may choose, shall constitute a committee to examine the candidate upon his motives and mental and moral qualification, and, if they are satisfied, to license him to preach, catechise, baptize, and celebrate the rites of matrimony among those of his own race, according to the usages of our Church, until the next regular session of Synod thereafter, when said committee shall report. This license, however, does not authorize them to preach in our churches, or take part in our ecclesiastical meetings; nevertheless they are permitted to worship with us as heretofore, yet we advise them to erect houses for themselves in which they may worship.

Resolved 2. That we will use every reasonable means to aid them in organizing and building up congregations.

Thomas Fry, a freedman, having frequently expressed a desire to preach, the President, in compliance with the resolution given above, appointed Rev. P. C. Henkel and Rev. J. M. Smith as the clerical half of a committee to examine and, if found qualified, to license him.

This year, only about half of the ministers reporting, 322 infants and 20 adults were baptized, and 217 confirmed.

Synod adjourned to meet in Cedar Grove Church, Lexington District, South Carolina, on Thursday before the fourth Sunday in September, 1867.

Forty-seventh Session.

This meeting was held in Cedar Grove Church, Lexington District, South Carolina, commencing September 19, 1867.

The officers elected were: Revs. A. J. Fox, president; J. R. Peterson, secretary; Daniel Efird, corresponding secretary; and David S. Henkel, treasurer.

Revs. J. H. Bailey, E. Kaughman, A. W. Lindler, and Prof. J. P. Smeltzer, of the South Carolina Synod, were received as advisory members.

Sardis Church, Catawba County, North Carolina, was received in connection with Synod.

Rev. Prof. Smeltzer addressed the Synod in regard to the interests of Newberry College and Theological Seminary, South Carolina. Synod took favorable action relative to these institutions.

The President stated in his message, that he had extended the license of D. S. Henkel, and that he had given Rev. J. M. Wagner an honorable dismissal to the Holston Synod. These acts were approved.

The commissioner, appointed to attend the Southern Lutheran General Synod, which was held in Staunton, Virginia, in 1867, reported. It seems he fully carried out his mission, and kept within the limits of his instructions. He spoke in the highest terms of the manner in which he was received and treated by that body. He appeared to be well satisfied with the sentiments of that Synod, as expressed during his sojourn among its members. He then submitted the following report of a committee, appointed by said General Synod, to confer with the said commissioner:

The committee, appointed to confer with the Rev. Dr. Fox, as a commissioner from the Evangelical Lutheran Tennessee Synod, have advised with him in reference to a union of that Synod with this body.

We, with pleasure, report that the interview afforded us satisfactory evidence of the truly Christian character of the Synod which Dr. Fox represents, and the high principles of integrity and church love which animates them in the propositions made to this General Synod; therefore,

Resolved, That we will cordially receive said Synod as an integral part of this body on the truly Lutheran basis which we have adopted, and in accordance with which we feel bound as an ecclesiastical body to withhold our sanction or *imprimatur* from any religious publication of whatever form, which shall inculcate principles opposed to the doctrines of the Augsburg Confession as construed and defended by our Church in her Symbolical writings.

Resolved, That we feel ourselves in like manner bound to appoint or employ no Professor in our Theological schools who shall teach doctrines at variance with our time honored Confession.

In regard to this report, a committee was appointed to give an expression relative to it. The committee submitted the following:

Inasmuch as the question of a union between this body and the General Synod in North America is one of very grave importance, and should be well and maturely considered, your Committee upon the Report of the Commissioner to the General Synod have examined the matter in all its bearings; and inasmuch as but a very small number of our ministers are present, and comparatively few congregations represented in this meeting; and inasmuch as our brethren residing in Virginia may fail to effect an organization in that State, we would therefore recommend that a Committee of five, three ministers, of whom the President shall be one, and two laymen, be appointed to collect all the facts they can in relation to this contemplated union, and report them to the next annual meeting of Synod, that decisive action may then be taken.

The foregoing report was adopted, and the following committee appointed: Revs. J. R. Peterson, P. C. Henkel, A. J. Fox, and Messrs. A. Costner and M. L. Cline.

Feeling the great necessity of making suitable religious impressions upon the minds of the children of our congregations; therefore, it was

Resolved, That the ministers of our connection be requested to endeavor to get up and encourage Sunday schools in all their congregations, and report their success to the Committee on the State of the Church, some time previous to each annual meeting of Synod.

License was granted M. L. Fox, M. D., to perform the functions of the ministry.

The Parochial Report shows 340 infant and 14 adult baptisms and 257 confirmations.

Synod adjourned to meet in Salem Church, Lincoln County, North Carolina, September 24, 1868.

Forty-eighth Session.

Synod assembled, pursuant to adjournment, in Salem Church, Lincoln County, North Carolina, September 24, 1868.

The election of officers resulted in favor of Rev. J. M. Smith, president; Rev. C. Moretz, recording secretary; Rev. A. J. Fox, corresponding secretary; and Rev. T. Moser, treasurer.

Rev. G. D. Bernheim, of the North Carolina Synod, was received as an advisory member.

During the meeting of the Southern General Synod, at Newberry, South Carolina, in 1868, the Holston Synod was admitted.

It appears from the proceedings of this session of the Tennessee Synod, that the Northern General Synod, at its meeting in Harrisburg, Pennsylvania, in its twenty-third session, adopted the Augsburg Confession. The committee of the Tennessee Synod, in reporting on the Minutes of the said General Synod, say the General Synod may have made advances in the right direction, but it does not yet seem to reach the sound Lutheran faith.

Well, it may appear rather singular that a general body, claiming to be Lutheran, should have failed to adopt the Augsburg Confession till its twenty-third session. Is it any wonder that there was a continual conflict between it and the Tennessee Synod, which was and is strictly confessional?

Rev. Miles J. Stirewalt, Augusta Station, Indiana, received an honorable dismission to the English District of the Joint Synod of Ohio.

The President, in his message, calls attention to the condition of the Church in the Valley of Virginia, caused by an attempt to organize a new synod in that section, called the Concordia Synod of Virginia, and recommends a suitable committee to be appointed to investigate that matter, and report the result of their investigation. The committee was appointed, and submitted the following report:

We, the committee, appointed to take into consideration the relation sustained by the body claiming the title of "Evangelical Lutheran Concordia Synod of Virginia," to the Evangelical Lutheran Tennessee Synod, and to give an expression of Synod in regard to this matter, beg leave to submit the following:

Whereas, In the year 1866, application was made to our Synod by the brethren in the Valley of Virginia, to form a synod in that locality; and, whereas, such request was granted to these brethren, accompanied with a promise contained in a preamble and resolution passed by our Synod in regard to this matter, that, as soon as an organization should be effected in accordance with said preamble and resolution, an honorable dismission from our Synod would be granted these brethren; and, whereas, an effort was made to form a regularly constituted synod, but the object contemplated failed; and, whereas, the Revs. H. Wetzel, G. Schmucker, and J. E. Seneker, with several congregations, united themselves into a body, styled "The Evangelical Lutheran Concordia Synod of Virginia," thereby disturbing the peace and prosperity of the Church in that section of our Synod, the other brethren dissenting; and, whereas, the Rev. H. Wetzel has denied the jurisdiction of our Synod over him, and as no request has been made by the other brethren, who entered the said organization, for an honorable dismission from our Synod; therefore, be it

Resolved, That this Synod disapprove of the course pursued by these brethren in this matter, and that their names be retained in our clerical catalogue until they properly apply for an honorable dismission, or announce their withdrawal from it.

This report was received and adopted.

Several years afterwards, efforts were made to make an impression on the public mind, that a difference in doctrine between the ministers in the Valley of Virginia, in connection with the Tennessee Synod, gave rise to the organization of the new synod formed in the Valley of Virginia, and called the Concordia Synod of Virginia. But these efforts failed. For the fact is, there was not, at the time of its organization, one word said about differences in doctrine, and all the ministers of the Tennessee Synod, in the Valley of Virginia, with delegates representing their congregations, were notified of the time and place agreed upon for such organization, and invited to be present and participate in its organization; and when the time came for such organization, and none of the ministers in Virginia, of the Tennessee Synod, except Revs. H. Wetzel, J. E. Seneker, and George Schmucker, appeared, Rev. H. Wetzel, be it said to his praise, opposed the contemplated organization, but was overruled. Since that time, all the churches in the Valley of Virginia, except two, which went into that organization, have returned to the Tennessee Synod, and now stand in its connection. One of the churches that did not return, now stands independent of any synod, and is served by a Missouri Synod preacher, whilst the other one stands in connection with what is called the Concordia District of Ohio. Rev. H. Wetzel was ultimately received again in connection with the Tennessee Synod, and Rev. J. E. Seneker, a year or so before his death, spoke of returning to this Synod; and even Rev. George Schmucker finally expressed a preference for this Synod, stating that he neither could conscientiously, nor would he, submit to some of the regulations of the new order of things.

That Concordia Synod, having changed its tactics a time or two, finally drifted into what is now called the Concordia District of Ohio, and so far as the material taken from the Tennessee Synod is concerned, it consists of several congregations in West Virginia, a few fragments in Virginia, and a few of the fragments in North Carolina which were broken off by the withdrawal of Rev. Adam Miller, Jr., who was resting under grave charges of immorality, and was in the very act of being suspended by the Synod when he withdrew.

With respect to the President's recommendation, that an effort be made to reunite all the ministers and congregations who have formerly been in her connection, with those now in it, with a view of forming the Synod into district synods, and out of these district synods, a joint synod, and that a committee be appointed to take this matter into immediate consideration, the committee on his message recommended, that such committee be appointed to give that matter proper attention. The committee suggested was appointed, and consisted of Revs. P. C. Henkel, A. J. Fox, and T. Moser, Messrs. A. Costner and F. L. Herman.

Rev. N. Aldrich presented his credentials as a delegate from the North Carolina Synod, and was received as such. Rev. J. M. Smith was chosen as a delegate to the next convention of the North Carolina Synod.

On the reception of Rev. N. Aldrich, there were mutual, fraternal greetings, upon which Rev. G. D. Bernheim made some of the most eulogistic remarks respecting the character and high orthodox standing of the Evangelical Lutheran Tennessee Synod, and the indebtedness of Lutheranism in America to her.

Revs. S. Henkel, J. Stirewalt, and J. Killian were appointed a committee to report on the Book of Worship, at the next meeting of Synod.

With respect to re-districting North Carolina into conferences, Synod voted unanimously, that the conference embrace all ministers and churches in North Carolina, belonging to the Tennessee Synod, and that its name be the North Carolina Conference of the Tennessee Synod.

The committee, on union with the General Synod of North America (Southern General Synod), not having had time to give the matter proper attention, were continued.

Rev. L. A. Fox received an honorable dismission to the Southwestern Virginia Synod.

Messrs. John S. Bennick and William H. Swaney were received as Licentiates.

The Committee, appointed to prepare a plan for the reconstruction of the Evangelical Lutheran Tennessee Synod, from the limited time they had to consider the matter, did not feel themselves fully prepared to mature a plan which would fully meet the necessity of the case, but respectfully submitted that it is the opinion of the Committee that a committee of one be appointed to open a correspondence with some of the most prominent members of the Holston Synod upon this subject, and that Synod be respectfully invited to consider this matter in her next annual convention; and that this committee of one report the result of his correspondence to the next meeting of this Synod; and that the Virginia Conference be requested to take up the subject of organizing themselves into a branch synod, and lay the same before the next meeting of this Synod.

As recommended above, Synod appointed the Corresponding Secretary a committee of one to open the correspondence with prominent members of the Holston Synod.

The committee, Rev. S. Henkel, Rev. T. Moser, and Mr. A. Costner, appointed to report in reference to the publication of the Epistles, contained in Dr. Martin Luther's Church Postil, now in manuscript in the English language, and in the possession of parties at New Market, Virginia, submitted the following:

In regard to this subject, we recommend, that a call be made by the Synod on those parties, to make arrangements for the publication of those sermons in what they may conceive to be the most judicious and practicable manner, at as early a period as possible, and that the Synod give such enterprise their heartfelt co-operation and support in the circulation of the work.

The Parochial Report shows 454 infant and 29 adult baptisms, and 343 confirmations.

The place and time for the next meeting were Emmanuel Church, New Market, Virginia, and Friday before the first full moon in October, 1869.

Forty-ninth Session.

Synod convened, in its forty-ninth session, in Emmanuel Church, New Market, Shenandoah County, Virginia, October 15, 1869.

The officers for this meeting were: Revs. T. Miller, president; S. Henkel, recording secretary; A. J. Fox, corresponding secretary; and J. S. Bennick, treasurer.

Rev. D. M. Henkel was received as delegate from the Pennsylvania Synod. On motion, the following resolution was adopted:

Resolved, That this Synod hail with joy the appearance of Dr. Luther's Church Postil on the Epistles, in the English language, published by the New Market Evangelical Lutheran Publishing Company, New Market, Virginia, and that each minister is hereby earnestly requested to recommend this work to his people.

The Committee on Union with the General Synod South, was continued.

The Committee on Joint Synod not being prepared to make a report, recommended that a committee of five, three ministers and two laymen, be appointed to take charge of the matter.

A committee of two ministers and one layman was appointed, to report at some future session of this meeting in regard to that matter. The following is the report of this committee:

Your committee, Revs. A. J. Fox and J. Killian, on the subject of a Joint Synod or Branch Synods, have examined the matter, as far as we have had opportunity, and regard such an organization as very desirable, provided some safe ground of union can be traced out, and we regard this as at least possible. We regard the calling of a convention of all concerned, at as early a day as practicable, as the best plan, and would, therefore, propose to our brethren of the Evangelical Lutheran Holston Synod, to meet us, in convention, as soon after the rising of this Synod in the year 1870, as may be convenient, in Grace Church, Catawba County, North Carolina, as this is one of the most central points. And that they then enter into a free conference with us, upon this subject, and endeavor to agree upon some safe plan by which the end may be consummated.

Resolved 1. Therefore, that a copy of this report be forwarded by the Corresponding Secretary of this Synod to the chairman of the committee appointed by that synod to correspond with us upon this subject.

Resolved 2. That the committee of the Holston Synod, charged with this matter, be requested to furnish the Corresponding Secretary, as soon as possible after the rising of their Synod, with a copy of their proceedings.

Resolved 3. That, if our proposition to call a convention is complied with, the time of the meeting of this convention be fixed upon at the next meeting of this Synod.

A church paper, called the *Lutheran and Missionary*, was recommended.

Rev. William H. Cone, delegate from the North Carolina Synod, was prevented from attending.

The President having announced, in his report, the death of Rev. Jacob Stirewalt, and that of Rev. E. E. Smyre, the following was adopted by a rising vote:

Resolved 1. That we have learned, with feelings of the deepest sorrow, of the death of our dear and well beloved brethren and fellow servants of our Lord and Master, Jacob Stirewalt and E. E. Smyre.

Resolved 2. That, in the death of these brethren, we have lost two of our most esteemed and worthy workmen in our Redeemer's cause upon earth; and that the Church has sustained a loss not easily repaired; nevertheless, we feel ourselves fully resigned to this very painful dispensation of Divine Providence, and earnestly pray God to speedily fill their places with others equally good and true.

Resolved 3. That this Synod hereby expresses her deep and most sincere sympathy with the family of brother Stirewalt, and also the relations and other friends of brother Smyre.

The committee, Revs. J. Killian and A. Efird, appointed to prepare a plan for Beneficiary Education, and submit it to this session of Synod, submitted the following:

1. That, owing to the want of sufficient time, we find it impossible to mature such a plan as we think would be necessary to enable us to operate successfully in this important enterprise of the Church. We, therefore, respectfully ask Synod to continue the committee to the next convention of Synod, so that we may have sufficient time to mature it.

2. That we respectfully recommend to Synod the importance and necessity of urging our ministers to take up collections, at an early day, to raise funds to enable J. Stirewalt and others to prosecute their studies for the Gospel Ministry.

3. That whatever money may be raised by the Synod for beneficiary purposes, be deposited in the hands of the Treasurer of Synod, and that he pay out the money, upon the order of the President of Synod, countersigned by the Secretary.

4. That the Treasurer be requested to report, to the next meeting of Synod, the amount of money coming into his hands, and the amounts paid over by him to the beneficiaries of the Synod, with proper vouchers.

5. We further recommend, that the officers of the Synod be appointed an Executive Committee, to decide upon the merits of the applicants for aid from the funds of the Synod.

6. We recommend further, that the beneficiaries of Synod be requested to report to Synod at her next meeting, a certificate from their teachers, of their moral standing and progress and proficiency in their studies.

This report was adopted, and this seems to be the first direct formal action of this Synod in regard to beneficiary education.

Mr. John N. Stirewalt, of New Market, Virginia, and Mr. M. A. Aderholt, of North Carolina, were received as students of theology.

Rev. William H. Swaney was honorably dismissed to the English District of Ohio.

The Parochial Report shows that during the year 408 infants and 39 adults were baptized, and 298 persons were confirmed.

Synod adjourned to meet in St. Peter's Church, South Carolina, November 5, 1870.

Obituary of Rev. Jacob Stirewalt.—Rev. Jacob Stirewalt was born near Salisbury, Rowan County, North Carolina, on Saturday, August 17, 1805, and departed this life, at his residence, in New Market, Shenandoah County, Virginia, on Saturday the 21st of August, 1869, at the age of 64 years and 4 days.

He was the second son, the third and youngest child of Capt. John and Elizabeth Stirewalt; was baptized in infancy, and eventually confirmed to the Evangelical Lutheran Church. By his pious parents he was trained up and educated, and acquired that firmness of Christian character and those habits of persevering and systematic labor which marked his entire life. In his day the advantages for acquiring an education were not equal to what they are now, still by close study and personal application he attained an eminent degree of literary and theological knowledge.

He was married to Henrietta Henkel, the daughter of Elias Henkel, at New Market, Virginia, on the 8th day of January, 1833. Two of his sons, John N. and Jerome Paul, are now actively engaged in the work of the Gospel ministry.

He was ordained Deacon, September 14, 1837, and preached his first sermon at Mt. Calvary Church, Page County, Virginia. On September 14, 1838, he was ordained Pastor, in Lincoln County, North Carolina. On the same day of his ordination to the office of Pastor, the Evangelical Lutheran Tennessee Synod, of which he was a most faithful member, "Resolved, That Revs. A. Henkel, Jacob Killian, and Jacob Stirewalt, be requested to compile a Liturgy for the use of our church, and present it to the next session of the Synod for examination." This duty was performed; the Liturgy was adopted, published, and is yet extensively used in our church.

As evidencing the energy and devotion, with which he discharged the duties of the office of Pastor, it may not be improper to state that, in the 32 years of his ministry, he preached 3132 sermons, of which 560 were funeral discourses; he confirmed 708 persons, and baptized 1259, and united in marriage 171 couples in the same period.

As if to complete the circle of his life, just three months before his death, he preached his *last* sermon in the same county and near the same place, at which he preached his *first*. A life of such protracted usefulness, and crowned with such fruits, may well lead us to ponder upon the character and habits of the man, and studying the means by which he accomplished so much, we may find in his example many useful hints to ourselves.

His character, like his features, was clearly defined and individual. Regulating his own life, even in its minor details, by the sternest and most critical rules of the severest discipline, he always had a charitable word for the faults and errors of others. Proclaiming the enormity of sin and the eternal punishment of the ungodly with terrible distinctness, he delighted most in picturing the absolute perfection of the character of Christ, and wooing by the sweet inclinings of a Savior's boundless love. He never denounced the evil without presenting the remedy; never threatened with punishment, that he did not more forcibly offer the rewards which attend the good. To him the Christian religion was an active, controlling principle—indispensable to man's happiness, not only in the world to come, but in the every day affairs of life. He did not merely *preach* in the pulpit; he so lived in *practice* that his whole life was but a continued application to his sermons.

The Bible and the works of Luther were his almost daily study, and the churches to whom he ministered listened as he preached, with that confidence and inclination to belief which generally follow the knowledge that the preacher has given to his subject the full benefit of all his ability, energy, and research. His opinions and conclusions were firmly formed after he had thoroughly examined and carefully and prayerfully studied his subject.

Just before his departure, the sainted subject of this notice called his son to his bedside and requested him to repeat the Lord's Prayer,—this being done, he quit this earthly habitation, to be present with the Lord. Rev. Ireneus Conder improved the visitation of Providence by preaching an eloquent discourse on the uncertainty of life and the certainty of death. "Blessed are the dead which die in the Lord from henceforth: yea, saith the Spirit, that they may rest from their labors and their works do follow them."

Fiftieth Session.

This session met in St. Peter's Church, Lexington County, South Carolina, November 5, 1870.

The election of officers resulted in favor of Revs. A. J. Fox, president; S. Henkel, recording secretary; J. R. Peterson, corresponding secretary; and T. Miller, treasurer.

Rev. A. R. Rude, D. D., Prof. J. P. Smeltzer, J. A. Sligh, and J. N. Derrick, of the South Carolina Synod, and Rev. Austin, of the Georgia Synod, were received as advisory members.

Rev. C. H. Bernheim, corresponding delegate from the North Carolina Synod, expressed his desire, in a letter, to be present, and renders feebleness of health as his excuse for absence.

The committee, appointed at the previous session, to prepare regulations for Beneficiary Education, submitted their report, which was adopted.

The President having announced the death of Revs. Ambrose Henkel, Christian G. Reitzel, and Adam Efird, the following resolutions were unanimously passed by a rising vote:

Resolved, That, by the death of these, our beloved

brethren in the ministry, their families and their relatives have lost most affectionate heads, who were examples of domestic, social, and moral virtues—sound in faith and doctrine; the Church and the Synod, to which they belonged, devout and faithful members.

Resolved, That we humbly submit to the dispensations of God, "who does all things well," and be encouraged while we are spared to labor in our Master's vineyard, to be more faithful in the work before us.

Resolved, That we deeply sympathize with the bereaved families and relatives of our beloved co-laborers in the ministry; and that a copy of these resolutions be sent to them.

The following is the report of the committee on union with the Southern General Synod, which was adopted:

We, the committee, to whom was referred the subject of a union of this Synod with the Evangelical Lutheran General Synod in North America, have given the subject much study, and while we have found many things in connection with it which would make such union desirable, we have also found many other things which seem, to your committee, to indicate that union with that ecclesiastical body is, at present, of such doubtful propriety, that we are wholly unprepared to recommend such a connection, and therefore, most respectfully ask that your committee be excused from the further consideration of this matter.

At the instance of Rev. S. Henkel, Junius S. Koiner, Waynesboro, Virginia, and J. Paul Stirewalt, New Market, Virginia, and at that of Rev. J. M. Smith, Adolphus Yount, Newton, North Carolina, and Wilburn T. Miller, of Newton, North Carolina, were received under the care of Synod, with a view to the ministry.

The Parochial Report, only nine ministers reporting, shows 29 adult baptisms, 417 infant baptisms, and 326 confirmations. It was

Resolved, That Synod adjourn to meet in Philadelphia

Church, Gaston County, North Carolina, on Saturday before the third Sunday in October, 1871.

During this decade, there were 11 applicants for the ministry, 3 ordinations, 7 licentiates, 5 dismissions, 3 died, 8 churches received, 5,261 infant baptisms, 256 adult baptisms, 40 slaves, and 28 colored, and 2,735 confirmations. It is to be regretted, that not more than two-thirds of the ministers furnished reports, and frequently not that number.

During this decade, there were many difficulties to encounter, obstacles to surmount, and disasters to overcome. The Civil War, of four years, between the States, North and South, which commenced in April, 1861, and continued till April, 1865, exerted a very depressing, disastrous, and demoralizing influence, not only over the country generally, but also over the Church. In the South, a large majority of the able-bodied men were in the army. Ministers were sometimes arrested, and others "refugeed," as the term went, when the Northern army invaded the country. Anxiety prevailed. Residences, mills, saw-mills, barns, &c., were burned by the hundreds. Horses, cattle, and other stock and property were driven up North by parties who followed the armies for the purpose of plunder. Churches were frequently occupied for weeks and months as hospitals and rendezvouses. The whole labor system was subverted and demoralized. The currency was vitiated and rendered worthless. Millions of slaves, that had been regarded as property, were set free, and required immediate care and attention, not having been trained during their state of slavery to provide for themselves.

For five years, the ministers in Virginia and Missouri, belonging to the Tennessee Synod, were prevented from meeting in the synodical conventions with their brethren in North and South Carolina. But notwithstanding this condition of things, there never was a truer and more faithful set of men. They worked in season and out of season. They attended as faithfully as possible to the spiritual wants of their people; they advised, encouraged, and cheered the wives and children whose husbands and sons and brothers had entered the army, often performing manual labor. Nor were the people generally less faithful. Strong faith prevailed. The exclamation was, Christ will take care of His Church, and God will provide for His people, and ultimately overrule all things for the best. It is almost miraculous how the people passed through the war as well as they did, and how soon they emerged from its ruins and devastations, both as to spiritual and temporal matters. Surely no one who knows anything about the conditions of things in the South, during the war and a few years after its close, can doubt the intervention of the hand of Providence. The lessons of faith, hope, and charity were learned. The people learned to depend on God, rather than on themselves. It is easy to talk about faith when peace, plenty, and prosperity prevail, but it is quite different when all these are removed.

Obituary of Rev. Ambrose Henkel.—Rev. Ambrose Henkel, the fourth son of Rev. Paul and Elizabeth Henkel, was born in Shenandoah County, Virginia, near Solomon's Church, 8 miles northwest of New Market, on the 11th day of July, 1786, and was initiated into the church through the Holy Sacrament of Baptism, in his infancy, and, at a more mature age, entered into full communion with the Evangelical Lutheran Church, through the ancient and solemn rite of Confirmation.

In 1802 he started, on foot, to Hagerstown, to learn the printing business. After working with Mr. Gruber, of Almanac reputation, and at Reading and in Baltimore, for three or four years, he purchased the bed and irons of a Ramage press and some old type, and, in 1806, established the first printing office in New Market, Virginia. With these old type, and cuts made by himself, he published a pictorial German spelling-book of his own arrangement. In 1807, he commenced the publication of a weekly German paper, called the "*Virginia and New Market Popular Instructor and Weekly News*," which continued for two years—and suspended for want of advertising patronage. The office was, however, continued as a Book and Job office by him, until he sold to his brother Solomon, about 1817.

He entered the ministry in the year 1823, and preached his first sermon in German, in Mt. Calvary (Hawksbill) Church, Page County, Virginia, on the 23d day of November, 1823, from 1 Corinthians 10, 1-12, and continued actively, faithfully, and successfully in the ministry till

1860. He preached his last sermon in Bethlehem Church, Augusta County, Virginia, in the year 1868. He was engaged in the office of the ministry 47 years. His labors in all the departments of his ministerial office, were extensive. He preached 3,995 sermons, of which 402 were funeral discourses; he baptized 1,625 persons, of whom 90 were adults; he confirmed 1,952 persons in the Church, and united in the holy estate of matrimony 400 men and women.

In 1838, under order of the Evangelical Lutheran Tennessee Synod, he prepared and published the Church Hymn-Book, which has now passed into its 4th edition.

In 1833 he was appointed, by the same body, chairman of a committee to prepare a Liturgy or Book of Forms and submit it to the Synod; which was done, and it was approved and published in 1843.

He also aided in the preparation of a purely literal translation of the Augsburg Confession, the Apology, the Smalcald Articles, the Appendix, and the Articles of Visitation, which appeared in print in the Christian Book of Concord, in the year 1851.

In the years 1857–8, he prepared a similar translation of the first volume of Luther's Church Postil on the Epistles, as extant in Plochman's edition, which work, after having been carefully compared with the original German, revised, transcribed, and prepared for the press, was issued in serial numbers. He was, perhaps, the oldest practical printer and editor in the State—having edited a newspaper in New Market 62 years before his death.

As a writer and translator, he was noted for the precision and accuracy of his style, rather than ornament. He was a profound thinker, an earnest student, and a forcible speaker.

He was married three times. His first wife was Miss Catharine Hoke, daughter of Frederick Hoke, Esq., of Lincoln County, North Carolina. His second one was Miss Mary Kite, daughter of Mr. Martin Kite, of Page County, Virginia, and his third one was Miss Veronica F. Heyle (Hoyle), daughter of Peter Heyle, Esq., of Lincoln County, North Carolina.

He departed this life on the 6th day of January, 1870, at 1 o'clock, A. M.; aged 83 years, 5 months, and 26 days. He left 6 children, a number of grand-children and great-grand-children.

His funeral services were rendered by Rev. Jacob Killian, in the presence of an unusually large concourse of people, in Emmanuel Church, New Market, Va., near which his body awaits the resurrection.

Obituary of Rev. Adam Efird.—And again another. The Rev. Adam Efird, of Lexington County, South Carolina, September 13, 1870. And all his days were forty-nine years, four months, and twenty-three days.

He was born in Stanley County, North Carolina, April 20, 1821, confirmed in St. Martin Church, by Rev. A. J. Fox, April 6, 1839, and ordained to the ministerial office, in St. Peter Church, Sullivan County, Tennessee, in October, 1847. He removed to Lexington County, South Carolina, in October of 1854, and took charge of several churches in connection with the Tennessee Synod. Actively engaged in the work of his Lord, beloved by his people, and honored and respected by the community, he proved himself to be a workman that needed not to be ashamed. His health, however, failed, and he, unable from bodily infirmity to continue his labor in the sacred office, finally offered his resignation; but his people would not give him up. He was unanimously re-elected, though unable to officiate. His five churches clung to him while he lived, and though his demise was not generally known, he was followed to his last resting place by a large multitude of mourning and attached people.

He served, during the war, as a member of the Legislature for two years, and filled the office of Probate Judge for Lexington County, at the time of his death. He had held the office for nearly six years. He left a wife and six children to watch, wait, and follow in the narrow path. One son had gone before him, to the happy land on high. Rev. Dr. Rude, of Columbia, performed the funeral services.

Obituary of Rev. Christian G. Reitzel.—Christian G. Reitzel was born March 30, 1805, in Guilford County, North Carolina. On the 15th day of November, 1827, he entered into the holy estate of matrimony with Miss Delilah Ingold, with whom he had eleven children.

September 17, 1835, he entered the ministry as a Deacon. September 16, 1841, he was ordained to the office of Pastor, in Rader's Church, Rockingham County, Virginia.

In the year 1841, he located in Catawba County, North Carolina, and took charge of St. Peter's, Miller's, and Zion's congregations, in that county, and of Friendship Church, in Alexander County, and served them till 1849.

On the 4th day of February, 1850, his first wife departed this life. A few years after this event, he married a second time. By this union he had six children.

On the 25th day of October, 1870, he departed this life; aged 65 years, 6 months, and 26 days. He was buried at St. Peter's Church, Catawba County, North Carolina. His funeral services were rendered and a sermon was preached by Rev. J. M. Smith, on 2 Tim. 4, 7, 8.

Whilst he was a plain, humble, common man, he possessed excellent native talents and fine mental capacities and powers. He was well indoctrinated in the teachings of Divine Revelation and the sound principles of the Confessions of the Evangelical Lutheran Church, derived from the Holy Scriptures. He was very exact and rather critical. He was a faithful, zealous preacher, a devout Christian, a good neighbor, a reliable citizen, an affectionate husband, and a kind father.

SIXTH DECADE.

Fifty-first Session.

Synod met in its fifty-first session, in Philadelphia Church, Gaston County, North Carolina, October 14, 1871.

The officers elected were, Revs. S. Henkel, president; I. Conder, recording secretary; J. M. Smith, corresponding secretary; and A. J. Fox, treasurer.

Rev. Prof. L. A. Bikle, corresponding delegate from the North Carolina Synod, was received.

On a letter of honorable dismission from the Pennsylvania Synod, Rev. L. A. Fox, who formerly had been a member of this Synod, was received into connection with it.

With regard to union, Synod passed the following resolution; be it

Resolved, That it is the sense of this Synod, that, at the present time, union, in the form of a Joint Synod, or Branch Synods, is preferable to that of one by consolidation.

The committee, appointed to meet with a similar committee appointed by the North Carolina Synod, for the purpose of preparing a basis for union between the Tennessee and North Carolina Synods, met in Mount Pleasant, Cabarrus County, North Carolina, April 25, 1871, and, after due consideration and considerable discussion, agreed on a basis, which was afterwards adopted by the North Carolina Synod, and, during this session, by the Tennessee Synod, with slight explanations. This basis is appended to the Minutes of this meeting. It is too long for insertion here.

The edition of the Hymn-Book, used by Synod, being exhausted, Revs. S. Henkel and A. J. Fox and A. Costner, Esq., were appointed a committee to examine various hymnbooks and liturgies, and report at the next session of Synod.

M. L. Fox, M. D., and Mr. A. L. Crouse, having sustained examinations, were ordained to the pastoral office, and Mr. John N. Stirewalt was ordained to the same office by the Virginia Conference of this Synod.

A church paper, called the *Evangelical Lutheran*, having been revived, and published by Rev. N. Aldrich, Charlotte, North Carolina, was recommended.

The committee on the synod, called the Concordia Synod of Virginia, submitted the following, which was adopted:

While we still regard the action of our misguided brethren, Revs. Wetzel, Seneker, and Schmucker, as irregular and schismatic, yet, as we can see no advantages that can accrue to our Synod by the retention of their names in our clerical roll, we recommend that their names be stricken from our list of pastors.

The committee, appointed to prepare resolutions on the death of Rev. Jacob Killian, submitted the following, which were unanimously adopted by a rising vote:

Whereas, It hath pleased the Almighty Disposer of all events, in the righteous dispensation of an all-wise providence, to call the Rev. Jacob Killian, a member of this Synod, from his labors on earth to his reward in heaven, be it, therefore,

Resolved 1. That in this painful dispensation, we recognize the hand of our Heavenly Father, who doth all things well; and bow with filial resignation to his chastening hand.

2. That we deeply lament the loss of a devoted friend, an earnest and efficient laborer in the work of the ministry, and of one manifesting the liveliest interest in the prosperity of our beloved Zion.

3. That we will ever cherish his memory, endeavor to imitate his many virtues, and emulate his bright examples, in an untiring devotion to the welfare and prosperity of the church, which he so much loved.

4. That we sincerely condole with the family of our deceased brother, in their sad bereavement and deep affliction.

5. That the Secretary of Synod forward a copy of these resolutions to the family of the deceased.

According to the Parochial Report, 504 infants and 38 adults were baptized, and 271 confirmed.

Rader's Church, Rockingham County, Virginia, was agreed on as the place for the next meeting of Synod, and Saturday before the first Sunday of September, 1872, as the time.

Obituary of Rev. William Hancher.—We make up the following in regard to this venerable minister, from an address delivered by Rev. A. J. Brown, D. D., before the Evangelical Lutheran Holston Synod of Tennessee:

Rev. William Hancher, born in Frederick County, Virginia, September 7, 1788, venerable alike for his years and his long and successful work in the ministry, is entitled to special mention and honor on this memorable occasion. He was ordained to the full work of the ministry in 1836, and died in 1870, at the advanced age of four score and two years, minus only two days. From the time he entered the ministry, till disabled by disease, embracing a period of nearly forty years, he labored constantly and assiduously in this calling. He occupied during this time, for much of it almost alone, an extensive, and an important and fertile field in the territory of the Holston Synod, and faithfully and successfully did he cultivate and develop its resources. His labors were confined principally to Sullivan County. He was for years the pastor of the principal churches now composing the charges of his son, brother J. K. Hancher, his grand-son, Rev. William G. Wolford, and Rev. A. J. Brown. It was at an important and critical time in the history of the Lutheran Church in this country. It was in the midst of her transition state from German to the English language. At the time of his ordination, father Hancher was perhaps the only minister in the Tennessee Synod who could speak the English language only. Under the difficult circumstances by which he was surrounded, when so much valuable material was lost to the Lutheran Church in many other sections of country, he not only retained in the church in the field of his operations the old members, but also brought into it most of their children, and many others whose proclivities were by education and early associations anything else rather than Lutheran. To his labors are we largely indebted for the firm hold of Lutheranism in Sullivan County, and for its prosperity in after years.

Father Hancher was a man for whom nature had done much, and had he enjoyed in early life the advantages of thorough, mental culture, he might have attained distinction in any of the great departments of human activity and interest. But such was not the case. His youth, his early manhood, and much of his riper years, were spent in manual labor. We speak of him now particularly as a minister of the Gospel. Much as we may regret his want of education, it may have been the best for the church at that particular juncture in its history . . . . While it is important, if not absolutely necessary, for the minister to be in advance of his people generally in education and general intelligence, it is not best that he should be too far in advance of them in these respects. For if so, they will fail to appreciate his labors and to be benefited to the fullest extent by them. But I am wandering from the subject, and will return.

For his work father Hancher had many fine, and some rare natural endowments. He was a ready speaker, and had a soft, mellow voice of sufficient volume and compass to address with ease to himself large audiences in the open air, and there was in his mental organism a deep, pathetic vein, which was clearly seen in his preaching, and seldom failed to be deeply felt by his hearers. We have witnessed moving scenes under the influence of his preaching.

Father Hancher was not a systematic sermonizer. While he attached great importance to soundness in doctrine, and gave prominence in his preaching to the distinctive doctrines of the Lutheran Church, his preaching was mostly practical and hortatory, and looked to the immediate conversion of sinners. His themes were generally such as treat of the deep innate depravity of the human heart, of repentance toward God and faith in the Lord Jesus Christ, the glories and felicities of heaven, the shortness and uncertainty of human life, and the importance and wisdom of making immediate and speedy preparation for death and judgment. He preached as a dying man to dying men, deeply impressed with the importance of his mission and the tremendous responsibility which it involves. And he was successful in bringing many souls to Christ, which shall adorn his crown when the Master comes to make up his jewels.

During his life he received many evidences of the esteem and love of his brethren, and when he died, he died deeply lamented. Like a ripe sheaf, he has been gathered home into the heavenly garner, full of years and of honors.

Obituary of Rev. Jacob Killian.—Rev. Jacob Killian was born of a well-known, influential, Christian family, in Lincoln County, North Carolina, June 8, 1818. He was dedicated to God in infancy, and, at a more mature age, he entered into full communion with the Evangelical Lutheran Church.

After securing a respectable education, he commenced the study of theology, with a view to the ministry. May 11, 1836, he entered the ministry, in connection with the Evangelical Lutheran Tennessee

Synod. In the year 1837, he located near Waynesboro, Augusta County, Virginia, where he took charge of Koiner's Church, and other congregations in that section, and lived and labored there, till he was called from time into eternity. He entered into the estate of holy matrimony with Miss Julia A. Koiner, daughter of George Koiner, Esq., of near Fishersville, Augusta County, Virginia.

He was a large, portly man of commendable bearing and extensive influence, commanding general respect and esteem. He was possessed of fine native talents and excellent oratorical powers. He was an influential speaker, and frequently grew quite eloquent in the delivery of his sermons. His voice was clear, strong, and forcible. He was a faithful and zealous laborer in the vineyard of his Lord and Master, true and faithful to the doctrines and usages of the Church, and strictly conservative. He made a good impression wherever he went. He was well acquainted with the history and doctrines of the Church, and always inculcated them in the best and most impressive manner.

He was a good, reliable citizen, a kind neighbor, and an affectionate husband and a loving father.

After spending a useful, successful, Christian life, in the Church, the Family, and the State, he departed this life, July 5, 1871; aged 53 years and 28 days, and entered his rest in the upper Sanctuary, leaving four children,—three sons and one daughter, with numerous relatives and friends to lament their irreparable loss. He was buried at Bethlehem Church, near his residence, Revs. J. I. Miller, D. D., and I. Conder officiating, in the presence of an unusually large and sympathetic concourse of relatives and friends.

"At length released from many woes,
How sweetly dost thou sleep;
How calm and peaceful thy repose,
While Christ thy soul doth keep."

Fifty-second Session.

Synod assembled in Rader's Church, Rockingham County, Virginia, on Saturday before the first Sunday in September, 1872.

The election for officers resulted in favor of Revs. A. J. Fox, president; L. A. Fox, recording secretary; S. Henkel, corresponding secretary; and J. S. Bennick, treasurer.

Revs. J. A. Snyder and Prof. J. I. Miller, of the Virginia Synod, and J. P. Stirewalt and J. S. Koiner, theological students, were received as advisory members.

A committee was appointed to prepare a fuller parochial table.

The Staunton, Virginia, Female Seminary, Rev. Prof. J. I. Miller, president, was recommended.

The committee of correspondence with members of the Evangelical Lutheran Holston Synod in regard to a union of that synod with this Synod, submitted the following:

We have had some correspondence with the president of that synod, and from his letters learn that the synod is likely to sever her connection with the Southern General Synod at her next convention, and that she is favorably disposed towards a union with this Synod, with the ultimate design of uniting with the General Council.

The committee recommended, that a delegate be appointed to attend the next meeting of the Holston Synod, and, if possible, make arrangements for the union of these two synods in a joint synod.

With a view of securing a higher degree of attainment on the part of those who intend to enter the ministry in connection with this Synod, both in regard to literature and theology, a committee was appointed to prepare a course of studies for theological students, who do not take a regular course in a theological seminary.

The committee, S. Henkel, A. J. Fox, and A. Costner, submitted, among other things, in their report, the following:

After a careful and conscientious examination of different hymn-books and liturgies now in use, (among them the Book of Worship—a work of decided merit) we would, under the circumstances and in view of the highest considerations, recommend to congregations in need of hymn-books or books containing the service of the Church, "The Church Book for the use of Evangelical Lutheran Congregations. By authority of the General Council of the Evangelical Lutheran Church in America." This book we regard as a work of the highest merit, strictly churchly in all its features.

The principles on which this was constituted were not

the taste of any individual or committee, but the *consensus* of the Lutheran Church in its purest periods, in all countries. Great care and labor have been bestowed on this work, in order to attain the highest degree of perfection. We are assured on the highest authority, that it is in its final shape as far as it goes—the forms for Baptism, &c., (*Actes Ministeriales*) remain to be added. The work will not be changed —the forms will simply be appended to later editions. The work is equally as cheap as the Church Hymn-Book. If any of our ministers should need a book containing the *Actes Ministeriales* before the later editions of the Church Book are published, we refer them to the "Book of Forms by Rev. J. A. Seiss, D. D.," published about fourteen years ago, and to the old Liturgy of the Pennsylvania Synod.

The President having recommended in his report the propriety of reviving the ancient custom of installation, it was

Resolved, That it be the duty of the President, with the consent of the pastor-elect and the congregation, to appoint a committee of installation, in all succeeding changes in the pastoral relations in our Synod, to perform this ceremony.

The Committee on the Revision of the Constitution of Beneficiary Association, was discharged, and another, consisting of Rev. S. Henkel and Mr. A. M. Bowman, was appointed in place of the former.

The corresponding delegate to the North Carolina Synod, presented, among other things, in his report, the following:

The only thing done in which this Synod is directly interested, was in regard to the contemplated union of this Synod with that in a joint body. The subject elicited much discussion, was fully ventilated, and was disposed of by the adoption of resolutions referring the matter to the next convention of the Synod for further action. These resolutions were ordered to be forwarded by the Corresponding Secretary to the President of this Synod.

In regard to this, Synod took the following action:

Resolved 1. That we heartily endorse the sentiment of the North Carolina Synod, expressed in these resolutions, viz.: "That a union of the two Synods in a Joint Synod is both practicable and desirable."

2. That we entirely approve the action of the North Carolina Synod in reference to this union.

3. That this Synod is ready to meet the North Carolina Synod in a joint convention at any time and place, and on any basis of lay representation that may be agreed upon by the Presidents of the Synods interested.

The following report was adopted:

The committee, consisting of Revs. S. Henkel and I. Conder, appointed to reply to the communications of Revs. P. C. Henkel and J. R. Moser, of Missouri, to this Synod, submitted the following:

Whereas, We learn from the communications of these brethren, that the prospects for building up the Church in the West are favorable, and that these brethren, in connection with others, have taken preliminary steps for the organization of the Evangelical Lutheran Synod in the State of Missouri; be it, therefore,

Resolved 1. That we hail with pleasure this information.

2. That their efforts put forth for the organization of a Synod, meet our approbation.

3. That, in order to aid them in publishing the proceedings of their conference, and their proposed constitution in connection with their discussion of "Doctrinal Theses selected from the Symbols of the Evangelical Lutheran Church, showing the principal distinction between the Lutheran Church and other ecclesiastical Communions," we request our ministers at once to bring the matter before their respective congregations and secure subscriptions to said work, which your committee presumes will cost fifteen cents per copy, and send the amount to Rev. P. C. Henkel or Rev. J. R. Moser.

Appropriations were made for the benefit of four beneficiary students. Messrs. M. L. Little and W. C. Holler were received as applicants for the ministry.

During this synodical year, 392 infants and 43 adults were baptized, and 284 confirmed.

Synod adjourned to meet in Zion Church, Lexington County, South Carolina, on the third Sunday in October, 1873.

Fifty-third Session.

Synod met in Zion Church, Lexington County, South Carolina, October 16, 1873.

Rev. J. M. Smith was elected president; Rev. J. R. Peterson, recording secretary; Rev. L. A. Fox, corresponding secretary; and Rev. J. N. Stirewalt, treasurer.

The following course of study, for private students in theology, was recommended: Horne's Introduction, Hutter's Compend, Book of Concord, Krauth's Conservative Reformation, Knapp's Christian Theology, Mann's Schmidt's Christian Ethics, Kurtz's Sacred History, Kurtz's Church History, Ripley's Sacred Rhetoric, Vinet's Homiletics, Vinet's Pastoral Theology. Instruction must be given in Exegesis, Catechetics, Liturgics, and Ecclesiastical Polity.

It is presumed that every minister who undertakes to give instructions, will be able to point out and guard his students against such things in any of the books given above that is un-Lutheran. The most objectionable one has important features not found elsewhere.

Special attention is to be given to the study of the New Testament in Greek, and when the minister is able to teach Hebrew, to the study of the Old Testament in Hebrew.

St. James Church, Summit, South Carolina, was received.

The Virginia Conference of the Synod was requested to examine, and, if found qualified, to ordain J. Paul Stirewalt.

M. L. Little and J. C. Moser, after examination, were

licensed as ministers. Mr. W. P. Cline and Mr. D. L. Crouse were received as theological students.

Arrangements were made to establish a regular synodical fund. Heretofore, there was no such fund in this Synod. The amounts necessary for printing Minutes, traveling expenses, &c., were raised by voluntary contributions from individuals and congregations, nearly every congregation having a treasury.

The following action was taken relative to *Our Church Paper:*

Resolved, That we hail with much pleasure the appearance of *Our Church Paper*, a religious journal, published at New Market, Virginia. The respectability of its appearance, the ability with which it is conducted, and the soundness of the doctrines and practices which it inculcates, are just what we think they ought to be, and we therefore regard it our duty, as far as possible, to encourage its circulation among the people of our congregations, and that we exert ourselves to introduce it into every family of our connection.

The Constitution and By-Laws of Synod were ordered to be appended to the Minutes of this session.

Messrs. J. F. Moser and A. B. Efird were received as beneficiaries, with a view to the ministry. Appropriations were made for four beneficiaries. Corresponding delegates were appointed to different synods.

The following action, taken by the North Carolina Synod, relative to union: "That all action in regard to union with all other ecclesiastical bodies be postponed for five years,"—seems to have put that matter to rest for that period at least.

According to the report, there were 599 infants and 34 adults baptized, and 447 confirmed.

Synod adjourned to meet in Pilgrim's Church, Davidson County, North Carolina, Thursday before the first Sunday in October, 1874.

Fifty-fourth Session.

This meeting was held in Pilgrim's Church, Davidson County, North Carolina, beginning October 1, 1874.

The officers elected were: Rev. L. A. Fox, president; Rev. A. L. Crouse, recording secretary; Rev. J. M. Smith, corresponding secretary; and Maj. A. Koiner, treasurer.

Rev. W. Kimball, corresponding delegate from the North Carolina Synod, was received.

Letters of honorable dismission were granted Revs. P. C. Henkel and J. R. Moser to the Missouri Conference of the Lutheran Church.

Crouse's Mission, Alabama, Morning Star, Page County, and St. Jacob's Church, Shenandoah County, Virginia, were received.

For sufficient reasons, the name of Christian Moretz, Jr., was erased from the clerical catalogue of Synod.

Rev. C. H. Bernheim, of the North Carolina Synod, was received as an advisory member.

During its meeting in 1874, the Holston Synod resolved to unite with the General Council of the Lutheran Church in America.

The Synod being notified of the fact, that the said General Council appointed a committee to co-operate with similar committees from other general bodies, and from synods not in connection with any general body, in arranging for a general colloquium of all Lutherans in America, who accept unqualifiedly the Augsburg Confession, the following action was taken:

Resolved, That we cordially approve this move of the General Council.

During this year, there were 384 confirmed, and 39 adults and 497 infants baptized.

Synod adjourned to meet in Mt. Calvary Church, Page County, Virginia, Thursday before the first Sunday in September, 1875.

Fifty-fifth Session.

Synod assembled in Mt. Calvary Church, Page County, Virginia, September, 1875.

Its officers were Rev. J. R. Peterson, president; Rev. I. Conder, recording secretary; Rev. J. N. Stirewalt, corresponding secretary; and Rev. S. Henkel, treasurer.

Rev. C. H. Bernheim, corresponding delegate of the North Carolina Synod, was received.

Mr. J. W. Hausenfluck was received as an applicant for the ministry, and, at his request, placed under the direction of Rev. S. Henkel.

Rev. J. M. Smith, in a letter, informed Synod that the congregations in Catawba County, North Carolina, had decided to establish a high school of a strictly Lutheran character. Synod approved of that move and heartily commended the enterprise.

Relative to the death of Rev. Godfrey Dreher, of Lexington County, South Carolina, the following preamble and resolutions were adopted by a rising vote:

Whereas, God, in his all-wise Providence, has been pleased to call from time to eternity Rev. Godfrey Dreher, pastor of Lutheran congregations, Lexington County, South Carolina, hereby

Resolved, That we express our high appreciation of his services and success; that we bow in humble submission to the will of him that doth all things well, cherish the memory of Rev. Dreher, and pray the Master to send in his stead faithful and worthy ministers of the New Testament.

Resolved, That a copy of these resolutions be published in *Our Church Paper*.

On motion, the congregation in Monroe, Union County, North Carolina, was received.

A committee was appointed to prepare a constitution and regulations for Home Missionary operations, and report to the next meeting.

On motion, Rev. S. Henkel was required to secure all

the minutes and pamphlets of the different sessions of our Synod, and have them bound, and also to collect such other material as may be of interest to the Church.

Appropriations were made for the benefit of two beneficiaries.

There were 484 infant and 48 adult baptisms, and 359 confirmations, reported at this convention.

Synod adjourned to meet in St. John's Church, Lexington County, South Carolina, on Thursday before the second Sunday in October, 1876.

Obituary of Rev. Godfrey Dreher.—Rev. Godfrey Dreher departed this life at the residence of his son-in-law, Rev. Daniel Efird, at Pine Ridge, Lexington County, South Carolina, July 28, 1875; aged 85 years, 7 months, and 24 days. Funeral services were rendered and a sermon preached at the said residence, by Rev. H. W. Kuhns, from 1 Thess. 4, 14, in the presence of a very large, sympathizing congregation. His earthly remains were then conveyed, in solemn procession, to St. Michael's Church, twelve miles distant, where another sermon was preached by the same minister from Psalm 71, 9, at the request of a large assembly, which had gathered there, to pay the last tribute of respect to departed worth. His body was then placed in the grave, to await the final resurrection, in rear of the pulpit of St. Michael's, between the graves of Revs. Wingard and D. Dreher, the place which he had selected and which had been reserved for that purpose,—a pulpit which he had filled with so much acceptance.

He entered the active services of the ministry in connection with the Evangelical Lutheran Synod of North Carolina, in the year 1811, and confined his labors chiefly to ministerial services in Lexington County, South Carolina, in a community generally known as "Dutch Fork," where he labored with acceptance and success. He was one of the first ministers who preached in the English language in that community. He was present at the conference which met in St. Michael's Church, Lexington County, South Carolina, in 1824, where and when the Evangelical Lutheran South Carolina Synod was organized, and elected as president of that synod. At that time the parochial reports show that he had six churches in his charge. From that time till 1835, he was elected treasurer of synod, successively each year. In that year, the constitution of the synod was so changed as to require a layman to fill that office. About the year 1834, some difficulties and differences arose in the synod which were not satisfactorily adjusted. In 1837, he met a committee appointed by the president of the synod, to meet at Lexington Court House, South Carolina, to adjust the differences. After some consultation, he was, at his request, permitted to withdraw from the synod in an amicable manner. Eight congregations went with him. These congregations he faithfully and zealously served, aided occasionally by visiting ministers and such other assistance as he could command, till 1851, preaching as many as two sermons on three of the Sundays in each month, although his congregations were situated a very considerable distance from his place of residence, and from five to eight miles distant from each other. From 1851 to 1854, he was permanently assisted by Rev. Daniel Efird. In 1854, he received an attack of paralysis. This ended his ministerial career.

He was always regular and punctual in his attendance at his appointments. The inclemency of the weather never prevented him from filling his engagements and complying with his obligations. It seems he was prompt in all the relations of life, and strong in his convictions. He was true and faithful, zealous and energetic in the performance of his duties. He was a man of excellent native powers and abilities, firm and indomitable. As a minister, he was earnest and effective, and often, and especially when he spoke on his theme in which he most delighted, "Justification by Faith," he grew most eloquent and pathetic. He wielded a very decided and beneficial influence in the community in which he labored. He contributed liberally of his temporal means towards the establishment of the theological seminary of the South Carolina Synod, first erected at Lexington Court House, South Carolina. As a man, he was generous, liberal, just, kind, and affectionate in all the departments of life. "He now rests from his labors, and his works do follow him."

Fifty-sixth Session.

Synod convened in St. John's Church, Lexington County, South Carolina, October 5, 1876.

The officers chosen were: Revs. S. Henkel, president; J. M. Smith, recording secretary; J. R. Peterson, corresponding secretary; and A. J. Fox, treasurer.

Rev. J. C. Moser and H. A. Meetze were received as advisory members.

St. Matthew Church, King's Mountain, the church at Hickory, North Carolina, St. Thomas Church, South Carolina, and St. Mark's, Luray, Virginia, were received.

A committee of three, consisting of Revs. J. M. Smith, J. R. Peterson, and A. J. Fox, was appointed to examine

A. L. Yount, and, if necessary, to ordain him. There was also a committee appointed to ordain J. W. Hausenfluck, if found qualified.

Rev. J. P. Smeltzer, D. D., of the South Carolina Synod, was received as a corresponding delegate from that synod.

The committee, appointed to prepare a paper relative to the death of Rev. Thomas Crouse, submitted the following, which was adopted by a rising vote:

Whereas, God, in his wise Providence, has called from his labors on earth, Rev. T. Crouse, a faithful minister of our Synod, to his rest and reward on high; therefore,

Resolved, That we recognize the hand of God herein, and humbly bow to his righteous ways, that we cherish his memory, and pray God for grace, that we may meekly submit to his dispensation.

Resolved, That these resolutions be published in "*Our Church Paper*," and a copy be sent to the family of the deceased.

The action of Synod in 1864, creating the license system, was rescinded, a committee of three was appointed to prepare and submit to the present convention of this Synod, a plan by which the requirements of our Constitution in regard to the candidates for the ministry in their period of probation, can be complied with.

This committee, not being able to submit a plan, for the want of time, Revs. A. J. Fox, J. R. Peterson, and S. Henkel, were appointed a committee to give this matter proper attention, and report at the next meeting.

The license system having been rescinded, Messrs. J. A. Cromer and E. L. Lybrand, who applied for license, were requested to labor, for the time being, under some regular pastor or pastors.

The committee appointed at the last session to prepare Regulations for Missionary Work, submitted the following:

ARTICLE I. There shall be elected, annually, by Synod, an Executive Committee of three, or five, or more members, as the nature and extent of the work may require, who shall hold office until their successors shall be appointed. Of this committee, the Committee on Vacancies shall be a member.

ARTICLE II. This Executive Committee shall have charge of the Missionary work between the conventions of Synod. They shall elect one of their number Treasurer, who shall hold and disburse the missionary moneys according to the directions of the committee. The Executive Committee may establish or discontinue missions, may employ or dismiss missionaries, and shall have the superintendence and control of all missionary operations during their time of office.

ARTICLE III. This committee shall hold at least two meetings during the year. It shall keep a clear and correct account of all its transactions, and especially of all moneys received and disbursed, and report annually to Synod, and be prepared with vouchers to sustain the same, which report shall be recorded by the Secretary of Synod.

ARTICLE IV. All moneys collected from congregations or otherwise, and donations for the purpose of missions, shall be paid over to the Chairman of the Executive Committee, for which he shall give his receipt.

ARTICLE V. Diligent and rigid inquiry shall be made as to the condition of every community, and the prospects of establishing a self-sustaining congregation or pastorate whenever application shall be made for aid, and where these are not favorable, no money shall be expended as a mere venture.

ARTICLE VI. Every pastor in connection with this Synod shall be required to take up collections in each of his congregations, annually, in the most judicious manner, for missions.

ARTICLE VII. These regulations shall be subject to amendment at any meeting of Synod after giving one day's notice of the proposed amendment, and with the concurrence of two-thirds of the members present.

Your committee, in submitting the above plan, would call the attention of the Synod to the importance of concentrated effort. It is a lesson learned after a dear experience by other bodies, and they are now centering their labors upon a few places until they make them self-supporting. It is found to be far better to make large appropriations to one point and assist in building a church than to scatter a small fund among many.

With respect to the Southern General Synod's suggestion, that this Synod reconsider its actions declining to unite with that synod, the following action was taken:

Resolved, That under existing circumstances, we regard it inexpedient to take any steps either toward uniting with or in any way committing ourselves to any one of the General Lutheran Bodies in this country.

The following preamble and resolution were passed:

Whereas, Prof. Ben. Hyde Benton, President of Polytechnic Institute, at New Market, Virginia, has kindly tendered to this Synod three free scholarships in that Institute, one for the congregation of this Synod in South Carolina, and two for our Churches in North Carolina, upon condition that the candidates are over 14 years of age, and come with a recommendation from one of the ministers of this Synod,

Resolved, That we highly appreciate this kind offer and most cheerfully accept it, and tender our most sincere thanks to the kind donor.

The baptisms reported were 544 infants and 56 adults, and 325 confirmations.

Synod adjourned to meet in Coble's Church, Guilford County, North Carolina, November 8, 1877.

Obituary of Rev. Thomas Crouse.—Rev. Thomas Crouse died April 11, 1876, at 12.30 P. M. He was born in Davidson County, North Carolina, June 6, 1822.

His paternal ancestors came from Germany to Pennsylvania, thence to Forsyth County, North Carolina, where Andrew Crouse, the father of the deceased, was born. He married a Miss Daniels, whose parents came from Ireland. They afterwards settled in Davidson County, North Carolina, where the subject of this sketch was born. He was baptized in infancy, in Beck's Evangelical Lutheran Church, where he afterwards received religious instruction, and was confirmed.

He received his literary education at Prof. Dusenberry's school, Lexington, North Carolina, and his theological training under the direction of tutors. He entered the ministry in connection with the Evangelical Lutheran Tennessee Synod, in 1845, and continued in its work until his death, having been engaged in the Master's service about 31 years.

Soon after he began his work, he moved to Randolph County, North Carolina, where he married Barbara Fox, a descendant, through her maternal line, from one of the Electors of Saxony. She died in about eight years, leaving four children. He afterwards married M. C. Fox, youngest sister of Rev. A. J. Fox, M. D., by whom one son was given him.

As a theologian, he was a sound and firm defender of the doctrines and customs of the old type of Lutheranism. As a preacher, he was attractive, because of his earnestness of manner, clearness of thought, force of style, and persuasive voice.

He labored in Guilford and Alamance, and organized Melanchthon, the only Lutheran Church in Randolph County.

In 1873, he moved to Davidson County, and rebuilt Beck's, the church of his youth, of which, with three other congregations, he was pastor until his death. His last sermon was preached in Beck's Church, ten days before he died.

Surveying his work, we are convinced that he was a "workman that need not be ashamed," and that he has many jewels in his crown.

Fifty-seventh Session.

Synod assembled in Coble's Church, Guilford County, North Carolina, November 8, 1877.

The election for officers resulted in favor of Revs. S. Henkel, D. D., president; J. Paul Stirewalt, recording secretary; M. L. Little, corresponding secretary; and D. Efird, treasurer.

Rev. P. C. Henkel, having been called back from Missouri to Conover, North Carolina, to lead in the permanent establishment of a school of a high grade, at the latter place, was unanimously received into Synod.

Rev. C. H. Bernheim, corresponding delegate from the North Carolina Synod, was received.

On Sunday, the new church erected to take the place of the old Coble Church, was dedicated, Rev. S. Henkel, D. D., preaching the sermon, and Rev. P. C. Henkel leading in the dedicatory services.

It was moved, that when Synod adjourn, it adjourn to meet in St. Matthew Church, Shenandoah County, Virginia, on Thursday before the first Sunday in September, 1878.

Rev. C. H. Bernheim, corresponding delegate of the North Carolina Synod, conveyed to this Synod in a few pertinent remarks, the fraternal greetings and kindly feelings of the North Carolina Synod, and was appropriately replied to by Rev. S. Henkel, D. D.

Rev. A. L. Yount, having left the bounds of this Synod, having received a call from a congregation at Murphysboro, Illinois, was requested to return to Synod the amount he had received from it as a beneficiary, not having labored in the bounds of the Synod anything like the length of time the regulations of the Beneficiary Society of Synod required from its beneficiaries. This he did; that is, refunded it in due time.

On motion, the President appointed a committee of three to prepare rules and regulations for the government of beneficiaries, to report at the next meeting of Synod. Committee—Revs. A. J. Fox, J. M. Smith, and Mr. M. L. Cline.

The reports show that during this year 585 infants and 56 adults were baptized, and 471 persons were confirmed.

Synod adjourned to meet at the time and place already indicated.

Fifty-eighth Session.

This meeting convened in St. Matthew Church, Shenandoah County, Virginia, August 29, 1878.

The officers of this convention were Revs. P. C. Henkel, president; L. A. Fox, recording secretary; A. J. Fox, corresponding secretary; and J. Paul Stirewalt, treasurer.

The congregation at Conover, Catawba County, North Carolina, was received.

A committee of three was appointed to prepare a plan for missionary work. A committee was appointed to examine Mr. A. R. Yoder.

Rev. V. R. Stickley, corresponding delegate of the North Carolina Synod, was received.

Rev. A. J. Fox, M. D., read the Regulations for the Government of Synod in the work of Beneficiary Education. It is too long for insertion here. It may be found in Minutes of 1878.

The committee, appointed to prepare resolutions on the death of Rev. Henry Goodman, presented the following, which was adopted, the Synod rising:

Whereas, It has pleased Almighty God, in his wise Providence, to remove Rev. Henry Goodman from his labors on earth to his reward in heaven,

Resolved 1. That in the death of Father Goodman, the Church has lost an earnest, faithful, and zealous laborer in his Master's vineyard;

Resolved 2. That we bow in humble submission to him who doth all things well;

Resolved 3. That a copy of these resolutions be sent to "*Our Church Paper*" for publication;

Resolved 4. That a copy of these resolutions be sent to the relatives of the deceased family.

Rev. Thomas Miller having asked for an honorable dismission to the Virginia Synod, it was granted.

Rev. V. Stickley conveyed to this Synod the fraternal greetings of the North Carolina Synod, and was replied to in a few pertinent remarks by Rev. P. C. Henkel.

Messrs. Eli Lot Lybrand and James Albert Cromer, Columbia, South Carolina, and Jacob Killian Efird were ordained. A committee was appointed to prepare an obituary on Rev. H. Goodman.

The reports show that 438 infants and 103 adults were baptized, and 178 persons confirmed.

Synod adjourned to meet in St. James Church, Summit,

Lexington County, South Carolina, Thursday before the third Sunday in November, 1879.

Obituary of Rev. Henry Goodman.—The subject of this notice was the son of Michael and Elizabeth Goodman (Guthmann), born April 9th, 1798, was baptized in infancy, and in the year 1819, entered into full communion with the Evangelical Lutheran Church, by the imposition of hands and prayer, by Rev. Daniel Scherer, at St. John's Church, Cabarrus County, North Carolina.

He was licensed to preach by Revs. Daniel Moser and David Henkel, on the 29th of November, 1830, and preached his first sermon on the 19th of December, following, at his uncle's, George Goodman, in Cabarrus County, North Carolina.

He was ordained by Revs. Philip Henkel, Adam Miller, and Daniel Moser, in Buehler's Church, Sullivan County, Tennessee, September 13th, 1832.

During the whole of his ministry, as also before entering the ministry, he labored faithfully in defence of the pure Confessions of the Evangelical Lutheran Church; often, especially in the early struggles of the Evangelical Lutheran Tennessee Synod for the pure faith of the Church of the Reformation, sacrificing much time as well as other means, to forward the work in this great crisis.

He preached his last sermon on the 4th Sunday of November, 1877, in Sharon Church, Iredell County, North Carolina, from 1 John 5, 7, 8.

The subject of the above notice died at his late residence in Iredell County, North Carolina, on the morning of the 26th of January, 1878; aged 79 years, 9 months, and 17 days; his consort having been called to her reward October 17th, 1876; aged 74 years, 8 months, and 22 days.

His perishable remains were deposited in the cemetery at St. Martin's Church, Iredell County, North Carolina, on the next day after his departure from this life; and notwithstanding the day was very rainy, a large concourse of people assembled to take a last view and to sympathize with the many relatives whose faces were bathed in tears, but in hopeful resignation to the will of Him who had taken His faithful servant home.

After the burial service ended, the many relatives and friends of the deceased repaired to the church to hear the funeral sermon, by Rev. P. C. Henkel, based on 2 Tim. 4, 7, 8.

Fifty-ninth Session.

This convention met in St. James Church, Summit, Lexington County, South Carolina, November 13, 1879.

In the election for officers, the following were chosen: Revs. J. R. Peterson, president; M. L. Little, recording secretary; J. M. Smith, corresponding secretary; S. Henkel, treasurer; and T. Moser, treasurer of beneficiary fund.

St. Michael's Church, Cleburne County, Alabama, and St. Andrew's Church, Richland County, South Carolina, were received.

Rev. J. Hawkins, corresponding delegate of the South Carolina Synod, was received, and Rev. A. D. L. Moser, of the same synod, was invited to a seat.

On motion, a committee was appointed to report some plan by which the Synod's Mission Work may be transferred to the Conferences. Committee—Revs. J. C. Moser, E. L. Lybrand, and P. Killian, Esq.

On their report, the Mission Work of the Synod was transferred to the Conferences in connection with the Synod.

Messrs. Thomas E. Armentrout, McGaheysville, Virginia, and D. A. Sox, Reeder's Store, Lexington County, South Carolina, were received as beneficiary students; and appropriations were made for their benefit.

The retiring president having recommended the propriety of Synod giving an expression in regard to the "Four Points," as they are called, the committee on said report, Revs. S. Henkel, J. M. Smith, and A. Costner, Esq., submitted the following relative to these matters, which was adopted:

Whereas, This Synod is invested only with advisory power; and

Whereas, The general policy of this Synod has not been to encourage such doctrines, worship, or fellowship, be it

Resolved 1. That this Synod, as we have, so far as we know, no minister now in affiliation with such societies, we advise all who may be looking to the office of the ministry in connection with this Synod, not to associate or hold fellowship with any societies that practice a deistic worship or service, to the disparagement of the adoration due Jesus

Christ, or that comes in conflict with the orthodox worship of the church, or that set up a plan of salvation coming in conflict with that set forth in Divine Revelation, through the Savior, the Lord Jesus Christ, as the Mediator between God and man; as it is the sentiment of this Synod that such could not be received.

2. That we regard these matters as subjects for investigation and instruction, and our ministers are advised to give such information as they may deem proper, when it is desired.

With respect to altar and pulpit fellowship, it is the sentiment of this Synod, that our ministers and people adhere to the practice set forth in the Confessions of the Church, using all necessary precaution, prudence, and judiciousness in the exercise of such privileges, lest the sacredness of the altar and pulpit be violated, or the consciences of any be oppressed, and reference should always be had to the preparation designated in the Augsburg Confession, Article eleven, and in Luther's Catechism, where it is said, "Let a man examine himself," etc., and "He only is truly worthy and well prepared, who has faith in these words," etc.

In regard to Chiliasm, we would simply say, it is clearly rejected in the 17th Article of the Augsburg Confession.

IV. Relative to the allusion in the President's report, to certain articles in the Constitution of Synod, we would simply remark, that organic laws should be seldom changed, and as no proposition has been made, in accordance with the 8th Article of said constitution, for any change or alteration, no action is required on the part of the Synod.

V. With respect to the matter of revising and publishing our Church Hymn-Book, we deem the action taken by our Synod last year, all that we could recommend.

This paper is usually designated the Summit Rule.

Sixtieth Session.

This meeting of Synod was held in St. Peter's Church, Catawba County, North Carolina, commencing November 11, 1880.

The officers, elected for the ensuing year, were Rev. S. Henkel, D. D., president; Rev. J. C. Moser, recording secretary; Rev. J. R. Peterson, corresponding secretary; and Rev. J. M. Smith, treasurer.

Candidates W. P. Cline, D. J. Settlemyre, W. A. Smith, J. A. Rudisill, and J. B. Fox, were invited to seats as advisory members.

Appropriations were made for beneficiaries.

Rev. C. H. Bernheim, of the North Carolina Synod, was received as an advisory member.

Amendments to the Constitution having been proposed on the day previous, a committee of four was appointed to take into consideration the proposed amendments.

After this committee reported, and several of the amendments had been considered, the matter was postponed until the next meeting of Synod.

Rev. C. H. Bernheim, of the North Carolina Synod, having presented a letter of honorable dismission from that synod to this Synod, was unanimously received as a member of Synod.

The following action was taken with respect to the reception of Concordia High School, located at Conover, Catawba County, North Carolina:

Whereas, The trustees of Concordia High School, Conover, North Carolina, have made a proposition to Synod to take this Institution under her care and supervision, and

Whereas, It is the desire and wish of this Synod to have an institution of learning in her connection, therefore,

Resolved, That a committee of three, on the part of Synod, be appointed to confer with the trustees of said school, and prepare an agreement which may serve as a basis upon which said school may become the recognized institution of Synod, and that this committee be required to report to the next session of Synod.

Resolved, further, That we hereby recommend Concordia High School to the members of our Church, and to the public generally, as a school of meritorious character.

The President appointed the following persons on this committee: Revs. J. C. Moser, J. R. Peterson, and C. H. Bernheim. On motion, A. Costner, Esq., and Mr. C. T. Sigman were added to this committee.

The Missionary Work of the Synod having been transferred to the Conferences of the Synod, the regulations of the Synod relative to such work, were repealed.

During this synodical year, 641 infants and 27 adults were baptized, and 227 persons confirmed.

The time fixed for the next meeting was Saturday before the second Sunday in September, 1881, and the place, Emmanuel Church, New Market, Shenandoah County, Virginia.

During this decade, there were 12 applicants for the ministry, and 6 beneficiaries received, 12 ordained, 4 received on letters, 3 dismissed to other synods, the names of 4 dropped, 1 church dismissed, 2 ministers licensed, 1 minister died, 13 churches were received, 5,432 infants and 497 adults baptized, and 3,378 confirmed. The reports in regard to baptisms and confirmations were not generally full.

SEVENTH DECADE.

Sixty-first Session.

This session of Synod convened in Emmanuel Church, New Market, Shenandoah County, Virginia, September 10, 1881.

The officers elected were Revs. A. J. Fox, M. D., president; L. A. Fox, D. D., secretary; J. M. Smith, corresponding secretary; and S. Henkel, D. D., treasurer.

Rev. J. A. Snyder, of the Virginia Synod, and Rev. H. Wetzel, were received as advisory members.

A committee was appointed, on motion, to inquire into the expediency of placing monuments at the graves of Rev. Ambrose Henkel, at New Market, Virginia, and Rev. Philip Henkel, at Richland Church, Randolph County, North Carolina. Committee—Revs. A. J. Fox and S. Henkel.

Prof. J. S. Koiner was invited to a seat within the bar of Synod.

The committee on reception of Concordia High School not being prepared to report, the committee, consisting of Revs. J. C. Moser, S. Henkel, D. D., C. H. Bernheim, and Messrs. A. Costner and C. T. Sigman, was continued.

Appropriations were made for two beneficiary students.

The consideration of the proposed amendments to the constitution, was postponed till the next convention.

Prof. J. S. Koiner, after sustaining a regular examination, was ordained.

The committee, appointed to report on the recommendation of the Committee on the President's Report, in regard to awaking a greater interest in Beneficiary Education, submitted the following:

That a committee of one be appointed in each conference, whose duty it shall be to call, by correspondence or otherwise, attention to the duties relative to this important matter, urging the congregations, through the ministers, or in any other way, to consider the propriety of aiding with their substance this much needed work, by contributing liberally; or to devise some systematic plan for raising means for such purpose, putting them in remembrance of these duties and privileges.

Relative to the colored people, or freedmen, the following action was taken:

Resolved, That the ministers of this Synod make all efforts in their power to educate religiously the colored people, by preaching, lecturing, and catechisation, with a view sooner or later of getting men of their own color to look after the spiritual interests of their race in connection with the Lutheran Church.

During this year, the Parochial Report shows 494 infant and 32 adult baptisms, and 168 confirmations.

Synod adjourned to meet in St. Jacob's Church, Lexington County, South Carolina, Saturday before the third Sunday in October, 1882.

Sixty-second Session.

This meeting was held in St. Jacob's Church, Lexington County, South Carolina, commencing October 14, 1882.

The officers elected were Revs. S. Henkel, D. D., president; J. Paul Stirewalt, secretary; J. M. Smith, corresponding secretary; and M. L. Little, treasurer.

The committee, appointed at the last session, to ordain D. A. Goodman, if found qualified, reported that they had ordained him; and so too, in regard to the ordination of W. P. Cline. The names of Goodman and Cline were ordered to be enrolled in the clerical catalogue of Synod.

The consideration of the amendments proposed to the Constitution, was postponed to the next meeting of Synod.

The President having called, in his report, attention to the death of Rev. John S. Bennick, a committee was appointed to prepare suitable resolutions relative to that matter. At the proper time the following paper was presented and adopted:

We, your committee, appointed to prepare suitable resolutions, have adopted the following:

WHEREAS, It hath pleased Almighty God, in his all-wise Providence, to remove our lamented brother, J. S. Bennick, from his work on earth to his reward in heaven; be it

Resolved 1. That we bow in humble submission to the will of Him who doth all things well.

Resolved 2. In his death, the Church militant has lost a most efficient and faithful laborer.

Resolved 3. That a copy of these resolutions be spread upon the face of the Minutes, and that one page be devoted to his memory.

Resolved 4. That a copy of these resolutions be sent to his bereaved family.

St. Stephen's Church, Shenandoah County, Cedar Point Church, and Alma Fairview Church, Page County, Virginia, and Killian's, Catawba County, North Carolina, were received.

Rev. P. Miller conveyed to Synod the fraternal greetings of the South Carolina Synod, and, at the request of the President, Rev. A. J. Fox replied in a few pertinent remarks.

Rev. A. L. Crouse offered the following :

Resolved, That we recommend "Grades in the Ministry," a book by the late Rev. Jacob Stirewalt, to the careful study and impartial examination of our people, both clerical and lay.

Synod having been informed, that a committee of two ministers and one layman, was appointed to meet and confer with a similar committee from this Synod, in regard to such territory as may be in dispute between the two Synods, Revs. A. J. Fox, P. C. Henkel, and Mr. A. Costner, were appointed to confer with a committee, appointed by the North Carolina Synod, in regard to such territory as may interlap between the two Synods.

The following resolutions were passed :

Resolved, That it be the duty of our ministers to obtain the number of baptized persons, infants and adults, as well as that of the communicant members, and report the result of their efforts to the next session of Synod, with a view to arranging our Parochial Report, so as to give the whole strength of our Synod, by adding a column for the insertion of such members.

Resolved, That until otherwise ordered, at the future meetings of this Synod, Sunday afternoons shall be devoted to Sunday-school work ; and the *pastors loci* where synodical meetings are held are charged with the duty of making the necessary arrangements, to give interest and effect to these services.

Whereas, It is meet and right, that the dignity, sacredness, and solemnity of the ministerial office be preserved and perpetuated, and in order that it may not be lowered and disparaged, be it

Resolved, That Synod recommend, that all applicants for examination and ordination, and for whom there are petitions to Synod from a congregation, or congregations, praying for such examination and ordination, and extending a call or a request for pastoral services on the part of the subject of such petition or petitions, appear at some session of this Synod, prepared to submit to such examination, and, if found qualified, to receive such ordination, and be it further

Resolved, That it is the sentiment of this Synod, that this recommendation should be acquiesced in, in all possible cases, as the order of Synod in all ordinary cases.

Mr. J. P. Price, of Lexington County, South Carolina, was received as a student for the ministry. Appropriations were made for two beneficiaries.

The following paper was read before Synod and discussed to a limited extent:

Whereas, The Evangelical Lutheran Tennessee Synod has in time past held aloof from direct connection with other Lutheran bodies in this country, from reasons patent and well known to all persons acquainted with her history; and since said reasons have been dispelled by other bodies, planting themselves on the same basis as ourselves; and

Whereas, In union and co-operative energy there is resistless strength; therefore, be it

Resolved, That the Evangelical Lutheran Tennessee Synod, now in convention assembled, do adopt the Constitution of "The Evangelical Lutheran General Synod in North America," and do elect a delegation, proportioned according to Article II. of said Constitution, to represent this Synod in the next regular convention of said General Synod, to sit in the city of Charleston, in April proximo.

In regard to it the following action was taken:

Whereas, A paper is before Synod, asking Synod to take into consideration the propriety of effecting some connection with the Southern Evangelical Lutheran General Synod; and

Whereas, This is a matter which requires careful and matured consideration, hence, in view of the late hour of this session of Synod, in which the said paper was offered, be it

Resolved, That this paper be deferred to our next annual session of Synod, for consideration.

A motion was made, and prevailed, to enroll all the churches in connection with this Synod.

During the past year, according to the Parochial Report, 38 adults and 675 infants were baptized, and 361 persons confirmed.

Synod adjourned to meet in the Chapel of Concordia College, Conover, North Carolina, October 13, 1883.

Obituary of Rev. John Silvanus Bennick.—Rev. John Silvanus Bennick, after several days confinement to his bed, departed this life at 8 P. M., on March 22, 1882; aged 44 years, 5 months and 29 days.

He was born, a son of Philip J. and Susan (*nee* Henkel) Bennick, in Catawba County, North Carolina, and came to New Market, Shenandoah County, Virginia, in the year 1859, where he entered the New Market Academy, and pursued a literary course with a view to the Gospel ministry.

In September, 1861, he entered the Confederate Army, in the infantry service, in which he continued till the surrender. As soon as he returned from the army, he resumed his literary branches, and entered on a theological course of study under the supervision of Rev. S. Henkel, D. D.

He entered the ministry of the Gospel in the year 1866, still, however, pursuing his regular course of studies under the direction of his preceptor, until he was well indoctrinated. After the death of the late, lamented Rev. Jacob Stirewalt, he received a regular call to that charge, and continued to labor in it most successfully and efficiently till June, 1880, when his health and strength partially failed. From this date, his charge being unwilling to accept his resignation, he continued to serve it, with occasional interruptions, however, till August, 1881. In September, 1881, he tendered his resignation, after which he performed few ministerial acts. He was most actively and energetically engaged in the work of the ministry for 15 years. Besides serving his large charge, he performed considerable missionary labor, often preaching on week days.

Three excellent church edifices of modern style were erected in his charge during his ministry, and one congregation organized, and an ordinary church erected for its occupancy. His ministerial acts, in regard to baptisms—infant and adult—confirmations, funerals, &c., were numerous. The number of marriage ceremonies performed was one hundred and sixty-five.

He was a grandson of Rev. David Henkel, one of the founders of the Evangelical Lutheran Tennessee Synod, and a nephew of Revs. P. C. Henkel, D. D., and S. Henkel, D. D.

He was naturally endowed with all the traits, qualities, and faculties so essential to the office of the ministry, and these with liberal attainments and indomitable energy, fidelity, and perseverance, gave him that success which so signally crowned his efforts.

On December 22, 1867, he entered into the holy estate of matrimony with Miss Elizabeth Emma, only living daughter of the late Peter J. and Elizabeth Wise of Rockingham County, Virginia.

His funeral services were rendered in Emmanuel Evangelical Lutheran Church, New Market, Va., and his body appropriately interred in the cemetery of said church, in the midst of a large and sympathizing concourse of people from the town and country. The services were rendered and a suitable sermon preached by Rev. J. Paul Stirewalt, accompanied with appropriate remarks and prayer by Rev. J. A. Snyder.

Thus a faithful laborer in the vineyard of Christ has been removed from the church militant to the church triumphant, to enjoy that crown of life secured by the Savior for all the faithful.

Sixty-third Session.

This session of Synod convened in the Chapel of Concordia College, Conover, North Carolina, October 13, 1883.

The officers were Revs. J. R. Peterson, president; A. L. Crouse, secretary; C. H. Bernheim, corresponding secretary; and J. N. Stirewalt, treasurer.

Revs. A. L. Yount, of the Pittsburgh Synod, and M. J. Stirewalt, of the Indiana Synod, were received as advisory members.

The following candidates for the ministry, J. A. Rudisill, D. J. Settlemyre, D. A. Sox, Prof. J. F. Moser, and P. C. Wike, were invited to seats.

Rev. H. M. Brown, of the North Carolina Synod, and Mr. W. S. Shepherd, student of the South Carolina Synod, were invited to seats.

The committee, appointed to meet a similar committee of the North Carolina Synod, to make some arrangements to prevent conflicts in church work, submitted the following report, which was adopted:

Your committee beg leave to submit the following: After some epistolary correspondence between the chairmen of the respective committees, in regard to the duty assigned them—the members of the committees from their respective synods, met in the town of Hickory, Catawba County, North Carolina, in the Evangelical Lutheran Church in that place, on the 27th day of March, 1883. An organization was effected by electing Rev. A. J. Fox, M. D., President, and Rev. L. A. Bikle, D. D., Secretary. The meeting was a very cordial one—the discussions fraternal and respectful, and the decisions prompt and unanimous.

The following paper was presented, carefully considered, and adopted by items, and then with great readiness and unanimity, it was adopted as a whole:

"We, the undersigned committees, appointed by the North Carolina and Tennessee Synods, at their sessions in 1882, respectfully submit the following as the conclusions and results of our deliberations at Hickory, North Carolina, on the 27th of March, 1883, relative to the important matter placed in our hands. The object of our meeting being to mature and to submit, for the consideration of and the adoption by said Synods in convention assembled, some expedient, judicious, equitable plan, or policy, to prevent—between these Synods in their efforts to extend the Redeemer's Kingdom in the occupancy of places, the establishment of missions, the erection of church edifices, the organization of congregations, etc.,—conflicts calculated to disparage the efforts at and the prosperity of such places, establishments, erections, organizations, etc., as are already occupied and inaugurated by the one or the other of these Synods, and in process of existence, we submit the subjoined plan or policy as practicable and effective:

1. That inasmuch as the aforesaid Synods confess, and teach in accordance with the confessional basis of the Evangelical Lutheran Church, as set forth in her Symbols, and so long as these Synods shall thus confess and teach, neither Synod, in its efforts to promote the Gospel and cause of Christ, shall occupy places, erect churches, establish missions, organize congregations, etc., where such things have already been done or instituted by the other, in villages or towns whose inhabitants do not exceed 2,000; and, so too, in regard to churches and church work in the country or communities, as due respect should be paid to locations at a reasonable distance, in order to prevent conflict of interest by the inauguration of such efforts too nearly contiguous.

2. That in towns or cities the number of whose inhabitants shall exceed 2,000, or shall be large enough to support two or more Lutheran Churches, it may be advantageous and proper for both Synods to operate without any view of conflict or infringement.

3. That when or where the one Synod has a member or members residing in a community, village, or town, already occupied by the other Synod, it shall be the duty of that Synod, having such member or members, to advise the same to unite with those of the Lutheran faith already engaged in the Redeemer's work in such town or village.

4. That in all proper efforts to promote the interests of the Church, friendly Christian relations between the two Synods shall be maintained and cherished, each respecting the rights of the other, as it becomes Christians to do in the dissemination of the Gospel, and in the promotion of the Church.

This paper was subscribed by each member of the respective committees, as follows: L. A. Bikle, S. Rothrock, D. R. Hoover, Committee of North Carolina Synod; A. J.

Fox, P. C. Henkel, Ambrose Costner, Committee of Tennessee Synod.

Inasmuch as the Evangelical Lutheran Synod of North Carolina has, in her late annual convention, adopted these articles of agreement, your committee most respectfully recommends their unanimous adoption by this Synod.

In regard to a letter, signed by G. L. Hunt, M. L. Carpenter, D. C. Huffman, C. H. L. Schuette, making a formal request to meet in a free conference the members of this Synod, or as many as are willing to meet with them, in or near Conover, on or about the 16th proximo, leaving it to this Synod to fix the exact time and place of meeting, a committee of two was appointed to meet the undersigned individuals of said letter, and ascertain the direct aim and purpose of such proposed conference, and that said committee report early to this Synod. This committee reported as follows:

We, the committee, appointed to convey the action of this Synod in regard to a certain paper, addressed to this Synod, signed by E. L. Hunt and others, requesting a free conference, submit, that we conveyed the said action of this Synod relative to this paper, and had a short interview with them, and that they furnished us no definite response, but intimated that, as their meeting had adjourned, it was too late at this time for such conference.

The Lutheran Church at Newton, and that at Antioch, North Carolina, were received.

The Secretary was ordered to add a column to the Parochial Report, in which he shall place the number of souls, as far as reported, and that all our ministers be requested to report annually the whole number of souls belonging to their charges, that is, all entitled to commune, as well as all who are baptized—and not confirmed, in their respective charges.

The following report of the Committee on the Reception of Concordia College was received, considered, and adopted:

We, the committee, appointed by Synod to confer with the Trustees of Concordia College, and prepare an agreement which may serve as a basis upon which said school may become the recognized institution of Synod, present the following report:

A meeting of the Board of Trustees having been called, the following resolution was adopted:

Whereas, There seems to be a general desire to establish proper relations between Concordia College and the Evangelical Lutheran Tennessee Synod, and

Whereas, It is generally believed that such relations would inure to the interest of this school, as well as to the good of the Synod or Church, at a meeting held in said institution on October 15th, by the Board of Trustees, the Faculty, and others immediately interested, the following action was taken:

Resolved, That, with a view of establishing proper relations between Concordia College, situated at Conover, North Carolina, and the Evangelical Lutheran Tennessee Synod, we, in meeting assembled, agree, 1. that whenever a vacancy, or vacancies, occur, either by death, resignation, or removal, in the Board of Trustees or in the Faculty, the said Synod shall have the right as well as the privilege to recommend a suitable person, or persons, to fill such vacancy, or vacancies; 2. that the Synod shall have the right to appoint a Board of Visitors, whose duty it shall be annually to visit said school, and make such report of the condition of the school to each session of the Synod, as may be deemed most advantageous; 3. that it shall be the duty of the President of the Faculty to make a report annually to Synod, relative to the moral and literary condition of the school, which report shall also be signed by the secretary of the faculty; 4. that the President of the Board of Trustees shall also make an annual report to Synod, in regard to the financial condition of the school, which report shall likewise be signed by the secretary of the Board of the Trustees; 5. that this school shall be continued and conducted as a church institution, under such rules and regulations, as may be instituted by the Board of Trustees, in accordance with the charter, and the Confessions of the Church as set forth in the Christian Book of Concord, each teacher, instructor, or professor, taking an obligation not to teach anything in said school that is contrary to said Confessions.

These stipulations or propositions shall be valid and in force, provided the said Synod shall acquiesce, and is disposed to lend said institution its fostering care and encouragement, as well as its influence and moral force; provided, that if the Synod shall fail, after notice, to recommend, in due time, a suitable person or persons to fill such vacancy or vacancies, the proper authorities of said institution, shall proceed to fill such vacancy or vacancies.

The following was offered and adopted:

Resolved, That we, as a Synod, accept the propositions made to us by the Board of Trustees of Concordia College, and that in consideration of the rights and privileges therein granted, we will lend to said institution our fostering care, influence, and moral support.

The Committee on Amendments to the Constitution and By-Laws submitted a report, which was adopted. The Constitution as revised and amended, reads as follows:

Constitution of the Evangelical Lutheran Tennessee Synod,

(As Revised in 1883.)

ARTICLE I. The name of this Synod shall be THE EVANGELICAL LUTHERAN TENNESSEE SYNOD.

ARTICLE II. The Holy Scriptures, the inspired writings of the Old and New Testaments, shall be the only rule and standard of doctrine and church discipline.

As a true and faithful exhibition of the doctrines of the Holy Scriptures, in regard to matters of faith and practice, this Synod receives the three Ancient Symbols: the Apostolic, Nicene, and Athanasian Creeds; and the Unaltered Augsburg Confession of Faith. It receives also the other Symbolical Books of the Evangelical Lutheran Church, viz.: The Apology, the Smalcald Articles, the Small and Large Catechisms of Luther, and the Formula of Concord—as true Scriptural developments of the doctrines taught in the Augsburg Confession.

ARTICLE III. This Synod is an association of congregations. Its conventions shall be composed of regularly ordained ministers in their connection, and their lay-delegates.

Each one of these congregations shall have the right to appoint one such delegate, who shall have equal rights and privileges with the ministers transacting the business of Synod.

Every minister desiring to be received into connection with this Synod, shall, on his reception, be required to subscribe this Constitution.

No minister, in connection with this Synod, shall be allowed to teach any thing, nor shall Synod transact any business contrary to the confessional basis as set forth in Article II.

ARTICLE IV. The business of this Synod shall be to employ the proper means for the promulgation of the Gospel of Jesus Christ, to impart its advice in matters of Christian faith and life, to detect and expose erroneous doctrines and false teachers, to recommend orthodox liturgies, hymn-books, catechisms, parochial and Sunday-school books, to engage in missionary work, domestic and foreign, to aid indigent young men in preparing for the work of the ministry, and to investigate charges of false doctrines, wrong practices, and immoralities of life, preferred against any of its ministers, and, finding them guilty, to suspend or expel from Synod such as are deemed unworthy to bear the office, and advise their pastorates to sever their official relations with them.

Upon application to examine candidates for the ministry, this Synod shall make the necessary provisions to attend to such application, and, after due approval, appoint one or more pastors to consecrate such candidate to the office of the ministry, by the laying on of hands and prayer.

Synod shall require a probationary period of not less than one year, during which time all candidates for the ministerial office shall be taken on trial.

Upon application, this Synod may receive congregations in its connection, provided they subscribe this Constitution.

ARTICLE V. The officers of this Synod shall be a President, Secretary, Corresponding Secretary, and Treasurer. A majority of all votes cast will be required to constitute an election to any office. The duties of these officers shall be such as usually devolve upon the same in other public bodies, or as may be made obligatory upon them from time to time by Synod. They shall be elected by ballot, at the regular session, annually, and hold their offices until their successors are elected.

ARTICLE VI. Synod shall meet from time to time upon its own adjournments. Extra sessions may be called by the President, when requested for good and sufficient reasons, to do so, by two ministers and two lay-men in its connection.

ARTICLE VII. Synod may at any regular meeting, by a concurrence of two-thirds of all the members present, make such regulations and by-laws as may be deemed necessary, not inconsistent with this Constitution.

ARTICLE VIII. If anything contained in these articles should hereafter be deemed contrary to the Confessional Basis of this Synod, oppressive, or inexpedient, it may be altered or amended. But nothing contained in this Constitution shall be altered or amended unless a proposition for alteration or amendment shall have been laid before one of the sessions of Synod, in writing, and agreed to by two-thirds of all the members voting. The proposition thus agreed to, shall then be laid, in due form, by the Synod in its Minutes before the congregations in its connection, for ratification or rejection by them; and the ministers or vestries of these congregations shall, at some suitable time, before the next succeeding session of Synod, take the vote of these congregations, on the Constitution as amended, allowing the members to vote for its ratification or rejection and send a statement of the vote to that session of Synod. If, then, it shall be ascertained by Synod that a majority of these congregations have voted in favor of ratification, the amendment shall become and be declared by Synod on the face of its Minutes a valid part of said Constitution, and the parts thereof repugnant to such alteration, void.

Relative to districting the Synod, joint union, and union with the General Synod South, the following action was taken:

Whereas, The Committee on Letters and Petitions recommend, that the three State Conferences, composing the Evangelical Lutheran Tennessee Synod, be resolved into three synods, confined by State lines; second, that the Evangelical Lutheran Tennessee Synod, in order to perpetuate her history, &c., be denominated the Joint Tennessee Synod, and meet in triennial conventions on middle ground, composed of the above-named three district synods, and such other synods as may desire to unite with us, for the purpose of transacting and having the superintendence of the general church work of said joint synod; we, your committee, respectfully recommend, that this matter be referred to these Conferences for consideration, indicating their wishes.

Whereas, At its last session, a paper was laid before our Synod, asking it to take into consideration the propriety of effecting some connection with the Southern Evangelical Lutheran General Synod; and

Whereas, The following action was taken by our Synod, relative to that request,

Resolved, That this paper be deferred to our next annual session of Synod for consideration; and

Whereas, There is a desire, as well as an element at work, to establish a more general union among the Evangelical Lutheran Synods South, in the form of a General Lutheran Southern Synodical Conference, based on the Confessions of the Church, as extant in the Christian Book of Concord; be it, therefore,

Resolved 1. That in view of this aspect of things, we deem it inopportune to take any action at this time, in regard to that paper or request;

Resolved 2. That it is the sentiment of this Synod, if there be sufficient internal union to justify external, organic union, that union in the form of a General Southern Lutheran Synodical Conference, properly based on the Confessions of the Church, with only advisory power, and invested with the more general operations of the Church, is the safest, and most feasible, and churchly policy that can be inaugurated, under the present circumstances;

Resolved 3. That with a view of accomplishing this desirable object, this Synod appoint a committee, consisting of three from Virginia, four from North Carolina, and two from South Carolina, whose duty it shall be, provided the move meet with sufficient encouragement in their judgment, to co-operate with other similar committees, or individuals, who may favor such move, in appointing a suitable time and place for the assembling of such a diet, and to represent this Synod in such diet, to inaugurate such Southern Lutheran Synodical Conference, submitting the result of their efforts and actions to the different synods for their approval or disapproval; and, if deemed proper, appoint another time and place for the consummation of such conference.

We would further submit, that we rejoice to be able to state, that this sentiment is indicated in resolutions passed by the late sessions of the Evangelical Lutheran Holston Synod, as set forth in its Minutes, transmitted to our Synod, as well as in resolutions passed at the recent sessions of the Evangelical Lutheran Virginia Synod, communicated to us in session assembled, in which a time and place are designated for the holding of a diet or other conference for such purpose.

Appropriations were made for six beneficiary students. The following candidates for the ministry were, after examination, ordained: D. J. Settlemyre, J. A. Rudisill, and D. A. Sox. Prof. Junius B. Fox being absent, a committee was appointed to examine him, and, if found qualified, to ordain him.

The following were appointed as delegates to the proposed Diet: Rev. S. Henkel, D. D., Rev. A. L. Crouse, Maj. A. Koiner, from Virginia; Rev. P. C. Henkel, D. D., Rev. C. H. Bernheim, Rev. M. L. Little, A. Costner, Esq., from North Carolina; Rev. J. S. Koiner and H. A. Meetze, Esq., from South Carolina.

During this year, 588 infants and 36 adults were baptized, and 264 persons were confirmed.

Synod adjourned to meet in St. Mary's (Pine) Church, Shenandoah County, Virginia, September 27, 1884.

Sixty-fourth Session.

This meeting assembled in St. Mary's (Pine) Church, Shenandoah County, Virginia, September 27, 1884.

Its officers were Rev. C. H. Bernheim, president; I. Conder, secretary; A. L. Crouse, corresponding secretary; and J. N. Stirewalt, treasurer.

Rev. J. I. Miller, of the Virginia Synod, and Prof. J. D. Dreher, Ph. D., of Roanoke College, Virginia, were invited to seats.

St. John's Church, Rockingham County, Virginia, was received.

By means of a letter, Rev. F. W. E. Peschau, corresponding delegate of the North Carolina Synod, conveyed the fraternal greetings of that synod to the members of this Synod.

The committee to draft and submit articles on the death of Rev. A. J. Fox, M. D., presented the following:

Whereas, Our Lord God has again wisely chastened us by the removal from our midst of Rev. Alfred J. Fox, and reminded us of his over-ruling providence in calling his servant from his labors here to his rest in heaven—

Resolved, That in the death of Father Fox, we recognize the loss of a noble and successful servant in the Master's earthly work; an earnest, zealous co-laborer, and a warm-hearted friend and brother.

Resolved, That we bow, humbly, to the call of Him who never errs and only wounds to heal.

Resolved, That our sympathies are extended to the bereaved widow and family, and that, while we mourn with them, we cherish upon the altar of his memory fond recollections of his virtues.

Resolved, That this feeble tribute be placed upon a separate page of our Minutes, one copy sent to the widow of our brother, and one be published in *Our Church Paper*.

After a satisfactory examination, Rev. H. Wetzel and Rev. Prof. J. I. Miller, D. D., were received and enrolled as members of this Synod.

Having sustained the required examination, Messrs. David I. Offman, of New Market, Virginia, and John Q. Lippard, of North Carolina, were received as students with a view to the ministry.

There having been a call at the previous session for the publication of the Christian Book of Concord in its third edition, Henkel & Co., New Market, Virginia, were appointed to give that matter proper attention.

D. D. Seitz, President of the Board of Trustees of Concordia College, and Rev. P. C. Henkel, D. D., President of the Faculty of said College, presented favorable reports relative to that institution.

Mr. L. L. Lohr, of Gaston County, North Carolina, was recognized as a student of theology.

The High School at Dallas, Gaston County, North Carolina, Rev. Prof. M. L. Little, principal, was recognized as a church institution and favorably commended.

The following persons, in addition to those already in office, were elected Trustees of Conover College: Rev. A.

L. Crouse and Hon. A. Koiner, of Virginia; Rev. R. A. Yoder, of North Carolina; Maj. H. A. Meetze and Mr. D. H. Wheeler, of South Carolina.

Appropriations were made for seven beneficiaries.

The time and place for the proposed Church Diet was agreed upon, by those concerned. The time was November 12, 1884, and the place, Salisbury, North Carolina.

According to the Parochial Report, 650 infants and 41 adults were baptized, and 381 persons confirmed.

Synod adjourned to meet in St. Peter's (Meetze's), Lexington County, South Carolina, October 31, 1885.

Obituary of Rev. A. J. Fox, M. D.—Died on the 10th day of June, 1884, at his home in Lincoln County, North Carolina, after an illness of one week, Rev. A. J. Fox, M. D.; aged 66 years, 9 months, and 4 days. On the day following, his remains were buried at Salem Church, Lincoln County, North Carolina, Rev. R. A. Yoder rendering the funeral services, assisted by Rev. J. M. Smith. Notwithstanding the inclement weather and in the midst of harvest, there was a very large congregation present, to pay a last tribute of respect to an aged and venerable minister of the Gospel. Rev. R. A. Yoder addressed the congregation, basing his remarks on Numbers 23, 10: "Let me die the death of the righteous!"

The Rev. Dr. A. J. Fox was married to Lydia Bost in the year 1842. He leaves a widow and 11 children, 7 sons and 4 daughters.

He entered the Lutheran ministry in 1837, and labored constantly in that work until within a few days of his death; extending over a period of 47 years. He labored during this whole period in connection with the Evangelical Lutheran Tennessee Synod; while his work was confined within the limits of the Tennessee Synod, his influence was felt in the whole Lutheran Church of this country, as he was frequently corresponding delegate to other Lutheran bodies. He always held positions of honor and trust in his Synod, and was for many years one of her leading spirits. He gave direction and counsel in all her interests, and was an able advocate and defender of the pure doctrines of the Church of the Reformation.

He was a man of extraordinary energy and physical strength. He served as many as eight or nine congregations at the same time, in addition to his professional duties as physician, and the cares and duties of a large household.

Two of his sons are in the Lutheran ministry—one Rev. L. A. Fox, D. D., is an eminent scholar, and an able professor in Roanoke

College, Salem, Virginia. The other, Rev. J. B. Fox, is laboring in connection with the Evangelical Lutheran Holston Synod, in East Tennessee. Two of his sons are following the medical profession with eminent success. One, Dr. A. C. Fox, lives in Waynesboro, Virginia; the other, Dr. Frank Fox, is at the old homestead and was practicing in connection with his father. Of his remaining sons, one is a farmer, and the other two are boys at home with their mother.

Of his four daughters, three are the wives who grace the homes of some of our best citizens, and one a widow.

An eminently successful career has closed with his life, and by his death, the State and community have lost a valuable citizen; the Church and Synod, an able, active, and energetic minister; and the family, a kind father and dear husband.

By his "works of faith and labors of love," he "being dead yet speaketh." The souls whom he has been instrumental in saving, the churches which he has helped to build, the brethren whom he has counseled, the voice of pen and pulpit, all speak:

"Blessed are the dead which die in the Lord from henceforth; yea, saith the Spirit, that they may rest from their labors, and their works do follow them." "Precious in the sight of the Lord is the death of his saints." "Mark the perfect man, and behold the upright; for the end of that man is peace."

He has been called to his reward, and is now in the fellowship of angels and saints, around the throne of God.

He "fought a good fight," he "kept the faith," and now he wears the victor's crown.

Sixty-fifth Session.

This meeting was held in St. Peter's (Meetze's) Church, Lexington County, South Carolina, commencing October 31, 1885.

The officers were Revs. J. M. Smith, president; R. A. Yoder, secretary; A. L. Crouse, corresponding secretary; and J. K. Efird, treasurer.

The proposed Diet having met at the time and place indicated, and adopted a basis for a more general union among the Evangelical Lutheran Synods in the South, as well as a constitution, the Synod adopted these documents, and appointed the following delegates to represent it in the next Diet: Revs. S. Henkel, D. D., A. L. Crouse, P. C. Henkel, D. D., C. H. Bernheim, M. L. Little, and E. L. Lybrand; and Messrs. A. Koiner, A. Costner, and W. A.

Meetze. Alternates—Revs. J. P. Stirewalt, J. S. Koiner, and J. K. Efird; and Messrs. Philip Killian, W. A. Mauney, and C. M. Efird.

A committee was appointed to ordain Mr. R. H. Cline.

The College Chapel congregation, Gaston County, North Carolina, was received.

The Secretary was ordered to make a complete roll of the congregations and preaching places in connection with Synod, and have it published in the Minutes.

The committee, Rev. A. L. Crouse, on monument for Rev. Ambrose Henkel, reported that the monument had been erected and paid for, out of funds collected in the Valley of Virginia for that purpose.

The President of the Board of Trustees of Concordia College, the President of the Faculty, and the Visiting Committee, submitted very favorable and encouraging reports in regard to that institution.

Rev. P. C. Henkel, D. D., President of Concordia College, Conover, North Carolina, having tendered his resignation relative to that office, the following resolution was adopted:

Resolved, That in the acceptance of the resignation of Rev. P. C. Henkel, as President of Concordia College, by this Synod, it does so with regret, and only under a sense of duty which is due under statements and representations made by him; and, in parting with him, the Synod desires to express its most hearty thanks for the sacrifices which he has made gratuitously for the institution, and prays God's richest blessings upon him.

Appropriations were made for six beneficiaries.

The report shows that during the year 741 infants and 63 adults were baptized, and 655 persons confirmed.

Synod adjourned to meet in College Chapel, Dallas, Gaston County, North Carolina, November 6, 1886.

Sixty-sixth Session.

This session was held in College Chapel, Dallas, North Carolina, commencing November 6, 1886.

The officers were Revs. R. A. Yoder, president; J. Paul Stirewalt, secretary; A. L. Crouse, corresponding secretary; and J. K. Efird, treasurer.

The committee, appointed to ordain Robert H. Cline, reported that they had attended to that duty.

Rev. J. P. Smeltzer, D. D., having presented an honorable dismission from the South Carolina Synod, and sustained a satisfactory examination, was received as a member of this Synod, and his name ordered to be enrolled in the clerical catalogue.

The following recommendation of the President in his report, was sustained: That "Sunday-schools be organized in all our congregations, and that sound Lutheran literature be used." In regard to this recommendation, it was suggested that where no such schools already exist, they be established, and that only the Holy Scriptures and sound Lutheran literature be used.

His recommendation, "that our people be advised to build no more union houses of worship," was adopted.

Rev. L. A. Fox, D. D., was granted an honorable dismission to the Southwestern Virginia Synod.

Holly Grove Church, Davidson County, Pisgah Church, Alexander County, North Carolina, Bethel Church, Rockingham County, Mount Calvary Church, Shenandoah County, Virginia, and Zion congregation, Jacksonville, Alabama, were received into connection with Synod.

The following is the report of the delegates to the Church Diet, held in Roanoke, Virginia:

"A second church Diet having been convened at Roanoke, Virginia, June 24, 1886, in accordance with the action of the Diet, held in Salisbury, North Carolina, November 12–13, 1884, and the Evangelical Lutheran Synods concerned having adopted the Basis for a more general union of these Synods and the congregations of which they are composed, and the Constitution designed for the government of such more general union, as set forth and agreed upon by the Diet which met in Salisbury, and the necessary preliminary regulations having been made, we, the undersigned delegates to said Diet, held at Roanoke, cast the vote of the Evangelical Lutheran Tennessee Synod, which we had the honor to represent, in accordance with her instructions, in favor of the establishment of the more general, organic union contemplated, and the action of the other synods concerned being favorable to such union, it was effected, on the Basis and Constitution indicated, under the name and title of the United Synod of the Evangelical Lutheran Church in the South. Thus with the Evangelical Lutheran Tennessee Synod and the Holston Synod, the Southern General Synod was merged into one general body.

We have reason to thank the Great Head of the Church, that the true Confessions have been thus again formally recognized and acknowledged. The Scriptural *premises* have, in this way, been laid down and agreed to, and by prudence, brotherly love, and the influences of the Holy Spirit, the conclusions must be, ultimately, inevitable. But it will require patience and much judicious work, to attain that higher and more churchly plain in regard to doctrine and practice.

After its organization, important business was transacted by the United Synod,—some of which will require the attention of our Synod; as, foreign missions, important home missionary work, &c. We trust Synod will take such action in regard to these, as she may deem proper.

S. Henkel,
A. Koiner,
A. L. Crouse,
E. L. Lybrand,
C. M. Efird,
C. H. Bernheim."

In regard to this report, the following resolutions were offered:

"1. That it be adopted.

2. That, in adopting it, as the Evangelical Lutheran Tennessee Synod rejects all ecclesiastical union and co-operation which is not based on the pure Lutheran teaching and faith; as, the Exchange of Pulpits, Promiscuous Communion or Altar Fellowship, Secret Society Worship, and Chiliasm, we, the ministers and lay-delegates, in Synod assembled, do hereby recommend or advise the Committee, or the Chairman of the Committee, appointed by the United Synod of the Evangelical Lutheran Church in the South to prepare by-laws for its government, in drafting such by-laws so to formulate them as to require every teacher or professor who may be appointed as a teacher or professor in any Theological Seminary that she may establish or put into operation, to take an obligation not to teach, practice, or inculcate anything that comes in conflict with these principles, or the doctrines of the Church.

3. That we trust the said United Synod will feel the importance of acquiescing in this precautionary request, with a view to the good of the Church; especially as this is desired only in work, for which each synod will be held responsible in its united efforts, and which it should be able to defend and maintain according to the pure doctrines and practices of the Evangelical Lutheran Church, as over against sectarian innovations and corruptions, leaving each synod in connection with the United Synod, in its individual, synodical transactions, so to shape its course, as ultimately to attain that higher plain in doctrine and practice, so characteristic of the true Church."

The above report and resolutions were received and adopted by a rising vote.

The following Regulations in regard to the Work of the United Synod of the Evangelical Lutheran Church in the South, were submitted to the said United Synod, at its meeting in Savannah, Georgia, November 24–29, 1887, in connection with By-Laws and Rules of Order, and ordered to be printed in the Minutes, and postponed till the next meeting of the United Synod, held in Wilmington, North Carolina, November, 1889, for consideration:

"I. Every important Home Missionary work or enterprise, undertaken by this Synod, shall be under its control and supervision, and the property of such enterprise shall be conveyed to trustees selected or designated by Synod, to be held for the use, benefit, and occupancy of the Evangelical Lutheran congregation worshiping at that place, and adhering to the Confessional Basis of said Synod, until the congregation is regularly transferred to an Evangelical Lutheran Synod in connection with this Body.

II. It shall not be the policy of this Synod to commence Missionary work at any place, unless the friends of the Church, residing at such point, are willing to do a reasonable part towards building up and supporting the contemplated congregation and the erection of a suitable church edifice.

III. Every minister, teacher, professor, or missionary, in any institution or enterprise under the supervision or control of this United Synod, before entering on the performance of the duties of his office, shall make an affirmation that he will inculcate nothing that is in conflict with the Doctrinal Basis of this United Synod as defined in its Constitution, but that all his religious teachings shall be in conformity with the same; and that he will not foster nor encourage intercommunion, or altar fellowship with non-Lutherans, or unionistic services, or any secret society of a doubtful or deistic character."

At the session of the United Synod, in Wilmington, North Carolina, in 1889, the By-Laws, Rules of Order, and Regulations in regard to Work, were again postponed till its next meeting.

The Committee on Church Institutions reported as follows:

"We, your committee, would respectfully report, that

we have had but one paper placed in our hands, from which we gather, that Concordia College, Conover, North Carolina, is in a flourishing condition, having had a larger enrollment of pupils than at any previous session.

Further, we, your committee, recommend:

1. That the Board of Trustees be the only authority, with the sanction of Synod, to elect or employ any of its professors or teachers that are in anywise connected with the said College.

2. That, as the Board of Trustees have the only authority, with the sanction of Synod, to elect teachers, or trustees for said institution, they elect two more members, who reside at or near Conover, North Carolina, to be added to the Board of Trustees, so that, in any case of emergency, a quorum may be had for the transaction of business.

3. That the advertisement of Concordia College be printed upon the last page of the cover of our Minutes."

The following resolution on Home and Foreign Missionary operations, was offered:

Whereas, In view of the connection which this Synod now sustains to the United Synod of the Evangelical Lutheran Church in the South, it will be her duty properly to aid in promoting the important home missionary operations, as well as the foreign, under the supervision of said United Synod, be it

Resolved, That our ministers be required to bring this matter before their respective congregations, and that the said congregations are advised to co-operate with their pastors in devising ways and means to raise not less than 10 cents per each communicant, by establishing congregational treasuries, or woman's societies, or whatever mode they may think the better for raising such amounts, and that the amounts be raised as soon as possible and sent to the Treasurer of our Synod, and the result be reported to the next meeting of our Synod.

The committee on the publication of the Book of Concord was continued till the next convention of Synod.

The committee on resolutions on Mr. Armentrout, submitted the following:

We, the committee appointed to prepare suitable resolutions, submit the following:

Whereas, It hath pleased God, in whose hands are the issues of life and death, to remove our lamented brother, T. E. Armentrout, from his labors on earth to his rest in heaven; be it

Resolved 1. That in the death of our brother we recognize the hand of God, and bow with resigned submission to His will.

Resolved 2. In his death, the Church Militant has lost a devoted member, an efficient teacher, and one who gave good promise of future usefulness in the Gospel Ministry, for which he had prepared himself, and in which he labored more or less for a year or two, as a candidate, with efficiency.

Resolved 3. That a copy of these resolutions be spread upon the face of the Minutes.

Resolved 4. That a copy of these resolutions be sent to the sad family of which he was a member.

After a satisfactory examination, Mr. P. C. Wike was ordained.

Appropriations were made for beneficiaries.

According to the Parochial Report, 51 adults and 690 infants were baptized, 474 persons were confirmed, and 1 ordained as pastor.

Synod adjourned to meet in Bethlehem Church, Augusta County, Virginia, August 31, 1887.

Obituary of Mr. Thomas E. Armentrout.—It is sad to part with our loved ones, and especially with those who are faithful servants of the Church, but, the rider upon the pale horse is no respecter of persons. He calls alike upon the noble and ignoble, and commits his solemn deed. He has made his visit in the person of Mr. Thomas E. Armentrout, who departed this life of malarial fever, after an illness of several weeks; aged 31 years, 9 months, and 11 days.

Mr. Armentrout two years ago went to Missouri, and remained there some two months, after which he went to Florida, and returned home to his father's the next spring, his health being somewhat improved. He was advised to go South again; he accordingly went to North Carolina. Shortly after his arrival there, he commenced teaching a school which was secured for him through the kindness of Rev. W. A. Lutz. He obligated himself to teach one month, and if his health would admit, at the end of said month, he proposed to continue the school through the winter season. As his health seemed to be sufficient for the task, he continued, and finished a five months' term.

After taking a rest of one or two months, he was requested by his patrons to teach a summer school of two months at the same place, which he consented to do, and having continued it within two weeks of its close, he was taken with malarial fever, accompanied with chills, but was not confined to his bed until the 18th of September, when he became very sick, and his hopes of recovery doubtful. He gradually grew worse until the evening of the 24th at 6.40 P. M., when his soul took its final departure into the presence of God, to receive its final reward.

His brother, C. F. Armentrout, arrived the second day before his death, but he was not conscious of his presence; he took charge of his remains and brought it back to his father's; from thence it was removed to the cemetery in McGaheysville, Va., accompanied with an unusually large number of persons, where it is to rest until the morning of the resurrection.

His character was without reproach, his piety unquestionable, and his love for the Church highly commendatory. We feel that we have lost a precious jewel in his departure, but we bow in humble submission to the dispensation of him who doth all things well, believing that our loss has resulted in his everlasting gain.

He pursued a regular collegiate course of studies in the New Market Polytechnic Institute, New Market, Virginia, and received the degree of A. B., and then pursued a post-graduate course, and received that of A. M. He was an excellent scholar and a close student.

Sixty-Seventh Session.

This meeting convened in Bethlehem Church, Augusta County, Virginia, August 27, 1887.

The officers elected were Revs. Prof. J. S. Koiner, president; J. Paul Stirewalt, secretary; Prof. R. A. Yoder, corresponding secretary; and J. N. Stirewalt, treasurer.

Revs. Prof. J. A. Willis, C. Beard, J. H. Barb, G. W. Spiggle, of the Virginia Synod, B. S. Brown, of the North Carolina Synod, and L. K. Probst, Secretary of the Board of Missions of the United Synod, were received as advisory members.

The report of the President of Concordia College, and that of the President of the Board of Trustees, were very favorable, showing that church institution in a healthy and prosperous condition.

Rev. L. K. Probst, at the request of the President, addressed the Synod and the congregation on the subject of Home and Foreign Missions.

The following is the substance of a paper submitted to Synod by Rev. F. W. E. Peschau, President and Corresponding Delegate of the North Carolina Synod, in which he conveys the fraternal greetings of that body, and asks prayerful and kind attention to an important petition which his Synod submits, as follows:

"The kind Christian greetings I bring you are the outgrowth of the kind and fraternal relations existing between the worthy pastors and faithful members of your honorable body, residing in the 'Old North State,' as our ecclesiastical neighbors; yea, brethren, with us in the same household of faith.

The petition I present is an earnest request that your honorable body will, in view of the forming of 'the United Synod,' and in view of the pleasant relations thus made between us, as sister Synods, and in consonance with the whole movement to bring about more harmony, peace, unity, and strength, both local and general, in our dear Evangelical Lutheran Church, South, grant the members of the North Carolina Conference, both clerical and lay, letters of honorable dismissal to the Evangelical Lutheran Synod of North Carolina, that they may be one with us, not only in point of a confessional basis, but also one with us in corporate organization.

Will your honorable body grant this request, and thus bring about a union of brethren long desired? May the Holy Spirit guide all in this important matter?"

In regard to this the following action was taken:

Resolved, That it is the sentiment of this body that such petition for transfer should proceed first from the North Carolina Conference of our Synod.

Resolved, That whilst we appreciate the cordial, fraternal spirit manifest in that action, it is the sentiment of this Synod, that, in view of the present condition of the Church in the South, and the relations which this Synod sustains to it, it would be inexpedient, as well as injudicious, to form such a union; especially, as it would result in disintegrating the Evangelical Lutheran Tennessee Synod—a Synod which has done so much towards sustaining and perpetuating the doctrines of the Church, and which, it seems, still has a mission to fill, and a history to perpetuate,—and particularly as there is no necessity for such union, since the relations between the two Synods are so fraternal as to prevent any conflict in the respective and legitimate work or operations of the two Synods, under the happy regulations established by them in the year 1883.

The committee, Rev. M. L. Fox, M. D., appointed to collect funds to erect a monument at the grave of Rev. Philip Henkel, in Randolph County, North Carolina, reported that he had succeeded in erecting a suitable monument at that place.

In regard to the publication of Luther's Small Catechism, the following action was taken:

Whereas, We learn that the last edition of Luther's Small Catechism, published by S. P. C. & C. C. Henkel, New Market, Va., is exhausted; and

Whereas, We need a good, reliable, Lutheran Catechism for our families, Sunday-schools, and catechumens; be it, therefore,

Resolved 1. That we recommend to Henkel & Co., New Market, Va., the propriety of publishing another edition of that Catechism;

2. That, in the event they publish such an edition, we advise our people, teachers, and ministers to use it in their

families, Sunday-schools, and catechetical classes, and to give it such other circulation as it deserves.

Rev. D. A. Sox having resigned the mission work in Alabama, it was recommended:

First, That said work in Alabama be made a special mission field of this Synod.

Secondly, That this Synod put into said field, *as early as possible*, a missionary, and sustain him.

Thirdly, That by adopting this, Synod pledges herself to pay her missionary $300.00 per year.

Fourthly, That the mission be required to raise the other $200.00 of a salary of $500.00.

The following delegates were elected to the United Synod which met in Savannah, Georgia, November 24, 1887:

Principals—Revs. S. Henkel, D. D., A. L. Crouse, J. P. Stirewalt, J. C. Moser, R. A. Yoder, P. C. Henkel, D. D., W. P. Cline, J. K. Efird, J. A. Cromer, and Messrs. D. S. Henkel, Wm. Coffman, Philip Killian, James T. Miller, John F. Moser, A. M. Huit, D. P. Boger, Maj. Henry A. Meetze, Dr. J. W. Eargle.

Alternates—Revs. John N. Stirewalt, I. Conder, H. Wetzel, M. L. Fox, J. R. Peterson, J. S. Koiner, J. A. Rudisill, Dr. J. P. Smeltzer, E. L. Lybrand, and Messrs. Ambrose L. Henkel, Isaiah Printz, Isaiah Bowman, C. T. Sigman, Tobias Barnes, F. L. Herman, D. M. Wyant, P. S. Fulmer, Lewis Shealey.

In regard to Theological Instruction at Concordia College, Conover, North Carolina, it was moved that Rev. Prof. J. S. Koiner continue to devote a portion of his time to such instruction, and that the College Board pay him in proportion to the labor he performs, out of the funds which have been or may be raised for such purpose, and paid into the hands of the Treasurer of College.

During this year, 49 adults and 453 infants were baptized, and 227 persons confirmed.

Synod adjourned to meet in St. Peter's (P. W.) Church,

Lexington County, South Carolina, on Saturday before the first Sunday in October, 1888.

Sixty-eighth Session.

This convention met in St. Peter's (P. W.) Church, Lexington County, South Carolina, December 1, 1888, the time having been postponed.

The election for officers resulted in favor of Rev. J. C. Moser, president; Rev. A. L. Crouse, secretary; Rev. W. P. Cline, corresponding secretary; and Rev. J. N. Stirewalt, treasurer.

All Lutheran ministers present were recognized and invited to seats within the bar of the Synod, with the privilege of debate. Revs. C. A. Marks, Z. W. Bedenbaugh, M. J. Epting, Prof. J. B. Fox, W. A. Julian, and J. A. Sligh were announced. Rev. Prof. A. G. Voigt, delegate from the South Carolina Synod, presented his credentials and was received.

Rev. W. A. Lutz, delegate from the North Carolina Synod, was announced as present. A motion was made to receive him, and pending its consideration Synod adjourned till the afternoon session.

Synod resumed the consideration of the reception of the delegate of the North Carolina Synod. On motion, it was postponed till some subsequent session of this convention.

The following was passed:

Whereas, At its recent convention, the Evangelical Lutheran North Carolina Synod took certain action in regard to the course pursued by the Evangelical Lutheran Tennessee Synod relative to the application of Rev. B. S. Brown for admittance; and

Whereas, That action may, in the future, be construed as a reflection on the Evangelical Lutheran Tennessee Synod; be it, therefore,

Resolved 1. That the Tennessee Synod pursued the same course in reference to the said B. S. Brown, as it has relative to other similar applicants, for more than three score years;

2. That this Synod can see no good reason for deviating from that policy, convinced that it is right and proper.

At a later date, Synod resumed the consideration of the reception of the North Carolina Synod's delegate, and the following action was taken :

Rev. W. A. Lutz having appeared as corresponding delegate of the Evangelical Lutheran North Carolina Synod, and presented his credentials as such, was received ; but it is to be regretted, that, in view of the following action taken by the North Carolina Synod at its late meeting, relative to the course pursued by our Synod in regard to the application of Rev. B. S. Brown, it would be incompatible for this Synod to continue such courtesy or correspondence in the future, without some modification or satisfactory explanation of the intention of that action, which, otherwise, is calculated to reflect on our Synod :

"*Resolved*, That we have heard with pleasure the very excellent and able address of Rev. B. S. Brown, regarding his non-reception into our sister Synod, the Tennessee Synod, and that we rejoice to find that he stood so firmly on the confessions of the church and refused to go beyond them in accepting opinions or practices that are nowhere required or distinctly stated in the symbols of our church."

The matter of establishing a mission at Asheville, North Carolina, was referred to the North Carolina Conference of the Synod for consideration.

A letter from Rev. L. K. Probst, Secretary of the Board of Missions of the United Synod, was read, in which attention was called to the apportionment of this Synod, due the United Synod, of $800 for Home Missions and $400 for Foreign Missions, as approximated by the Board.

The services of a pastor for the Alabama Mission were secured.

The request, made at the previous meeting of Synod, for the publication of another edition of Luther's Small Catechism, was complied with, Henkel & Co., of New

Market, Virginia, having brought out the new publication, in its fifth edition, in due time.

The committee on text-books for Sunday-schools recommended the following :

1. The Bible, or portions of it, and Luther's Small Catechism.

2. As helps to learning the contents of Bible and Catechism, Little Children's Catechism, My First Book, The Child's Book, Stories from Bible History ; and for Song, The Little Children's Book.

3. For more advanced scholars, also, Biblical History in the Words of Holy Scripture, Outlines of Church History ; and for Song, The Sunday-school Book.

Favorable action was taken in regard to the endowment of Concordia College, Conover, North Carolina.

With respect to the relation which the Tennessee Synod sustains to the United Synod in the South, the following action was taken :

Whereas, The relations of the different synods, composing the United Synod of the South, to each other, and to the United Synod, as defined in the Basis of Union and Constitution of the United Synod, are differently interpreted ; and

Whereas, There is some difference of opinion as to what rights, privileges, and courtesies should be accorded to each individual synod by the other synods ; and

Whereas, The principles involved in said Article III. are held by the Tennessee Synod ; and

Whereas, Said Article III. has not been adopted by the United Synod, but action upon it postponed to its next meeting ; therefore, be it

Resolved, That we, the ministers and delegates of the Evangelical Lutheran Tennessee Synod, do emphatically reiterate the principles set forth at Dallas, North Carolina, in 1886, as our position, viz.: "That in adopting it (The Report of the Delegates to the Diet at Roanoke, Va.), as the Evangelical Lutheran Tennessee Synod rejects all ecclesiastical union and co-operation which is not based on the pure Lutheran teaching and faith; as, the Exchange of Pulpits, Promiscuous Communion or Altar Fellowship, Secret Society Worship, and Chiliasm, we, the ministers and lay-delegates, in Synod assembled, do hereby recommend or advise the committee, or chairman of the committee, appointed by the United Synod of the Evangelical Lutheran Church in the South, to prepare By-laws for its government, in drafting such By-laws, so to formulate them as to require every teacher or professor who may be appointed as a teacher or professor in any theological seminary that she may establish or put into operation, to take an obligation not to teach, practice, or inculcate anything that comes in conflict with these principles, or the doctrines of the Church.

"That we trust the said United Synod will feel the importance of acquiescing in this precautionary request, with a view to the good of the church; especially as this is desired only in work for which each Synod will be held responsible in its united efforts, and which it should be able to defend and maintain according to the pure doctrines and practices of the Evangelical Lutheran Church, as over against sectarian innovations and corruptions, leaving each Synod in connection with the United Synod in its individual synodical transactions, so to shape its course as ultimately to attain that higher plain in doctrine and practice so characteristic of the true Church."

Resolved, That until such position is taken by the United Synod, by adopting the principles contained in Article III. of proposed By-laws, the Tennessee Synod cannot *co-operate* with the United Synod in her work.

J. P. Price having sustained a satisfactory examination in regard to his qualifications to bear the office of Pastor, was ordained.

J. T. Miller was examined and ordained to the office of Pastor, by a special committee, during this synodical year.

The President having called attention in his regular

report to the deaths of Rev. J. P. Smeltzer, D. D., and Rev. M. L. Fox, M. D., the following action was taken:

Whereas, In the providence of God, Revs. M. L. Fox and J. P. Smeltzer, D. D., have been called from their labors in the Church militant to their rest in the Church triumphant:

Resolved 1. That while the Tennessee Synod has lost able and efficient ministers of the Gospel, the families dear friends and kind husbands, and the States and communities honored citizens, we bow in humble submission to the will of Him who doth all things well.

Resolved 2. That we spread these resolutions upon the face of our Minutes as an humble tribute of respect to their memory, as an appreciation of their worth and merits, and as a token of esteem in which they were held.

Resolved, That a page, containing the name, the date of the death, and the age, be devoted to the memory of the deceased brethren.

Rev. S. Henkel having stated to Synod that there is a probability that another edition of the New Market, Va., edition of the Christian Book of Concord, or Symbolical Books, will be published in the near future, if the enterprise meet with proper encouragement, it was

Resolved, That Synod hail with pleasure that announcement, and shall give it proper encouragement.

So too, relative to the History of the Tennessee Synod, it was

Moved, That we have heard the statement of Dr. S. Henkel with reference to the publication of his History of the Tennessee Synod, and that we make earnest efforts to introduce the work among our people.

The report on the state of the Church is quite favorable and encouraging. The usual routine business was transacted in a regular way.

The following delegates were elected to the next meeting of the United Synod:

Principals—Revs. S. Henkel, D. D., A. L. Crouse, J. P. Stirewalt, J. C. Moser, J. S. Koiner, J. M. Smith, W. P.

Cline, J. A. Rudisill, J. K. Efird, E. L. Lybrand, and Messrs. Ambrose L. Henkel, Isaiah Printz, Philip Killian, A. M. Huit, Luther Mosteller, J. L. Yount, A. C. Lineberger, J. S. Lipe, C. M. Efird, Maj. H. A. Meetze.

Alternates—Revs. I. Conder, John N. Stirewalt, P. C. Wike, P. C. Henkel, D. D., M. L. Little, C. H. Bernheim, R. A. Yoder, D. J. Settlemyre, D. Efird, J. A. Cromer, and Messrs. Wm. Coffman, A. Dodson, D. I. Offman, D. M. Wyant, Wm. Yoder, G. M. Yoder, H. F. McCaslin, D. A. Coon, W. Henry Hare, D. C. Boland.

The reports on Literary Institutions were favorable.

The Parochial Report shows 31 ministers, 101 churches, 89 adult baptisms, 889 infant baptisms, 662 confirmations, 9,392 communicants, and 14,120 souls.

Synod adjourned to meet in Holly Grove Church, Ilex, Davidson County, North Carolina, November 8, 1889.

Obituary of Rev. Michael L. Fox, M. D.—At his residence in Randolph County, North Carolina, July 22, 1888, Rev. Michael L. Fox, M. D., departed this life; aged 63 years, 6 months, and 10 days.

He was a son of Christian and Charity Fox. In his infancy he was dedicated to God through the Sacrament of Holy Baptism, and at a more mature age he entered into full communion with the Evangelical Lutheran Church, through the rite of Confirmation, Rev. Henry Goodman officiating.

In early life he commenced the practice of medicine, and in that profession he proved most successful and efficient. His practice was extensive, not only in his own county, but also in adjoining counties. He represented his county, one session, in the State Legislature, with satisfaction to his constituents.

In 1871 he entered the office of the Gospel ministry, in connection with the Evangelical Lutheran Tennessee Synod, and, in that capacity, proved zealous, faithful, and efficient. He served acceptably, during his ministry, three congregations; one in Randolph County, one in Guilford County, and one in Alamance. Notwithstanding his practice as a physician was extensive and laborious, he never failed to meet his appointments, in an ecclesiastical point of view.

His remains were placed to rest, till the resurrection morn, in Melanchthon church yard, Rev. B. W. Cronk rendering the burial service in the midst of an unusually large concourse of relatives and sympathizing friends. In all the relations of life, he gained the highest esteem among all who knew him.

On the second Sunday of November, 1888, his funeral was preached at Melanchthon Church, Randolph County, N. C., by Rev. P. C. Henkel, D. D., from 1 Thess. 4, 13–18, in the presence of a very large congregation of relatives and affectionate friends, taking his position at the door of the church, as not more than one-third of the people could get room in the house.

He leaves a widow, two daughters, and five sons,—two of whom are practicing physicians,—to lament their irreparable loss of a kind husband and an affectionate father. Thus another true soldier of the cross has been promoted to the triumphant army in that better country.

Obituary of Rev. J. P. Smeltzer, D. D.—Dr. Smeltzer was born in Frederick County, Maryland, September 10, 1819. He received a liberal education, and about the time he reached manhood was ordained a minister of the Lutheran Church. He was for several years principal of a well-known and popular educational institution at Harper's Ferry, Virginia, and was at different times pastor of the churches at Shepherdstown, West Virginia, and Salem, Virginia. In 1861, so great had become his reputation as an instructor, that he was elected president of Newberry College, South Carolina. He removed to South Carolina, and conducted the affairs of this institution with signal ability when the college was located at Newberry, and after its removal to Walhalla until 1879, when the college was again taken back to Newberry. In that year he resigned the presidency of the institution, and established at his mountain home the Walhalla Female College, of which he was the head until 1885.

During his labors as a teacher, Dr. Smeltzer did not discontinue his work in the pulpit. Last spring, his health having given way under the ceaseless toil of many years, Dr. Smeltzer came to Charleston, where he spent the last few months of his life. Dr. Smeltzer was a very forcible preacher. He was possessed of profound powers of analysis, and preached with great effectiveness. For his theological learning the degree of doctor of divinity was conferred upon him by Erskine College.

He was one of the oldest as well as one of the ablest and most impressive preachers of his age.

Soon after the death of his wife, he resigned his position in Walhalla Female Seminary, South Carolina, and having received a call, he took charge of the Springhill, South Carolina, charge, and this charge being in connection with the Evangelical Lutheran Tennessee Synod, he received an honorable discharge from the Evangelical Lutheran South Carolina Synod, and was received into the said Tennessee Synod, October, 1886.

He died at the residence of his son, Mr. John B. Smeltzer, of Charleston, South Carolina, October 31, 1887; aged 68 years, 1 month, and 21 days. His funeral services were conducted by Rev. Dr. Muller and Rev. Dr. Horn. His remains were conveyed to Walhalla, and interred.

Sixty-Ninth Session.

This meeting convened in Holly Grove Church, Ilex, Davidson County, North Carolina, November 8, 1889.

The officers elected were Rev. A. L. Crouse, president; Rev. J. Paul Stirewalt, recording secretary; Rev. Prof. W. P. Cline, corresponding secretary; Rev. J. N. Stirewalt, treasurer; Rev. J. M. Smith, treasurer beneficiary fund; and Rev. S. Henkel, D. D., assistant treasurer beneficiary fund.

During this session, on proper petitions from congregations desiring ministerial services, and after sustaining satisfactory examinations, the following theological students were ordained to the office of Pastor, Rev. T. Moser preaching the ordination sermon: J. P. Miller, W. L. Darr, and David I. Offman.

Rev. Prof. J. G. Schaid, having received a letter of honorable dismission from the Evangelical Lutheran Synod of North Carolina, and sustained a satisfactory examination, was received into Synod.

Rev. J. F. Moser, who had been, according to resolution, examined and ordained, at a convention of the North Carolina Conference of the Tennessee Synod, during the synodical year, was received into Synod.

The following applicants for the ministerial office, were, after examination and approval, received under the care of the Synod: S. S. Keisler, J. T. Craps, G. E. Long, R. L. Fritz, D. F. Conrad, A. R. Beck, W. H. Roof, and A. V. Sherrill.

Mt. Tabor, Richland County, South Carolina, Mt. Olive, Catawba County, North Carolina, St. Luke's, Union County, North Carolina, and Bethel, Prince William County, Virginia, were received in connection with Synod.

The report of the committee on Missions, was quite favorable and encouraging, in regard to the work in Virginia, North Carolina, South Carolina, and Alabama.

The reports of the committees on the state of the Church and Literary Institutions, were commendable and gratifying.

Rev. Prof. J. S. Koiner having resigned, Rev. Prof. R. A. Yoder was elected as theological professor in Concordia College.

The President announced the following committee to secure $10,000 for the purpose of erecting new college buildings for Concordia College, Conover, North Carolina: Revs. Prof. W. P. Cline, Prof. J. F. Moser, P. C. Wike, Mr. A. M. Huit, and Mr. Jonas Hunsucker.

In regard to an effort being made, to establish a first-class female college, to be located in the city of Charlotte, North Carolina, which institution is to be conducted in accordance with the Confessional Basis of the Evangelical Lutheran Church, as contained in the Book of Concord, and in which Luther's Catechism and Lutheran training are to constitute part of the college curriculum, commendable action was taken.

Appropriations were made for three beneficiary students.

The following report, relative to a formula of distribution in the Lord's Supper, was ordered to be spread on the minutes, for consideration at the next meeting of Synod:

Resolved 1. That it is the sense of this body that the elements in the Lord's Supper must be distributed with the unfailing use of Christ's words;

2. That our pastors be, and they are hereby, instructed to use the formula of our Synod found in its liturgy, page 80, namely:

"Take, and eat; this is the body of your Savior, Jesus Christ, which is given for you; this do in remembrance of him."

"Take, and drink; this is the blood of your Savior, Jesus Christ, which is shed for you, for the remission of sins; this do in remembrance of him."

The words, "May it strengthen and preserve you in the true faith, unto life everlasting, Amen," may be used *after* the giving to the whole or any part of the communicants present at the altar, but never in the act of giving and receiving either element.

The committee, consisting of Revs. T. Moser, J. R. Peterson, and M. L. Little, appointed to report resolutions on the death of Rev. P. C. Henkel, D. D., submitted the following:

Whereas, It has pleased Almighty God in his wise providence to remove our dear brother from his labors in the Church militant to his reward in the Church triumphant, be it

Resolved 1. That in the death of Brother Henkel the Church has lost an able and valiant defender of her time-honored doctrines, the Synod a most faithful and devoted member, society an excellent neighbor and loyal citizen, and the bereaved family an exemplary Christian husband and father.

2. That we humbly submit to this dispensation of our Heavenly Father, that we devoutly cherish the memory of our beloved brother and fellow-laborer, that we hereby express our appreciation of his labors, toils, and sacrifices for the cause of Christ, and that we lay seriously to heart the solemn lesson addressed to us.

3. That we tender the family of the deceased our sincere sympathy in their sad bereavement, and commend them to the care of the Good Shepherd and Bishop of souls.

4. That a copy of these resolutions be sent the afflicted family, and that a page of our Minutes be inscribed to the memory of our departed brother in Christ.

Five churches were received.

Three ministers were ordained to the office of Pastor, and two were received, and eight applicants for the ministry were taken under the care of Synod.

In regard to the History of the Tennessee Synod, it was,

Resolved, That this Synod hails with delight the forthcoming History of the Tennessee Synod, by Rev. S. Henkel, D. D.; that it commends it to the hearty reception of its pastors and people; and that it make earnest effort to sell it among our people.

According to the Parochial Report, there were 35 ministers, 105 churches, 660 infant baptisms, 70 adult baptisms, 462 confirmations, 9,426 communicants, and 14,323 souls.

During this decade, which lacks one year of being full; that is, nine years instead of ten, there were 6,040 infants baptized and 469 adults, and 3,653 confirmed, and 8 ministers received.

Synod adjourned to meet in Mt. Calvary Church, Page County, Virginia, on Friday, 10 A. M., before the fourth Sunday in October, 1890.

According to the Parochial Reports, which do not, as heretofore indicated, give much more than two-thirds of the actual numbers, there were, from the organization of the Synod down to the close of its session in 1889, 42,150 infant baptisms, 6,542 adults, and 795 slaves, and 20,712 confirmed.

Obituary of Rev. Polycarp C. Henkel, D. D.—On the 20th of August, 1820, was born the oldest son of Rev. David and Catharine Henkel, in Lincoln County, North Carolina. That son was the Rev. Polycarp C. Henkel, D. D., who is a descendant of a long line of distinguished Lutheran ministers. He inherited very great physical and mental powers from both his parents.

He was early dedicated to God in Holy Baptism, and was received into full communion with the Evangelical Lutheran Church with St. Peter's congregation, Catawba County, North Carolina, having been catechised by Rev. Daniel Moser and confirmed by Rev. Adam Miller. On the 5th day of September, 1843, he was married to Rebecca Fox, of Randolph County, North Carolina, daughter of David Fox. The issues of this union were two sons and one daughter. The youngest son preceded his father into the spirit world. The other son, Hon. David S. Henkel, of New Market, Virginia, and Mrs. Catharine C. Lail, of Conover, North Carolina, and his aged widow, survive him, to mourn their loss.

He died at his late residence in Conover, North Carolina, on the 26th of September, 1889, after a few days of intense suffering, at the age of 69 years, 1 month, and 6 days, and was buried at St. Peter's Church, Catawba County, North Carolina, September 28, 1889. Rev.

J. M. Smith preached the funeral from 2 Tim. 4, 6-8, in the presence of hundreds of people who came from far and near. He was followed in brief, appropriate addresses, by the pall-bearers, Revs. Yoder, Schaid, Koiner, Bernheim, Little, and Rudisill.

Dr. P. C. Henkel was an extraordinary man, and unique in his character. He has been so long and so favorably known in this country, that anything like an attempt at a sketch of his life, would seem useless; yet we offer these few lines as a tribute of respect to his memory. As a husband and father, he was kind and devoted to his wife and children, anxious for their welfare, both temporal and spiritual, and supplied them with both precept and example.

As a neighbor and citizen, he was kind and obliging, always ready to do a favor, if it were in his power, frequently disobliging himself and family to oblige others.

Intellectually, he was a powerful man. He was an original thinker and a fine logician. He would clinch every argument, and in debate and controversy was a formidable antagonist. He would consider well, make up his opinion deliberately, and when once made up, was very decided. He was immovable from an opinion which was the result of long and careful consideration. He would never, for any consideration, go back on his word. His word was as sacred to him as a most solemn oath. In his manners he was humble and unassuming. Humility was manifest in all his intercourses with his fellow man. Integrity was also a salient point in his character. He was rigidly honest and truthful.

As a minister, he was a power. His style of preaching was expository, plain, and forciful. He entered the ministry of the Evangelical Lutheran Church of the Tennessee Synod in 1843, having been ordained in Green County, Tennessee. He preached for forty-six years without interruption, and wholly in the Tennessee Synod, except a few years, while in the State of Missouri, where he led in the organization of the English District of the Missouri Synod. He labored exceedingly hard in the vineyard of the Lord. At one time he had pastoral charge of fifteen congregations. He did an immense amount of missionary work, traveled thousands of miles, in cold and heat, and rain and storm, in obedience to the call of the Master to this work. He never shirked from duty, but was always punctual, and ready to speak the word of encouragement to the weak, the word of comfort to the sorrowing, the word of life to those seeking a knowledge of the way of life. He was an uncompromising antagonist of error, and boldly and fearlessly denounced it wherever he met with it.

As a theologian, he was very profound. His range of study was broad, and his investigations were intense and searching, and descended into the very depths of theological problems, perhaps as far as human mind could go. His chief text-books were the Bible and the Confessions of the Lutheran Church. On Dogmatic Theology he was an acknowledged authority, in the Lutheran Church in the South, at least.

As a writer, he showed the same originality of character as in other fields. His ideas were original, and his style bold and vigorous. His writings are not numerous, but the treatment of the subjects he handled is exhaustive. It is to be regretted that he could not devote more of his time to writing, and thus transmit to generations to come, the results of his deep researches in theology.

His influence in all the relations in which we have mentioned him, as husband and father, as neighbor and citizen, as a man and as a preacher, and as a theological writer, was very great. In the Lutheran Church of the South, he was, perhaps, the greatest man in its history.

He labored hard and made great sacrifices to establish our school, Concordia College, for the Tennessee Synod, in which the Word of God should be recognized as a factor in education, and in which the Bible and Luther's Catechism should be taught daily. His influence is felt far beyond the limits of his own Synod, even throughout the whole Southern Church. He was in the midst of his earnest labors, both writing and preaching, to raise the Lutheran Church of the South to a higher plain of doctrine and practice, when the Master called him to his reward. Thus ended his work. A good and great man has fallen.

Obituary of Rev. Henry Wetzel.—At his residence, near Calvary, about two miles west of Woodstock, Shenandoah County, Virginia, March 3, 1890, after a complicated illness of three or four months duration, Rev. Henry Wetzel departed this life; aged 74 years, 2 months, and 20 days.

His funeral services took place from Mt. Calvary Church, March 5, at 10 A. M., Rev. P. C. Wike officiating. His remains were then conveyed to Zion's Church, a distance of six miles, and laid to rest by the side of his consort who preceded him to eternity.

He was born in Southwest Virginia, near the Tennessee line, of Christian parents, who brought him up in the nurture and admonition of God. He prepared himself for the Gospel ministry, and was ordained to the office of pastor, by the Evangelical Lutheran Tennessee Synod, at its session held in Rader's Church, near Timberville, Rockingham County, Virginia, in the year 1841, and continued in the active services of the ministry until within a few months of his death, —a period of forty-nine years. During his ministry, he served congregations in Augusta, Rockingham, and Shenandoah Counties, Virginia, as well as congregations in West Virginia, doing much missionary work. He also served a congregation in Baltimore, Maryland, for several years.

He was a man of strong mind and indomitable energy, an able and impressive preacher, both in the German and English languages, sound in the faith, and ever ready to promulgate, maintain, defend, and perpetuate the true doctrines and usages of the church, in their purity and simplicity. He was an able, fearless, formidable debater, full of zeal and perseverance.

By assiduous effort and close application to study and investigation, he attained an eminent degree in literature and theology, as well as in church history and dogmatics. He was one of the ablest ministers in the Valley of Virginia. He possessed an extensive library, and he really used it. He took great delight in reading the Confessions of the Church and Luther's Entire Works. He was quite familiar with them, frequently making translations from them.

When the translation of the Christian Book of Concord, or the Symbolical Books of the Evangelical Lutheran Church, into the English language, was undertaken, he was selected to make a purely literal translation of the Epitome; so, too, when Luther's Church-Postil on the Epistles was translated for publication in the English, he was selected to prepare a similar translation of the third volume.

He was a son of George and Margaret Wetzel. He entered into the estate of matrimony with Miss Mary C. Staubus, daughter of Christian and Mary E. Staubus, of Augusta County, Virginia, December 5, 1839, with whom he had seven children,—six daughters and one son.

He leaves two daughters and several grand-children, with numerous other relatives and friends, to lament his departure. Having finished his course here, he has now gone to the spirit world, to enjoy, as we trust, that rest and those rewards prepared for the faithful.

As the following papers were submitted to Synod for its action, it was deemed proper to give them a place here.

Basis of Union of the United Synod of the Evangelical Lutheran Church in the South.

I. The Confessional Basis.

1. The Holy Scriptures, the Inspired Writings of the Old and New Testaments, the only standard of doctrine and church discipline.

2. As a true and faithful exhibition of the doctrines of the Holy Scriptures in regard to matters of faith and prac-

tice, the three ancient symbols, the Apostolic, the Nicene, and the Athanasian Creeds, and the Unaltered Augsburg Confession of Faith. Also the other Symbolical Books of the Evangelical Lutheran Church, viz.: the Apology, the Smalcald Articles, the Small and Large Catechisms of Luther, and the Formula of Concord, consisting of the Epitome and Full Declaration, as they are set forth, defined, and published in the Christian Book of Concord, or the Symbolical Books of the Evangelical Lutheran Church, published in the year 1580, (see EPITOME *of the Compendious Rule and Standard, and the Sol. Declaration—Preface*), as true and Scriptural developments of the doctrines taught in the Augsburg Confession, and in the perfect harmony of one and the same pure, Scriptural faith.

II. THE OBJECT AND AIM.

Outward expression of the spiritual unity of the Synods concerned; mutual strengthening in faith and confession; unification of all Lutherans in one orthodox faith, and mutual co-operation in the promotion of the more general interests of the Church; as, books of worship, liturgies, theological seminaries, charitable institutions, immigrant missions, foreign missions, and important home missionary operations.

III. ITS POWERS.

Its powers shall be only of an advisory and recommendatory character in all matters, except such as pertain to the general interests or operations of the Church, as already indicated. In regard to these, it shall be invested with such powers as the Synods composing it may delegate to it.

IV. ITS SPHERE.

In its operations, it shall not interfere with the legitimate work of the Synods in its connections.

V. ITS CONSTITUTION.

Its Constitution shall contain nothing that is in conflict with this basis of union.

Constitution of the United Synod of the Evangelical Lutheran Church in the South.

In the name of the Father, and of the Son, and of the Holy Ghost.

I. NAME.

The name of this body shall be The United Synod of the Evangelical Lutheran Church in the South.

II. DOCTRINAL BASIS.

The Doctrinal Basis of the organization shall be,

1. The Holy Scriptures, the Inspired Writings of the Old and New Testaments, the only standard of doctrine and church discipline.

2. As a true and faithful exhibition of the doctrines of the Holy Scriptures in regard to matters of faith and practice, the three Ancient Symbols, the Apostolic, the Nicene, and the Athanasian Creeds, and the Unaltered Augsburg Confession of Faith ; also, the other Symbolical Books of the Evangelical Lutheran Church, viz.: The Apology, the Smalcald Articles, the Small and Large Catechisms of Luther, and the Formula of Concord, consisting of the Epitome and Full Declaration, as they are set forth, defined, and published in the Christian Book of Concord, or the Symbolical Books of the Lutheran Church, published in the year 1580, (see the Epitome *of the Compendious Rule and Standard, and the Sol. Declarations—Preface*) as true and Scriptural developments of the doctrines taught in the Augsburg Confession, and in the perfect harmony of one and the same pure, Scriptural faith.

III. OBJECT AND AIM.

The object and aim of this Synod shall be outward expression of the spiritual unity of the Synods concerned; mutual strengthening in faith and confession; unification of all Lutherans in one orthodox faith, and mutual co-operation in the promotion of the more general interests of the Church; as, books of worship, liturgies, theological seminaries, charitable institutions, immigrant missions, foreign missions, and important home missionary operations.

IV. Components of the Body.

1. This body shall consist of delegates from all Evangelical Lutheran Synods, having adopted this Constitution, who may present themselves properly accredited by the presiding officers of their Synods.

2. These delegates shall be chosen in the following ratio: one Minister and one Lay-Delegate for every one thousand communicants or fraction thereof.

3. A majority of the delegates elected, provided a majority of the Synods are thereby represented, shall constitute a quorum.

V. Officers.

1. The officers of this Synod shall be a President, a Vice-President, a Secretary, and a Treasurer. They shall be elected by ballot. Ministers alone shall be eligible to the offices of President and Vice-President, but both clerical and lay-delegates to those of Secretary and Treasurer. No one shall be elected President for more than two conventions in succession.

2. The President shall act as chairman of the convention. He may give his opinion, and, whenever the delegates shall be equally divided upon any question, he shall have the casting vote. He shall subscribe all letters, written advices, resolutions, and proceedings of the body. In extraordinary cases, and by request of any one of the Synods belonging to this organization, made known to him in the form of a Synodical resolution, he may call special conventions of the body, of which not less than six weeks' notice shall be given.

3. If, for any cause, the President is unable to discharge his duties, the Vice-President shall take his place.

4. The Secretary shall keep a journal of the proceedings of this Synod, and write, attest, and take care of all its documents. He shall also make known the time and place of meetings through the Church papers, published

within the bounds of the body, at least three months beforehand. In case of special conventions, such as provided for in Section 2 of this Article, he shall make known the time and place of meeting as soon as informed by the President. Should the duties of the Secretary become too burdensome for one person, the President, at his suggestion, may appoint an assistant secretary.

5. The Treasurer shall keep an account of the receipts and expenditures of the body. He shall give receipts for all funds put into his hands. He shall make no disbursements except by resolution of the Synod and upon the written order of the President, attested by the Secretary.—At every convention he shall render an account.

6. Should any officer of this body, in the interim of its regular conventions, depart this life, resign his office, or become incapable of executing the same, then the other officers shall appoint some capable and faithful man to serve in his place until the next regular meeting—save in the case otherwise provided for in Section 3 of this Article.

VI. Powers.

The powers of the body shall be only of an advisory and recommendatory character in all matters, except such as pertain to the general interests or operations of the Church, as already indicated in Article III. In regard to these it shall be invested with such powers as the Synods composing it may delegate to it. In its operations it shall not interfere with the legitimate work of the Synods in its connection.

VII. By-Laws.

This body shall make such By-Laws as it may deem necessary. No By-Law, however, shall be adopted which conflicts with any article of this Constitution.

VIII. Amendments.

1. The Doctrinal Basis of this Constitution shall ever remain unaltered.

2. No alteration of other parts of this Constitution

shall be made except with the consent of two-thirds of the Synods connected with this organization. An exact copy of the intended alterations must be sent by the Secretary to the Presidents of the District Synods in connection with the body, with the request that they submit them to their respective Synods for decision. If, at the next convention, it shall appear that two-thirds of the District Synods are in favor of the alteration, it shall be declared adopted.

CHAPTER VI.

ITS POLICY.

IN VIEW of the clear teachings of the Augsburg Confession, article twenty-eight, in regard to church government, that "the two governments, the civil and the ecclesiastical, ought not to be mingled and confounded," but kept distinct from each other, and in view of the position taken by our Revolutionary fathers, based on the principle evolved in the Reformation of the sixteenth century, in the establishment of our State governments, and dreading whatever savors of the union of Church and State, the Tennessee Synod pursued a cautious and judicious course in her policy, lest it might give occasion for some of the evils and calamities with which the church had been afflicted in different ages and in different countries, by a combination of civil and ecclesiastical powers. So cautious was the Synod in regard to this matter, that several writers have presumed to charge it with adhering too closely to "the Jeffersonian principles of Democracy." Be this as it may, its policy seems to be, in many respects, closely in accord with the teachings of the Bible, as set forth in the twenty-eighth article of the Augsburg Confession. And possibly there was great reason for caution at that time, from the fact, that none of the Synods then recognized that article, and that there was a move to effect a union of the different, principal Protestant denominations, and have that recognized as the State Church.

1. In its policy, it took the position, in the outset, that the rules and principles of church government are contained in the Holy Scriptures, and that no Christian organization has the right to make any rules or regulations which are not strictly in accord with the Bible. It condemned and rejected all human traditions, or rules or regulations im-

posed on the Church as necessary to Christian fellowship, which are not well and clearly founded in the Holy Scriptures. It even denied the right of a majority to decide or control matters relative to doctrine and church discipline. The only standard by which such things can be decided, is the Word of God. The fact, that a majority might decide against a doctrine clearly taught in Divine Revelation, should be no sufficient reason that the minority should reject or denounce such doctrine.

2. Its position is, that synods are only advisory bodies, and that they have no right to receive appeals from the decisions of congregations, or to make rules or regulations which are absolutely binding on the congregations. Of course, synods may recommend certain regulations for the conduct of congregations, and advise them to adopt such rules, but they have no right to enforce them contrary to the will of the people. The chief business of synods, according to its position, is to impart useful advice, to employ the proper means for the promotion and perpetuation of the Gospel of Jesus Christ, to detect and expose erroneous doctrines and false teachers, and, on application, to examine candidates for the ministry; and if they sustain a suitable examination, and there are applications for their services in a congregation or congregations, to ordain them to the office of the ministry, in a regular, churchly way. Synods are composed of congregations, represented by ministers and lay-delegates; and when persons representing these classes are present, the one class shall not transact business without the presence and co-operation of the other. The right to examine and ordain candidates to the ministerial office, does not, however, belong exclusively to synods. Congregations have the right to choose fit persons for the ministry, and individual pastors have authority to ordain them to such office.

3. It was opposed to the incorporation of synods by civil government, or of their holding, as incorporated bodies, any institutions. For this would be blending of civil and

ecclesiastical authority. It would give synods power to sue and be sued, and to levy taxes on their members, and to compel them to pay them, just the same as any civil incorporation. It is amply sufficient for the best interests of the Church, for civil government to protect the property of the Church by its acts of legislation and incorporation of certain individuals as trustees, to hold its institutions, against damage and infringement, for the purposes for which they are intended. The incorporation of a synod, holding within its own corporate limits certain property, is one thing, and lending its influence and patronage in favor of colleges, or other institutions so incorporated and held by trustees, for certain purposes, without any legal claim on synods as incorporated bodies, is something very different, and can lead to no conflict between the Church and the State.

4. For the purpose of raising funds for the promotion of the Gospel and the extension of the Kingdom of Christ, the Synod suggested the propriety of each congregation having a treasury for itself, in which to deposit all the money that each member or other person might freely give. The moneys thus contributed were used to defray the cost of printing the minutes of the Synod, to aid traveling ministers, and for other purposes which would best enhance the interests of the churches or congregations. The manner, in which these treasuries were to be kept, and the disbursements, made, was left to the good judgment of the church councils and the ministers acquiescing. The moneys were to be gathered at every meeting, each month or every three months. At every meeting of Synod, the council of each church was expected to make a report of the amounts thus collected. The contributions were generally quite liberal, judging from the amount of printing that was done, and the extensive traveling expenses, and other matters, that were defrayed from such collections. It is true, there may not have been as much boasting about liberality during the former period of the Synod, as there is at the present age, but

the probability is, that there were more real charity and free giving.

Perhaps, it would not be wide of the fact to state, that possibly there is more time spent by the different denominations in collecting their dimes, through their innumerable societies, treasuries, and manipulations, which must be rung "from Maine to Georgia," than there is in teaching, preaching, and admonishing. Money, money, is the continual cry everywhere. Congregations are divided up into too many distinct societies or organizations, each one claiming a distinct organization. A house divided against itself cannot well stand long. Whither is the Church tending? Is there not too much extravagance and too little economy? The love of money is the root of all evil, and is not this evil cropping out in all directions? Every church member was expected to contribute to the pastor's salary and to the other expenses of the church, in the promotion of the Gospel, and where people are taught the pure doctrines of the Gospel and earnestly admonished according to the Scriptures, they are most likely to become liberal and perform their duties in the different relations of life.

5. In tracing the policy of the Synod in all its aspects and bearings, it will be found that it held that the power of the Church is founded in the eternal nature and relation of things, having its lodgment in the congregations—for wherever the Gospel is preached in its purity and believed, and the Sacraments are administered and received according to the Gospel, there is the true Church,—and that synods or councils are only advisory bodies, having only such powers as the churches may invest them with. They are not sovereign.

CHAPTER VII.

ITS FUTURE.

It required much care, investigation, attention, and thoughtful consideration to trace and present fairly and honestly the history of the Synod, in all its aspects and bearings, and possibly it will require more insight, thought, and conception to formulate anything like proper views in regard to its future. But the past may be often taken as a somewhat reliable index of the future. If truth, fidelity, courage, boldness, and indomitable energy characterize the past, there are reasonable grounds to hope that similar elements will manifest themselves in future efforts, and that a sound, churchly, positive policy will be maintained and perpetuated. A building that rests on a good and well arranged foundation, has a chief element of endurance, indicating, to a greater or less extent, its perpetuity in the future. A house built on a rock, is likely to stand against the forces of destruction, whilst one built on the sand, is most likely to fall, when ruinous forces come in contact with it. Matt. 7, 24–27. So, too, a synod based on the doctrines and principles of the Rock of Ages, as evolved from Divine Revelation, and set forth in the Scriptural Confessions of the Church during the sixteenth century, as they stand in the Symbolical Books of the Church, ought to be able to stand and perpetuate itself against all the storms of Pietism, Rationalism, fanaticism, and unionism.

The Tennessee Synod, based on that foundation, and having withstood the fierce storms of fanaticism, unionism, and so-called liberalism, which prevailed during the nineteenth century against it, cannot, in the future, deviate from its sound, tenable, Scriptural position in regard to doctrine and practice, without greatly and shamefully stultifying itself in the eyes of the Church and of the world. Notwithstanding the taunts, abuses, and persecutions it had to bear on account of its fidelity to the doctrines and practices of the Church, it adhered most tenaciously to the time-honored Confessions, proclaiming, teaching, and maintaining them in the family, in the catechetical class, from the pulpit, and through the press; yea, even anglicizing them, and thus leading the Church in North America in these churchly, Scriptural directions.

This Synod having proved so faithful and courageous for nearly three quarters of a century, and established a most enviable reputation for orthodoxy, or fidelity to the faith of the Church, and having accomplished so much in restoring the Church to her normal condition in doctrine and practice, it is not unnatural to conclude, that it will require a most abnormal change to induce it to forsake its Scriptural principles and to ignore its well-merited history. All the indications are favorable to its pressing forward with greater vigor, if possible, in its well founded position, in fully restoring the Church to her true, confessional position,—one of the chief objects for which it was organized. It is now in a better condition for work than it has been in any previous period. It is well organized. It is a unit in doctrine and practice,—all speak the same thing. It has quite a number of able ministers, in literature and theology, who are true to the faith of the Church,—men of energy, zeal, and perseverance, with their hearts in the cause. Its congregations are generally in a prosperous condition, adhering to the Confessions of the Church. Harmony prevails among the ministers and their people or congregations. Every effort is made to indoctrinate the rising generations in the sound, Scriptural principles and usages of the Church. Its literary institutions are being gradually built up. Its children are regularly dedicated to God, and instructed in the elementary principles of Christianity, as arranged in Luther's Catechism. Its prospects are brighter now than they were at any previous time. If it will, as all the aspects and bearings indicate, maintain its present position and policy, it has an important, a glorious mission before it, in the future. Let it determine then to *go forward*, according to the command of God, and it will be able to stem the currents of fanaticism, and to over-ride the obstacles of unionism, cant, and hypocrisy, and to fill the sphere for which it was designed, with honor and success. Who, that is honest in his investigation and observance of the work of this Synod, in view of the circumstances under which it was organized and labored, cannot see the hand of God in its work and accomplishments! Mere human force could not have accomplished what it did. Let us rejoice that God has brought us hither, and ask his guidance in the future. For, the true Church is built upon the Rock of Ages: "and the gates of hell shall not prevail against it."

APPENDIX.

Names and Addresses of Ministers Now in Connection with the Evangelical Lutheran Tennessee Synod.

REV. J. R. PETERSON, Dallas, North Carolina.
REV. T. MOSER, Mt. Pleasant, North Carolina.
REV. S. HENKEL, D. D., New Market, Virginia.
REV. C. H. BERNHEIM, Conover, North Carolina.
REV. D. EFIRD, Lexington, South Carolina.
REV. J. M. SMITH, Conover, North Carolina.
REV. L. A. BIKLE, D. D., Dallas, North Carolina.
REV. J. I. MILLER, D. D., Luray, Virginia.
REV. I. CONDER, McGaheysville, Virginia.
REV. J. N. STIREWALT, Stony Man, Virginia.
REV. A. L. CROUSE, Hickory, North Carolina.
REV. J. P. STIREWALT, New Market, Virginia.
REV. PROF. M. L. LITTLE, Dallas, North Carolina.
REV. J. C. MOSER, Hickory, North Carolina.
REV. J. K. EFIRD, Rightwell, South Carolina.
REV. J. A. CROMER, Columbia, South Carolina.
REV. E. L. LYBRAND, Summit Point, South Carolina.
REV. PROF. R. A. YODER, Conover, North Carolina.
REV. PROF. J. S. KOINER, Waynesboro, Virginia.
REV. D. A. SOX, Edwardsville, Alabama.
REV. D. A. GOODMAN, Happy Home, North Carolina.
REV. J. W. HAUSENFLUCK, Alma, Virginia.
REV. PROF. W. P. CLINE, Ilex, North Carolina.
REV. D. J. SETTLEMYRE, New Sterling, North Carolina.
REV. J. A. RUDISILL, Henry, North Carolina.
REV. R. H. CLINE, Orkney Springs, Virginia.
REV. P. C. WIKE, Maurertown, Va.
REV. D. C. HUFFMAN, Hickory, North Carolina.
REV. PROF. J. G. SCHAID, Conover, North Carolina.
REV. J. P. PRICE, Concord, North Carolina.
REV. J. F. MOSER, Monroe, North Carolina.
REV. W. L. DARR, Chapin, South Carolina.
REV. D. I. OFFMAN, Julian, North Carolina.
REV. J. P. MILLER, Conover, North Carolina.

List of Churches Now in Connection with the Evangelical Lutheran Tennessee Synod.

ALABAMA.

CLEBURNE COUNTY.—St. Michael's. CALHOUN COUNTY.—Zion.

SOUTH CAROLINA.

LEXINGTON COUNTY.—Zion, St. Peter's (M.), St. Paul's, Cedar Grove, St. James's, Immanuel, St. Peter's (P. W.), St. John's, St. Jacob's, Bethlehem, St. Thomas's.

RICHLAND COUNTY.—St. Andrew's, Mt. Tabor.

NORTH CAROLINA.

ALAMANCE COUNTY.—Mt. Pleasant.

ALEXANDER COUNTY.—Friendship, Salem, Shiloh.

BURKE COUNTY.—Luther, Lutheran Chapel.

CALDWELL COUNTY.—Philadelphia, Mt. Zion, Lutz's.

CABARRUS COUNTY.—St. Martin's, Lutheran Union.

CATAWBA COUNTY.—St. James's, Grace, Concordia, St. John's, St. Paul's, St. Peter's, St. Stephen's, Zion, Holy Trinity, Newton, Sardis, Bethel, St. Timothy's, Mt. Olive.

CLEVELAND COUNTY.—St. Matthew's.

DAVIDSON COUNTY.—Pilgrim, Beck's, Emmanuel, New Jerusalem, Holly Grove.

GASTON COUNTY.—St. Mark's, Philadelphia, Lutheran Chapel, St. John's, Antioch, Christ's, College Chapel, Mt. Holly.

GUILFORD COUNTY.—Coble's.

IREDELL COUNTY.—Sharon, St. Martin's.

LINCOLN COUNTY.—Daniel's, Trinity, Salem, Bethphage, St. Luke's, Sharon.

MECKLENBURG COUNTY.—Morning Star.

RANDOLPH COUNTY.—Melanchthon.

ROWAN COUNTY.—Mt. Moriah, St. Mark's, Phanuel.

STANLEY COUNTY.—St. Martin's.

UNION COUNTY.—Emmanuel, St. Luke's.

WATAUGA COUNTY.—Valle Crusis, Mt. Pleasant.

VIRGINIA.

AUGUSTA COUNTY.—Bethlehem, St. Paul's.

ROCKINGHAM COUNTY.—Bethany (St. Jacob's), McGaheysville, Trinity, St. Peter's, Rader, St. John's, Bethel.

PRINCE WILLIAM COUNTY.—Bethel.

PAGE COUNTY.—St. Paul's, St. William's (Fairview), Grace, Mt. Calvary, Morning Star, St. Mark's, Cedar Point.

SHENANDOAH COUNTY.—Emmanuel, Mt. Zion, Solomon's, St. Mary's (Pine), Powder Springs, St. Paul's, St. Jacob's, Zion, St. Matthew's, St. Stephen's, St. David's, Mt. Calvary, Morning Star.

MADISON COUNTY.—Mt. Nebo.

INDEX.

www.ingramcontent.com/pod-product-compliance
Lightning Source LLC
Chambersburg PA
CBHW030338270326
41926CB00009B/881

* 9 7 8 3 3 3 7 0 4 2 9 9 8 *